T0305458

DECOLONIZING CHILDHOODS
From Exclusion to Dignity

Manfred Liebel

First published in Great Britain in 2020 by

Policy Press
University of Bristol
1–9 Old Park Hill
Bristol
BS2 8BB
UK
t: +44 (0)117 954 5940
pp-info@bristol.ac.uk
www.policypress.co.uk

North America office:
Policy Press
c/o The University of Chicago Press
1427 East 60th Street
Chicago, IL 60637, USA
t: +1 773 702 7700
f: +1 773-702-9756
sales@press.uchicago.edu
www.press.uchicago.edu

© Policy Press 2020

British Library Cataloguing in Publication Data
A catalogue record for this book is available from the British Library

Library of Congress Cataloging-in-Publication Data
A catalog record for this book has been requested

ISBN 978-1-4473-5641-7 (paperback)
ISBN 978-1-4473-5640-0 (hardcover)
ISBN 978-1-4473-5643-1 (ePub)
ISBN 978-1-4473-5642-4 (ePdf)

The right of Manfred Liebel to be identified as author of this work has been asserted by him in accordance with the Copyright, Designs and Patents Act 1988.

Cover design by Robin Hawes
Front cover image: iStock-184317578
Printed and bound in Great Britain by CMP, Poole
Policy Press uses environmentally responsible print partners

Contents

Preface and acknowledgements   iv

Introduction   1

Part I   How to understand childhoods in the postcolonial context
1   Childhoods from postcolonial perspectives   9
2   Colonialism and the colonization of childhoods   33
3   Postcolonial theories from the Global South   53

Part II   Children under colonial and postcolonial rule
4   State violence against children in British Empire and   77
       former settler colonies
5   Racist civilization of children in Latin America   87
6   Pitfalls of postcolonial education and child policies   99
       in Africa

Part III   Children's rights and the decolonization of childhoods
7   Postcolonial dilemmas of children's rights   127
8   Beyond paternalism: Plea for the de-paternalization of   161
       children's protection and participation
9   Children's movements as citizenship from below   191

Epilogue: Childhoods and children's rights beyond postcolonial   217
          paternalism

References   223
Index   269

Preface and acknowledgements

The idea for the book arose from my many years of experience and studies with children in Latin America and Africa. My first significant experience was in the 1980s in a camp of Salvadorian refugees in Honduras and in a rural region of Nicaragua, where a cruel civil war was underway. There I experienced children who had to endure unimaginable suffering and fought for their survival in a way that astonished me, often on their own. These experiences turned a lot of what I thought I knew about children upside down. My thoughts about children of the Global South, especially those living in extreme poverty, were soon put to the test again, when I found an opportunity to volunteer for a 'social brigade' (as it was then called) to accompany children on the streets and markets of the Nicaraguan capital Managua (and other cities in the country). Here the children provided for their livelihoods and in some cases also for their families. I kept wondering where these children found the strength to cope with such oppressive living conditions without losing courage and even humour.

I began to understand that the children often drew their strength from taking care of themselves and others and taking responsibility, and – which I consider decisive – found recognition in their environment. Observing that the children often supported each other, together with my colleagues who tried to support the children, we came up with the idea of promoting the children's self-organization. I was familiar with this idea from the social movements of school and university students and young workers, who have rebelled in Germany and other countries since the late 1960s against authoritarian control and fought for a freer and self-determined life. Nevertheless, the idea of self-organization gained a new meaning in many respects in view of the living conditions of the children I was dealing with. It was not only about freedom and self-determination, but also, to a much greater extent, about social equality and justice. In Nicaragua and – as I have experienced since the 1990s – in other regions of the Global South, the idea of self-organization manifested itself in various social movements of young people against discrimination, disregard, poverty, exploitation and war and for a peaceful and secure life in which their human dignity is protected. Increasingly, the idea of children's rights, understood as the human rights of children, was also approached.

One of the social movements that influenced my thinking about children and childhoods to a particular degree is that of working children and adolescents, which began in Latin America, starting from Peru in the late 1970s, and appeared in Africa and Asia from the early 1990s. This movement, which has different local characteristics, shows an understanding of childhood that contradicts the concept of childhood that emerged in modern Europe in many respects. It is characterized by the fact that children do not live in a sphere separated from the world of adults, but want to participate in society as a whole and exert an influence on it. According to this understanding, children do not stop being children (for example, when they work or take joint responsibility in society), but it no longer excludes children from society and does not make them 'smaller' than they are and see themselves (which is sometimes referred to as 'infantilization'). The expectations associated with this can perhaps best be described as a new form of citizenship of children that comes from below and is not limited to preparation for 'real' citizenship.

The more intensively I dealt with this understanding of childhood embodied in children's lives, the more it became clear to me that children in the Global South are often met with incomprehension even by people and organizations who claim to help them. This incomprehension can even take on forms of enmity when, for example, children are persecuted and criminalized by the police at the insistence of international organizations simply because they help their mothers on the market (as I have seen in Nicaragua, Colombia, Peru, Paraguay and India). It can also lead to the degradation of children when they are displayed on posters as suffering and helpless beings (without being asked) in a kind of pornography of misery to collect donations for charity projects. Such and other forms of disregard have led me over time to see it as an unspoken continuation of colonial subjugation and conquest.

Through my intensive engagement with the history of colonialism, with so-called postcolonial theory and with studies that made visible colonial stereotypes, for example in development policy and development education, I wanted to reflect on and express in a more comprehensive and structured way my experiences and unease have grown over the years. I also had to experience how even well-meaning people who wanted the best for the 'poor little ones' – children and families who did not meet their standards – secretly met them with contempt and arrogance, even if they did not express this openly or wanted to admit it. This book is the result of all this.

It was helpful for my enterprise that I have been able to participate in several meetings of the movements of working children and adolescents over the years and that I kept in constant contact with many active and former active children and their adult collaborators. I was also able to exchange ideas with experts of different ages, backgrounds and professions at various workshops and conferences in Latin America, Africa and India. In Germany and some other European countries, I found the opportunity to reflect on this experience in solidarity groups to support the rights of working children as well as with students and colleagues of the master's programme 'Childhood Studies and Children's Rights' at Free University Berlin (established in 2007) and continuing at Potsdam University of Applied Sciences.

In particular, I would like to thank the following persons for their suggestions, stimulating conversations and critical remarks on individual parts of the manuscript: Rebecca Budde, Alejandro Cussiánovich, Elizabeth Dieckermann, Ina Gankam Tambo, Antonella Invernizzi, Andrea Kleeberg-Niepage, Bea Lundt, Urszula Markowska-Manista, Philip Meade, Brian Milne, Olga Nieuwenhuys, Iven Saadi, Giangi Schibotto, Peter Strack and Elisabeth Weller. Rebecca Budde and Courtney O'Connor in particular supported me in the elaboration of my thoughts in the English language. Finally, I would like to thank the anonymous reviewers and Sarah Bird of Policy Press for their critical comments on the book project and their suggestions for its revision.

Manfred Liebel
Berlin, September 2019

Introduction

It is one of the self-comprehensions of today's socio-scientific childhood research that children and childhoods cannot be considered as natural phenomena, but are shaped by the social conditions, social relations and cultural contexts they are part of. Moreover, no talk about children and childhood is ever perfectly matched to reality – it is always filtered through the visions and values of those who talk and write about children and childhood. In this book, children are seen as actors who are never unaffected and uninfluenced by predetermined social structures and cultural patterns, but who can nevertheless influence, shape and thus also modify these structures and patterns. This also applies to the development and appearance of what we call childhood. That is why it is important to emphasize that there is not only one childhood, but always different childhoods, be it with regard to the history, to each individual life course, or to different societies and cultures. In the context of the presentation of children and childhoods in this book, I aim to express children's perceptions and actions.

Why is this book devoted to childhoods in the postcolonial context, and what do I mean by that? The European colonialization of other continents, which has been going on since the 15th century, still has consequences for the power structures of today's world and people's ways of thinking in different parts of the world. These are postcolonial in the double sense that they follow the colonial epoch in time and challenge criticism of the aftermath of colonialization. The term postcolonial is thus used to criticize the existing unequal global power structures that are remainders of colonialism, and thus can also be described as neo-colonial. When I speak of childhoods in the postcolonial context or postcolonial childhoods, I want to express that even today's childhoods, and in reflections, talk and writings about them, the colonialization of 'alien' parts of the earth continues to affect them and therefore must be critically examined. In doing so, I will also show that the dominant understanding of childhood in Europe is closely interwoven with the process of colonialization.

One aspect of reflecting about postcolonial childhoods is that the people living in Europe (as involuntary descendants of the colonial powers) know little about children and childhoods outside Europe and

North America. One reason for this is that they have largely been seen in the light of a ' "Western" narrative of modernization' (Morrison, 2012: 3). The history of childhood in non-Western regions has been ignored for a long time or has been viewed in a very one-sided light due to existing stereotypes about childhood. In the media, but also in scientific representations, for example, children in Africa are almost exclusively regarded as AIDS orphans, street children, child soldiers or trafficked girls, often portrayed as helpless and needy victims in exceptional circumstances. They do not seem to have a 'normal' life or characteristics comparable to the lives of 'our' children. Their lives are being degraded, and they are also pushed to the brink of the world, made 'children out of place' (Connolly and Ennew, 1996; Invernizzi et al, 2017). On the contrary, I want to put these children, who represent the large and growing majority of children on earth, in the centre of this book and express their lives in their many facets.

Childhood research to date and the categories developed by it are largely based on children and childhood in the Global North. The categories are occasionally subjected to an ideological-critical deconstruction in which their role of legitimization is made visible (see, for example, James et al, 1998; Prout, 2005). In so far as childhood research refers to children and childhood in the Global South, it is usually restricted to ethnographic descriptions without questioning the categories themselves and without taking the postcolonial power constellation into consideration. In this book, which I also see as a contribution to the decolonization of research on childhood and children's rights, I will show how this constellation affects children in the former colonial territories as well as how they are perceived and dealt with.

A postcolonial constellation to me is an unequal material and ideological or epistemic power relationship that leaves little space for childhoods that do not correspond to the pattern of childhood that dominates the Global North. On the material level, the life of most children in the Global South, or the former colonial territories, is determined by the fact that they are cut off from vital resources and have to grow up under precarious conditions. These conditions result from the continuing economic and political dominance of the Global North and corresponding dependencies, disadvantages and multiple (mostly racist) discrimination. On the epistemological level, the lifeforms of childhood are made invisible, based on or influenced by inherited cultural traditions that appear to be unfathomable. This is all the more so since, in the dominant discourses, these modes of life are not valued as being childhood, children are at best mocked and bemused, sometimes feared, and labelled as 'children without childhood'. However, the postcolonial exercise of power does not merely replace the 'old' childhood with a 'new' childhood, but rather creates hybrid structures in which subversive potential can also be concealed. This potential cannot be raised if only one or more 'original' childhoods are sought. Such a search is necessarily caught up in myths and idealization. Yet it is also not worth denying them. For this reason, I am not concerned with searching for 'the' lost childhood, but instead with the most possibly precise appraisal of the childhood that has emerged from the postcolonial constellation and continues to emerge.

The investigation of childhoods in the postcolonial context can be understood as part of a global history that reconstructs the different and changing living conditions and lifestyles of children worldwide in their spatial-temporal dimensions. There are singular attempts to conceive such a global history, but these are either based again on the ideological pattern of 'Western modernism' (Stearns, 2006), limited to the 'Western world' (Fass, 2007; 2012; Fass and Grossberg, 2011) or the compilation of single contributions from previous childhood research (Morrison, 2012). With this book, I am also not pursuing the task of writing a comprehensive history of childhood(s) in their manifestations and appearances from precolonial, via colonial, to postcolonial periods. Instead, I focus on illuminating the lives of children in today's Global South in some aspects of the postcolonial constellation which seem important to me. Nevertheless, it must be borne in mind that this postcolonial constellation also has repercussions on the childhoods in the Global North, whether it is by migration processes and the corresponding problematizations of national and cultural identities, or growing doubts about the future of the 'Western' childhood pattern.

For the study of postcolonial childhoods, I try to use theories that are generally referred to as postcolonial and have been formulated since the 1970s in the Global North as well as in the Global South. This is not an easy task to do, since these theories rarely address questions of childhood. The topic of childhood is, at best, taken up in theories and studies which point to colonial paternalism as a kind of childhood project or understand paternalism as a colonization of childhoods.

Postcolonial theories do not form a homogeneous unity. Some emphasize cultural, others economic and social aspects. Basically, these are not strict theories that claim to provide a comprehensive explanation of today's postcolonial world constellation and its origins. All of them, however, contribute in their own way to making conceptions of civilization, progress and development disputable; these conceptions have emerged as myths since the 'discovery' of the Americas and the Enlightenment in Europe and serve as ideological justifications for the conquest of the extra-European world. However, postcolonial theories do not discard all the ideas and concepts of the European Enlightenment. They challenge the intercultural, international and intercontinental dialogue on equal terms.

This is immensely important for the understanding of postcolonial childhoods and the possible ways of their decolonization, as it encourages and facilitates the understanding of these childhoods as the result of different and often contradictory social and cultural processes. It has not been easy for me, and probably not always satisfactory, to reconstruct such childhoods and the notions of it in this complex way, especially since it cannot be understood as a kind of final product, but as a permanently changing and in itself differentiated and contradictory sociocultural phenomenon. Moreover, I have at least the ambition to make the children visible who are embodied in these childhoods as actors who influence the conditions of their lives, and thus also the postcolonial constellation.

Another difficulty arises from the fact that, as an adult who has grown up and lives in a European context, I am writing about children whose lives and experiences are very different from mine and which I can only know partially and from my own view. I mainly rely on my own observations and conversations, as well as on empirical research that has been carried out in different places with a theoretical and methodological approach directed to the actual life, reality and subjectivity of the children. In working through certain empirical studies and their conclusions critically, I am aware that I could not have done it better myself. A particular risk, however, is always present when I make childhood or child policy proposals and construct alternatives. Even though, as I hope, they are adequately justified, the smell of the European know-it-all is always attached to them, and they could fall under suspicion of reproducing colonial messages. This is particularly true when I refer to geographic areas and sociocultural circumstances that deal with colonial heritage. I can only hope not to be self-centred on standards and not to use them in a manner which I criticize as Eurocentric in the book.

I can certainly not completely escape the contradictions and ambivalences between universalistic and cultural-relativistic modes of reflection. In the book, it will become clear that I regard certain universalistic norms as indispensable, but I also feel that they must be scrutinized for their own historical and cultural prerequisites, and must not be politically instrumentalized and imposed on the people from 'above'. With regard to the decolonization of childhoods, this is especially true for the basic assumption that children are to be respected as *social* subjects who have the inalienable right to a worthy living future and the right to meaningful participation in all matters that concern them. I see it as an exciting yet also risky enterprise to find criteria for a good childhood or various good childhoods that are valid beyond the postcolonial constellation for all children of the world. When I discuss these and similar questions, I will try to use universal criteria in such a way that they remain open to cultural diversity without losing myself in cultural relativisms.

I will explain some of the terms commonly used in the book. When I speak of the *Global South*, and the *Global North*, I have a geopolitical, not geographical, meaning in mind, which takes into account the division and inequality between and within different regions of the world. These cannot be understood any longer as a mere inequality of economic and political power between the 'West and the rest' (Hall, 1992), if we look, for example, at China or the so-called tiger states in Asia, or at the so-called threshold countries in other parts of the world. But the colonialist conquests and the model of capitalist industrialization, which have emanated from Europe, continue to work to this day, and are manifested in the power structures of what we call globalization. The two terms largely correspond to what is also known as the *majority world* and the *minority world*, in order to express the fact that the vast majority of the world's population and particularly the world's children live in the Global South. However, it must be borne in mind that the Global South also extends into the Global North, especially through migration processes as well as the economically and politically induced marginalization of certain regions in Europe and North America itself. I explicitly avoid the term 'developing countries' – often used even in United Nations documents – as it implies that the so-called developed countries embody a generalized, particularly advanced ideal by which the state of other countries and the cultural level of other people can be measured.

In Part I, I explore various ways to understand childhoods in the postcolonial context. In Chapter 1, I discuss some key aspects of the postcolonial analysis of childhood, such as the question of the scope and limitations of the childhood pattern emerging in modern Europe, how social inequality that is aggravated by capitalist globalization impacts on children's life prospects as well as on the specific modes of agency emerging in children of the Global South, and how they are to be conceptually understood. In Chapter 2, I reconstruct the way in which the colonialization process and the ideologies that supported it have used the metaphor of childhood, and investigate the extent to which they are reproduced in processes of colonizing childhoods. In Chapter 3, which concludes Part I of the book, I sum up various contributions to postcolonial theory, which I have used to analyse postcolonial childhoods.

In Part II of the book, I reconstruct the life and experiences of children under colonial and postcolonial rule in different regions of the world emphasizing particular aspects. In Chapter 4, using case studies from the British Empire, the USA, Canada, Australia and New Zealand, I investigate the ways in which the emergence of nation states was connected with violence against certain groups of children and was legitimized with the alleged necessity of their civilization. In Chapter 5, with a view to the colonial and postcolonial history of Latin America, I examine how the discourse on 'illegitimate' and 'irregular' children led to racist arbitrariness against the children of indigenous and African origin. In Chapter 6, with a view to contemporary Africa, I examine some postcolonial pitfalls of education and child policy, and ask about the possibilities of overcoming paternalistic practices and amplifying children's participation.

In Part III of the book, I ask about the importance of children's rights and social movements for the decolonization of childhoods and portray some efforts into this direction. In Chapter 7, I address the question of how to deal with human rights in general and children's rights in particular in terms of global social inequality and postcolonial power relations. In Chapter 8, I discuss various forms of paternalism and ask how they could be overcome in the field of rights-based children's protection and participation. In Chapter 9, I show how child-led movements in the Global South can be understood as a form of citizenship from below that could pave the way for a childhood that emancipates itself from illegitimate dependencies and subjugations. The examples given are not only valid for the Global South, but own special characteristics caused by postcolonial inequality and oppression.

The book is an interim analysis of my studies on childhoods in the postcolonial context, mainly those of the Global South. They have a largely exploratory character. In further studies, it will be beneficial to deal with the concrete agency of children and young people of the Global South even more intensively than in this volume, and to get to the roots of its manifestations, conditions and impacts. At the end of the book, I formulate some questions and outline possible perspectives for further research and better child policies in favour of excluded and marginalized children and their liberation from postcolonial dominance.

PART I

How to understand childhoods in the postcolonial context

1

Childhoods from postcolonial perspectives

As I walked down our street, under the persistence of the yellow sun, with everything naked, the children bare, the old men with exhausted veins pumping on dried-up foreheads, I was frightened by the feeling that was no escape from the hard things of this world. Everywhere there was the crudity of wounds, the stark huts, the rusted zinc abodes, the rubbish in the streets, children in rags, the little girls naked on the sand playing with crushed tin-cans, the little boy jumping about uncircumcised, making machine-gun noises, the air vibrating with poisonous heat and evaporating water from the filthy gutters. The sun bared the reality of our lives and everything was so harsh it was a mystery that we could understand and care for one another or for anything at all. (Azaro, the little boy from the spirit world, in the novel *The Famished Road* by the Nigerian author Ben Okri, 1993, pp 160–1)

Introduction

Dutch anthropologist Olga Nieuwenhuys (2013: 4) explains the necessity of postcolonial perspective in childhood studies with three arguments: first, 'the dominance of the North over the South is inextricably linked to Northern childhood(s) representations against which Southern childhood(s) are measured and found wanting'. Second, the normative dominance of Northern childhood(s) translates 'in an overproduction of knowledge based in disciplinary strongholds that resist critique of their Eurocentrism'. Postcolonial thoughts could help subvert this process. Third, 'the analysis of children's agency, finally, while playing a seminal role in addressing the two first limitations, runs up against a lack of imagination about its wider social, political and ethical implications and risks missing its radical edge'. In a general sense, the postcolonial approach challenges otherwise unquestioned Eurocentric thought patterns, and can contribute to opening the intellectual arena for all those who are considered subaltern, or subordinate.[1]

Describing colonized people as possessing a lower rank than those coming from 'higher', European civilization shows, according to Nieuwenhuys, 'remarkable parallels with theories of child development that were emerging at the same time in Europe' (Nieuwenhuys, 2013: 5). Postcolonial thoughts do not reject constructs such as 'modern childhood' or 'children's rights', they rather question the supposed exceptionality or absolutism of these terms, by contextualizing them. They bring attention to the fact that, since the beginning of colonization, the colonial world was an integral part of, and even a prerequisite for modernization. The dominant perception of the child in Europe, as needing to be protected and supplied for, required the exploitation of the colonies. In rejecting the idea of modern childhood as a purely Western discovery or experience, the postcolonial perspective is able to inspire a generally positive tone, which, in place of an 'us versus them' attitude, opens the path for a conceptualization of childhood(s) as the unstable and uncertain result of an intercultural encounter.

From Nieuwenhuys' perspective, postcolonial approaches invite us to constantly re-invent concepts of childhood and to pay attention to the unexpected and uncertain insights which can arise from such encounters. Here it is important to 'put children's perspectives and experiences, including their artistic, literary and material culture, at the centre of analysis' (Nieuwenhuys, 2013: 6). This approach could in sum 'offer a wealth of new information and support endeavours to take children seriously and stand by their side' (Nieuwenhuys, 2013: 6). Thereby, children's creativity and sensibility with respect to social inequality, and their resistant practice, which is widely overlooked, can receive due attention again.

Another author I would like to pick up on is Kristen Cheney. Starting from a critique of international development politics in which she sees a 'colonization of childhood' at work, she argues 'for a *decolonization* of childhood research and practice – both in the conventional sense of confronting Western civilizing constructions of childhood and as a means to challenge the patriarchal underpinnings of the politics of knowledge production about children' (Cheney, 2018: 91–2; italics in original). According to her, a vitally inclusive co-production of knowledge with children that aims to resist or even rupture the status quo of adults as the primary holders of knowledge is necessary:

In keeping with other decolonization movements, including decolonial feminism, childhood studies could strive not only to decolonize the curriculum by diversifying its contents but also to actively question broader structures of research, policy, and practice to make space for epistemic diversity that will in turn help children's knowledge to be seen as more legitimate in the eyes of researchers, policymakers, and development practitioners. (Cheney, 2018: 100)

Based on the considerations of Olga Nieuwenhuys and Kristen Cheney, in this and subsequent chapters I will use postcolonial and decolonial thoughts for the study of the life and agency forms of children, principally those of the Global South.

First, I will follow some of the debates conducted in social childhood research, such as the question of whether a 'global childhood' has developed during the process of globalization. Then I will explain what I mean by postcolonial constellation and postcolonial childhoods, and illustrate it with some empirical data. Finally, I will look at which kinds of agency in children and young people of the Global South are to be found and how they are to be understood.

Limitations of the Eurocentric childhood pattern

The childhood pattern that prevails in the world today, emerging in modern Europe, confers on children a certain degree of autonomy, but on the condition that they are restricted to activities that have no significant current relevance for the formation of society. These are, on the one hand, activities which are imagined as not being purposive and have no direct impact on social life (understood as 'play') and, on the other hand, activities that prepare for later life and the pursuit of vitally important activities (understood as the 'production of human capital'). This encompassing of children's activities is accompanied by a strict division of childhood from adulthood and the corresponding attributes and spheres of action. It is assumed that children are, as a matter of course, inferior to adults and dependent on them.

This conception of childhood, often referred to as 'modern', comes from the claim that it is the culmination of a development into a better society and can be regarded as the yardstick for a good childhood. The childhood and children's rights researcher Bob Franklin (2002: 17–18) notes critically:

The modern conception of childhood, which in Europe dates from the sixteenth century and stresses the innocence, frailty and dependence of children, forcefully ejected children from the worlds of work, sexuality and politics – in which previously they were active participants – and designated the classroom as the major factor of their lives. Children were no longer allowed to earn money or to decide how to spend their time, they were forced into dependency on adults and obliged to study or play. … Cute and contented, but dependent on adults and denied autonomy in important decisions concerning their lives, children are encouraged to be 'seen and not heard'.

The prehistory of the modern conception of childhood sketched out here is certainly not free from romanticization by suggesting that children and adults could have had freedom of choice for work, sexuality, and politics, but it rightly points out that the supposed privileges of modern childhood had to be paid with a high price.

The childhood researcher Alan Prout, who contributed to the emergence of the New Childhood Studies, illustrates the central elements of this childhood conception in a simplified but concise way (see Table 1.1).

Table 1.1 Childhood and adulthood in modern times

Childhood	Adulthood
Private	Public
Nature	Culture
Irrational	Rational
Dependent	Independent
Passive	Active
Incompetent	Competent
Play	Work

Source: Prout (2005: 10)

It is acknowledged today that childhood can be imagined and 'constructed' differently, and that children must be 'listened to' (according to Art. 12 of the UN Convention on the Rights of the Child), but the basic pattern of separation and dependency is held. This is illustrated by a quotation from a UNICEF publication (UNICEF, 2005: 3):

What then do we mean by childhood? The quality of children's lives can vary radically within the same dwelling, between two houses on the same street, between regions and between industrialized and developing countries. The closer children come to being full-grown, the more cultures, countries, and even people within the same country differ in their views of what is expected of children and on the level of adult or legal protection they require. Yet, despite intellectual debates about the definition of childhood and cultural differences about what to expect for and from children, there has always been a substantial degree of shared understanding that childhood implies a separate and safe space, demarcated from adulthood, in which children can grow, play and develop.

It should not be disputed here that the distinction between children and adults is not limited to the 'Western' concept of childhood that has emerged in Europe. However, it is specifically Western if this distinction is conceived as strict separation and the quality of childhood is measured by whether the children are kept away from adult roles. This is illustrated by another UNICEF publication, entitled 'Children in adult roles' (UNICEF, 2006: 62; translated from German):

> Childhood should be a separate living phase, clearly separated from the adult world. Children should be able to grow, play, rest and learn. ... When children have to take over the role of adults, they are deprived of their childhood.

Such statements are made in order to prevent children from being overwhelmed, exploited or abused but, added together, they attribute passivity and a one-sided dependency relationship between children and adults. They leave no space for the imagination of childhoods or lifestyles of children, which are accompanied by the self-chosen assumption of tasks in the sense of shared responsibility or mutual support (reciprocity). This not only condemns and stigmatizes children's agency in such contexts as 'not childlike' or 'premature', but also imposes the Western image of a dependent and all-round cared childhood as the standard for the societies of the Global South. So they have a paternalistic and colonizing function.

Often, the emergence of the Western childhood pattern and its institutionalization in the 'developed' societies is attributed to the assumption that, because of the higher level of productive resources, the labour power of the children became unnecessary and a special learning phase has been required in which young people are prepared for their productive tasks. Such an explication assumes that the learning of abilities is in principle only possible beyond productive work. It is ruled out that the work at issue here is work that is subject to the maxims of economic exploitation and embedded in structures which hinder the development of abilities. The separation of a life phase of childhood from that of the adult has also become 'necessary' because the 'gravity of life', which is proverbial to childhood, is based on the exploitation of human labour, a circumstance that has changed its face but in essence continues to exist.

Already almost half a century ago, US-American women's rights activist Shulamith Firestone, in a text that influenced the women's movement, saw the 'oppression of the children' principally founded in economic dependence (Firestone, 1970: 95): 'Anyone who has ever observed a child wheedling a nickel from its mother knows that economic dependence is the basis of the child's shame.' Firestone exaggeratedly criticized the widespread notion that the fortune of children had improved and their exploitation had been overcome when they went to school instead of working. According to her, it is precisely the segregation of the world of adults that goes hand in hand with the school, which 'reinforces the oppression of children as a class' (Firestone, 1970: 94) and, as a result, the 'growing disrespect' and 'systematic underestimation of the abilities of the child' (Firestone, 1970: 83). With regard to so-called child labour, we should be aware, according to Firestone (Firestone, 1970: 96; italics in original)

> ... rather than that children are being exploited just *like* adults, is that *adults* can be so exploited. We need to start talking not about sparing children for a few years from the horrors of adult life, but about eliminating those horrors. In a society free of exploitation, children could be like adults (with no exploitation implied) and adults could be like children (with no exploitation implied).

Such considerations are more recent than ever. It is observed worldwide that children no longer live only in the separate worlds that the Western childhood conception provides for them. It is true that the time of children is increasing, especially that in which they stay at school, but at the same time they are increasingly involved in processes and activities that were previously reserved for adults. This applies in particular to the use of new digital communication technologies, which are already presented to children at an earlier age and which they usually use competently for themselves or for the area of the commodity world, where children as consumers as well as innovative designers participate. It can also be observed that children increasingly accept co-responsibility for daily life, whether they are forced to do so by material necessity, or that they want to make new experiences beyond the educational space provided for them and interfere into the world of adults.

Such trends have repeatedly prompted social researchers in recent decades to speak of a breakup of the strict separation between the fields of activity of adults and those of children. Some of them, like the US-American sociologist Neil Postman (1982), were disappointed in the 'disappearance of childhood', others, such as the British media researcher David Buckingham (2003) or the German culture researcher Heinz Hengst (2013), saw these tendencies as an emancipation of the children from the restrictions of the Western conception of childhood and a new kind of generational relations.[2] Alan Prout (2005: 7) expresses these tendencies in the following way:

> The distinction between adults and children, once firmly established as a feature of modernity, seems to be blurring. Traditional ways of representing childhood in discourse and in image no longer seemed adequate to its emerging forms. New ways of speaking, writing and imaging children are providing new ways of seeing them and these children are different from the innocent and dependent creatures that appeared to populate the first half of the twentieth century. These new representations construct children as more active, knowledgeable and socially participative than older discourses allowed. They are more difficult to manage, less biddable and hence are more troublesome and troubling.

In such observations, it is not always clear whether they refer to the real life of the children or rather to childhood images and the hopes and fears of the adults that are reflected in them. There is also the question of whether it is possible to speak of a worldwide harmonization of childhoods, as expressed in the popular speech of a 'global childhood'.

Unequal global childhoods

Looking at the history and at different parts of the world makes the idea that there is a single global form of childhood appear absurd. But it is also to be understood that the spatial and temporal concentration of the world through economic and technological processes as well as through international legal norms also influences the conceptions of 'good childhood' and the life of the children, bringing them closer together. That means in a certain way that they become 'globalized'. Karen Wells (2009: 3–4) describes this fact as follows:

> There is now a body of law and a group of international actors – intergovernmental, non-governmental and private – that is based on the presumption that childhood can be governed at a global level. One way of resolving the question of whether there can be a global form of childhood is by thinking of the global level, including international law and international actors but also global media, economic flows, war and politics, as a structure that shapes childhood at the local level. Thought of in this way the global becomes one of several structures – others would include the family, school and work – that shape the lives of children and concepts of childhood in any specific socio-cultural setting.

One question is how we can name the childhoods that result from their 'globalization'. Would it be justifiable to describe them as more vicious, modernized, secularized, legalized, scorned or consonant? In his attempt to conceive a global history of childhood, Peter Stearns (2005, 2006) argues that the childhoods outside Europe would not have become 'Westernized' but changed 'alongside' the Western model. It is hard to deny that in the course of colonialization, for example, the school following the Western model occupies more and more space in the life of children and gains greater importance for their further life. But with regard to other aspects of the globalization of childhoods, it must be borne in mind that they do not run the same way for all children, do not attain the same meaning and are even reversible. Classroom education, as well as the legalization of social relationships or the use of digital technologies, can be very differently conceived and practised. Any attempt to use certain concepts for the globalization of childhoods is at risk of making a definite (usually the dominant Western) point of view absolute and established.[3]

The following tendencies are emphasized in a contribution that relates global influences and local traditions to each other (Bühler-Niederberger and van Krieken, 2008). The international discourse on children's rights and, in particular, the UN Convention on the

Rights of the Child strengthened the tendency to measure the quality of childhood on the basis of universal standards, which were strongly oriented to the Western childhood pattern. Today, children are increasingly confronted with the spread and propaganda of consumer goods, which have created new preferences in consumer behaviour. Today, children spend more time outside of home privacy (as long as they were ever in the sense of the European-bourgeois small family) and are more visible. In some cases, they soon assume social responsibility. Global influences are picked up and processed in everyday practices, which are rooted in local traditions. Social inequalities are strengthened rather than reduced. The subordinate social status of children and the deprivation of girls against boys remains largely unaffected. Children show new forms of 'social agency', but their ability to express their own viewpoints is also more strongly undermined on the discursive as well as on the practical level by adult child experts.[4]

Perhaps the greatest challenge of social childhood research is to understand the connections and contradictions between the global and local dimensions of childhood and the lifestyles of children on the objective level, as well as at the level of subjectivity, thinking, feeling and acting. Children are also affected (if not in absolutely the same way) as well as adolescents and adults by what happens in other parts of the world, because there are no more isolated spaces. But the way in which they are influenced also depends on the parts of the world and under what conditions they live, and it is important to consider whether they are willing to be influenced at all. The globalization of childhoods is neither a one-sided nor an absolutely compulsive process, but implies many interdependencies (Twum-Danso Imoh et al, 2019). It does not produce a single uniform 'global childhood' but many, quite different 'global childhoods' (Cregan and Cuthbert, 2014). Lorenzo Bordonaro and Ruth Payne (2012: 371) bring this to the point:

> The notion of a 'global childhood' is based on an alleged natural and universal distinction between children and adults and has been formed in Western world imaginations and exported through processes of colonialism, the forces of globalisation, international development organisations and the United Nations Convention on the Rights of the Child. Whilst it is, therefore, limited in its understanding and conceptualisation of childhood; it has nonetheless become an ideal against which all childhoods should be measured.

Take, for example, the thesis of 'McDonaldization' or 'Coca-Colaization' in the world. Such pictorial descriptions are intended to show, among other things, the fact that the Global North is going through the world imposing certain thoughts and patterns of consensus which follow uniform prescriptions, are directed towards quick satisfaction, and ultimately reveal superficial and noncritical personalities (see Ritzer, 2007).[5] But even if we assume that almost every child has the desire to experience the atmosphere of a McDonald's location and to embrace a burger or a Coca Cola, this does not mean that the whole life of this child or even an entire generation is stamped by this experience. Children's lives always include other desires, experiences and challenges, which give them reason to think about their own lives and to make their own decisions.

However, it should not be overlooked that interdependencies are embedded in an extremely unequal global power structure in the development of global childhoods. How unequal these global interdependencies can be is shown most clearly by the widening gap between wealthy and poor regions of the world and the significantly lower chances of life for children in the poorer parts of the world, as the UNICEF annual reports on the situation of children in the world demonstrate tirelessly.[6]

For example, the 2016 UNICEF report on the situation of children in the world (UNICEF, 2016a: 9–11) reveals that the gap between the extent of child mortality in sub-Saharan Africa and South Asia, and wealthy countries has hardly diminished for a quarter of a century. Children born in sub-Saharan Africa are 12 times more likely to die before their 5th birthday than children in wealthy countries. For example, a child who is born today in Sierra Leone is 30 times more likely to die before they are five years old than a child in Great Britain. The proportion of children who die shortly after birth is larger. Almost half of the children die because of infectious diseases, pulmonary infections, diarrhoea, malaria, meningitis, tetanus, maize, blood poisoning or AIDS, all of which would be avoidable with better living conditions and better medication. According to the UNICEF report, the risk of dying from these diseases is particularly high among the most disadvantaged. In rural regions, life expectancy is particularly affected by the lack of access to land, credit and property rights. In cities, people living in informal or 'illegal' settlements and slums are particularly vulnerable to dangerous diseases due to overpopulation, lack of sanitation, high transport costs and discrimination practices. Climate change brings additional risks. Widespread water deficiency forces people to access unclean water, which leads to illnesses such as cholera and fatal diarrheal diseases. Climate change also has an impact on the spread of infectious diseases such as malaria and is associated with growing food insecurity, malnutrition and air pollution, which are particularly detrimental to the life expectancy and development of children.[7]

In another report, UNICEF (2016b) draws attention to the fact that 300 million children live in areas where air pollution is at least six times higher than internationally agreed limits. According to this report, 2 billion children are living in areas where fine dust pollution exceeds the annual limit of 10 micrograms per cubic meter (10 $\mu g/m^3$) set by the World Health Organization (WHO). Up to 88 per cent of all deaths caused by outdoor air pollution and over 99 per cent of all deaths caused by indoor air pollution occur in low- or middle-income countries. Asia is currently the worst continent for air pollution, while values in Africa are on the rise, due to intensified industrialization, urbanization and traffic. People in urban areas, where poverty is particularly high, are particularly vulnerable to air pollution. Poor families also have fewer opportunities to protect themselves from air pollution by using fans, filters or air-conditioning systems, which, however, would be associated with increased energy consumption.[8]

The high rate of child mortality highlighted in the UNICEF report on the situation of children in the world (UNICEF, 2016a) also logically coincides with poverty, to which people in the Southern world regions are condemned. It is true that the *proportion* of people living in absolute or extreme poverty has declined worldwide in the past two decades, but the *absolute* number of the poor and the gap between living conditions in poor and prosperous regions of the world has increased. The measurement of poverty is a complicated undertaking and must take into account other aspects, apart from income, that are equally important for quality of life, such as living conditions, educational opportunities, access to drinking water, sanitary conditions, and so on. But due to the fact that life, as result of capitalist production, today is largely monetarized in all societies, disposable income is particularly important.

The World Bank assumes that people who have less than US$1.90 a day to live on are considered extremely poor. According to UNICEF (2016a: 72), nearly 900 million people were living in extreme poverty in 2012, almost half of whom were children under the age of 18. The UNICEF report rightly points out that even children above the poverty definition of the World Bank are often severely restricted in their lives and have lower life expectancy. Let us consider, for example, a family that does not have access to housing, food, drinking water, sanitation, education, health services or information. Children in such a home are also affected, and even more so, by poverty. Taking into account these non-monetary aspects, UNICEF estimates that in 2015, 1.6 billion people lived in 'multidimensional poverty'. Particularly in sub-Saharan Africa, the results of research are alarming. Here, in 30 countries from which data was available, 247 out of 368 million children under the age of 18 had met at least two out of five poverty criteria that put their survival and development at risk (see Plavgo and de Milliano, 2014). Another study found for the years 2008 and 2009 that the life expectancy of 81 million children in Latin America and the Caribbean was limited by at least one poverty indicator (see ECLAC-UNICEF, 2010; UNICEF, 2016a: 78).

In the UNICEF reports, the reasons why high poverty, air pollution and child mortality are mainly affecting the people of the Global South are not or only vaguely named. It is clearer in other UN reports, in which not only poverty itself is depicted, but also the increase in worldwide material inequality over longer periods of time. For example, a United Nations Human Development Report (UNDP, 1999: 3) shows that:

> … the income gap between the fifth of the world's people living in the richest countries and the fifth in the poorest was 74 to 1 in 1997, up from 60 to 1 in 1990 and 30 to 1 in 1960. In the nineteenth century, too, inequality grew rapidly during the last three decades, in an era of rapid global integration: the income gap between the top and bottom countries increased from 3 to 1 in 1820 to 7 to 1 in 1870 and 11 to 1 in 1913. By the late 1990s the fifth of the world's people living in the highest-income countries had: 86% of world GDP – the bottom fifth just 1%.

In other investigations on the worldwide distribution of income and wealth (for example, Milanović, 2012; Piketty, 2014), it has been shown that material inequalities in the global context have long been extremely high and further growth is to be expected if those inequalities are not specifically politically counteracted.

The French economist Thomas Piketty (2014: 463) points out that wealth inequality is growing not only between states and regions, but is also reflected in an increasing privatization of assets, which he calls the 'oligarchic type of divergence'. That is a process in which all countries 'come to be owned more and more by the planet's billionaires and multimillionaires' (Piketty, 2014: 463) and therefore would not be available to the states, for example, for infrastructure, social or educational programmes. While assets are concentrated among a small minority of the super-rich, less than 5 per cent of the world's total assets are available to the poorest half of the world's population. According to a report published by Oxfam (2017), which is based on data from the Swiss bank Crédit Suisse, the richest 1 per cent of the world's population has as many assets as the rest of the world combined. In 2015, the 62 richest people on earth had as much as the poorer half of humanity – about 3.6 billion people. While the wealth of the rich grew by 44 per cent over the five years to 2015, the wealth of the poorest half fell by 41 per cent. The discrepancy between rich and poor has never been so great.

Growing social inequality reflects the unequal distribution of power between the Global North and the Global South, which arose in the colonial era, and which now exists in covert institutional forms. It no longer expresses itself openly in colonial expansion, conquest and dominance, but in the less visible dependence of apparently independent national states in the Global South, which in turn internally reproduce social and political inequality. The role of the former colonial powers has now been taken over by international institutions such as the International Monetary Fund, the World Bank and the World Trade Organization, which in turn are largely acting in the interest of rich countries and multinational corporations. The fact that their interventions are based on neoliberal maxims continually leads to increasing debt for the countries of the Global South. An important role in growing global inequality is played by free trade treaties pursued by the rich countries and state blocs such as the European Union, which push the former colonialized countries into the role of commodity suppliers and contribute to the destruction of their internal economies.

The unequal global power structure is evident not only on the material level. It is also reflected in the fact that the ways of life of these children and the childhoods in which they manifest themselves are devalued, disregarded and made invisible. The children are seen as existing 'outside childhood' (Ennew, 2005), and they are met with compassion at best. Kate Cregan and Denise Cuthbert (2014: 8) put it this way:

> The fact that geopolitical power was centred in the Global North over the course of much of the twentieth century – and that proceedings, policies and conventions in those global bodies were, as a result, infused with Global Northern

'world views' – has led to the domination of particular understandings of children and childhood that have often been at odds with the realities of children's day-to-day lives in local settings … of the Global South.

A further consequence of this power structure is that while the spread of schools and new digital media has expanded opportunities to gain information and knowledge, at the same time it depreciates and destroys the life-practical knowledge that the children in non-Western, precolonial cultures get through their proximity to nature and the inclusion in communitarian-family activities. This knowledge related, for example, to the characteristics of plants and animals and the need for their care and maintenance or to the handling of risks and dangers in the children's environment. It was a knowledge that resulted from practical experiences and participation in important tasks (not only 'homework' for the school). The anthropologist Cindi Katz (2004: 125) states:

> The links between practice and knowledge were extensive and durable. Most of what the children learned in their everyday engagements, whether among their elders or their peers, was important to both the contemporaneous reproduction of their community and its future.

These connections have been largely broken, and have, in particular, marginalized and discriminated against children in and from rural regions, as Cindi Katz (2004; 2012) exemplifies with the example of Sudan and Sarada Balagopalan (2014) with India. Nevertheless, children and young people remain important to their communities. They are often, with newly acquired knowledge and their better knowledge of the world, actors who show new ways, whereby not infrequently traditional knowledge and related lifestyles are updated (see Young Lives, 2016).

The destruction of traditional production methods, often connected with land robbery, leads to material hardship and often violent internal conflicts in the Global South. These have resulted in displacements and migrations within the countries from the countryside to the city, into neighbouring countries and into the richer Northern world regions. The migration movements caused by material hardship and social inequality lead to new forms of childhood, whether children themselves become actors of migration ('children on the move'), or that they return to their native places where they rely on themselves, relatives or neighbours. These movements are associated with separations, life-threatening risks and suffering, but they also create new identities, new experiences and new knowledge. Some communities and families in the Global South are dependent on the income and the newly acquired cultural and social capital (see Bourdieu, 1986) of their young migrants for their survival and progression. Transnational childhoods emerge, which have not existed so far, and they question 'how national boundaries and cross-bordering are produced and inscribed in social constellations of childhood' (Himmelbach and Schröer, 2014: 494). With regard to the children of immigrants living in the US, Cinthya Saavedra and Steven Camicia (2010: 33–4) speak of 'transnational bodies' with 'diverse and changing identities'. They advocate a 'geopolitics of childhood', which considers that the children with transnational biographies produce remarkable knowledge and trigger new cultural impulses.

Although suffering is growing with global inequality and migration, it also increases the challenges of dealing with this suffering and organizing it. Children are 'mature' earlier, they are part of the world. Syntheses from knowledge, acquired modes of life and the newly available information are the result. The Eurocentric understanding of childhood does not do justice to these changes and obscures them rather than nurtures them. On the normative level, that understanding of childhood spreads to the South, but is in conflict with the real-life conditions and lifestyle of the majority of children living there, and leads to hybrid childhoods as well as to distorted perceptions of the children's reality. It is a question of what makes this childhood pattern so appealing, 'that it gets anyhow more attention and interest than the real childhoods that it can produce, the social inequalities that it may strengthen, the conditions that make its implementation problematic' (Bühler-Niederberger, 2011: 67). Today's postcolonial childhoods of the Global South are, in any case, not 'autonomous' and 'separated' childhoods in the sense of the idealized Eurocentric childhood pattern, but childhoods closely linked to society and its existential challenges. And they are by no means confined to the Global South, but are spreading through migration processes, the precariousness of a growing number of people, and the dissolution of the strict separation of the working and reproduction spheres in the Global North (see Hunner-Kreisel and Bohne, 2016).[9]

Agency in childhoods

Here the question arises as to how the capacity for action and the forms of practice of the children in the Global South can be conceptually grasped and understood. The concept of agency customary in today's childhood research is, at all events, hardly suitable for this purpose as long as it is guided by the bourgeois concept of an individually acting, basically, male and 'white' subject (see Tisdall and Punch, 2012; Sutterlüty and Tisdall, 2019 for criticism).[10] According to Wyness (2015: 10), 'the individualistic strand of thinking has generated an over-romanticised conception of agency'. Measured against this conception, which is self-centred in Europe itself, the aggravated practice mentioned by Olga Nieuwenhuys (2013) can only appear distorted or remain completely invisible (see Valentine, 2011; Edmonds, 2019). This practice manifests itself neither in separate social spaces of a particular childhood world, nor in extraordinary, individualized heroic deeds. Nor is it aimed primarily at adults against whom children insist on their own childhood world or demand an upgrading of their own status (see James, 2011). It is more to be understood like the desire to reconstitute the social space with other people in similar social situations and facing similar problems, where common interests can be expressed.[11] This form of agency is, in my opinion, best understood as a materialization of *shared responsibility*.[12]

In studies on childhoods in the Global South, which are influenced by conceptual considerations on the social geography of children's worlds (see Holt, 2011; Kallio and Hakli, 2015; Kraftl and Horton, 2018)[13], and under the influence of feminist and other relational action theories, the key concept of agency is (self-)critically discussed by childhood researchers. In an anthology on this subject (Esser et al, 2016), the editors explain the 'almost dogmatic insistence on agency and its constitutive importance for Childhood Studies' (Esser et al, 2016: 2) as a critical response to the adult-centricity of almost all previous research on children and childhood. This research had seen children primarily as a result of socialization processes and as an appendix to a family. In contrast, agency has now been discovered as a specific property of children, which allows their emancipation. Their voice should be heard and their subordinate and marginalized position overcome. The 'new social movements' (see, for example, Laraña et al, 1995) and the Ariès' (1962) perspective on childhood as an invention of modern bourgeois society, or, in the words of Shulamith Firestone (1970), as an 'oppressed class', had a great influence on this new orientation.

Today, the agency concept is once again under criticism. The previously dominant concept of childhood as a development stage, with an adult imagined as perfect and the child imagined as vulnerable by nature, has been replaced by an essentialist version of agency. This has been hypostatized, on the one hand, as an anthropological fact opposite to the idea of the vulnerable, developing child, and, on the other hand, as the most advanced expression of 'modernity' (see Esser et al, 2016). By imagining the child in an absolute manner as an actor in itself, the link to the biological basis (body) and the social conditions of the life of children were lost or not sufficiently observed (see Prout, 2000). The relation to the generational order, another key concept of childhood research, has also been lost where the actions of children can have reproductive as well as transformative functions (see Närvänen and Näsman, 2007). This is now connected with the basic question of how children are individually and collectively positioned in different social contexts, making it necessary to introduce not just one, but different childhoods.

Another critique comes from feminist-oriented care concepts, which had already conceptualized interdependent relationships against the conceptions of an autonomous subject (see Wihstutz, 2016; Cheney, 2018). A theory of agency cannot simply assign the fictions of autonomy attributed to the (male) adult to children and thus negate their dependence on other people who care about them. In this context, relational social theories, in particular the Actor-Network-Theory founded by Bruno Latour (1993; 2005), have also had an influence on the re-conceptualization of agency (see Oswell, 2016; Raithelhuber, 2016; Spyrou, 2018). They are based on the assumption that agency is not an inherent personal property, but is always inherent in and interwoven with social relationships. Instead of hypostatizing agency as a quasi-natural property, it must be seen as part of a complex network of different human and non-human actors.[14] This could also refer to the concept of 'multidimensional agency', which Daniel Stoecklin and Tobia Fattore (2018) formulated with reference to the Capability Approach (Sen, 1999; Nussbaum, 2011). According to them, 'agency is constituted intersubjectively, within parameters set and enabled through structures represented in social space. Children's agency is thus always constituted through constraints and opportunities, whether they are accepted, negotiated or resisted' (Stoecklin and Fattore, 2018: 15; see also Stoecklin, 2013; Larkins, 2019).

The new theoretical reflection on the concept of agency is remarkably related to non-European contexts. In the past few years, various concepts of agency have been formulated in order to analyse, in accordance with the concrete conditions of life and in a culture-sensitive manner, the ability of children in the Global South to act. These concepts are to be critically appreciated here and linked with my own thoughts, which also form the basis of the following chapters.

Most attention so far has been paid to a concept developed by Natascha Klocker (2007) in research with children from rural areas of Tanzania working as domestic workers in homes of more or less well-off families. Klocker (2007: 85) distinguishes between 'thick' and 'thin' agency:

> 'Thin' agency refers to decisions and everyday actions that are carried out within highly restrictive contexts, characterized by few viable alternatives. 'Thick' agency is having the latitude to act within abroad range of options. It is possible for a person's agency to be 'thickened' or 'thinned' over time and space, and across their various relationships. Structures, contexts, and relationships as 'thinners' or 'thickeners' of individuals' agency, by constraining or expanding their range of viable choices. Between 'thick' and 'thin' agency there is a continuum along which *all* people (including rural young people) are placed as actors with varying and dynamic capacities for voluntary and willed actions.

The author justifies the concept by the fact that it was difficult for her to ignore the pressure on the girls, which is caused by poverty and various sociocultural factors. Above all, the girls were affected by 'powerful hierarchical age-structures' which largely restricted their options for action (Klocker, 2007: 85). Nevertheless, according to the author, among the child domestic workers, '*all* of the girls replied unequivocally that they had decided for themselves' (Klocker, 2007: 91; italics in original). This obvious contradiction, into which the author does not go further, points out that the distinction between 'thick' and 'thin' agency she has made does not meet the complexity of the contexts of action (Esser, 2016).

It is also apparent from other research in Africa and Middle East, as well as Latin America, that the material and sociocultural framework conditions do not necessarily lead to restrictions on the capacity to act, but can also become a kind of action provocation, which causes children and youths to take on new and independent actions. For example, studies on children in Ghana (Mizen and Ofosu-Kusi, 2010; Ofosu-Kusi and Mizen, 2012), Kenya (Omolo 2015) or Peru (Aufseeser, 2014a; 2014b) who live on the street show, in the words of Alderson and Yoshida (2016: 77), 'how children's self-reliant agency similarly keeps knocking against very hard contexts and discrimination against children'. A study carried out in a rural region of Mexico

(Carpena-Méndez, 2007: 45) concludes that boys and girls between the ages of 12 and 18 who are compelled to emigrate because of poverty are creating networks and behaviour patterns on their own initiative which become effective as 'social capital' and which also serve as an orientation for older people. These children 'are "juggling" and improvising with their own life trajectories as they intersect with rapidly changing social and economic contexts of development, where local, rural-urban, and transnational processes overlap' (Carpena-Méndez, 2007: 53).

Similarly, reference may be made to children involved in armed conflicts or participating in insurgency campaigns against repressive regimes. Although they are particularly in danger, they are also always looking for ways to make the situation the better for themselves and the people around them. Sometimes, as shown, for example, in the sometimes armed battles against apartheid in South Africa or the Intifadas against the Israeli occupation in Palestine, children are among the protagonists of the resistance (see Punamäki et al, 2001; Boyden, 2003; Brett and Specht, 2004; Rosen, 2005; 2014; 2015; Özerdem et al, 2017). In the civil war in Syria, children take over, for example, tasks to care for severely injured people in the improvised underground hospitals, or to encourage by singing their fellow citizens not to be put off (see Syrian Revolt, 2013; Taylor, 2016). All this does not diminish and even exacerbate the dangers that children are exposed to, but it also helps to reduce the psychological consequences of traumatic experiences and can make children more resilient (see Punamäki et al, 1997).

For children growing up under precarious conditions in the Global South, I therefore consider that a concept of agency, which Lorenzo Bordonaro and Ruth Payne (2012) call 'ambiguous' (see also Bordonaro, 2012), is more appropriate. It is based on the observation that children must assert themselves in situations for which there are no clear or definitive solutions and for which there are usually no legal ways. Or that children are in situations which are not envisaged in the dominant Western childhood concept, with the result that they are sometimes regarded as victims, sometimes as perpetrators, delinquents, disturbers or transgressors. They act out of the self-contradictory situation and their actions cannot be judged to be clearly 'good' or 'bad' (such as children in street situations, children in armed conflicts, working children). Michael Gallagher (2019: 197) speaks in a similar sense of the fact that agency is always 'ambivalent': 'it does not have intrinsic ethical value'. With regard to the everyday practice of children who live on the streets of Dhaka, the capital of Bangladesh, and seek to achieve their livelihood and a minimum of security, Sally Atkinson-Sheppard (2017) coined the concept of 'protective agency'. The children considered here can be understood neither as helpless victims, nor as individuals who can act as they please or who can find a flawless answer to all the problems which are charged to them.[15]

In a similar way, Ruth Payne (2012b) speaks of 'everyday agency' in the context of so-called child-headed households. The term is intended to underline the fact that, in the case of children whose lives do not correspond to the prevailing pattern of childhood, agency is not developed solely from crisis situations or related to their coping, but is part of their daily life. The behaviour arises from the life situation, and it pragmatically aims to cope with daily needs in order to achieve a minimum of social reliability and security. The children support each other, look for allies, and create networks that they can access in special emergency situations. This type of children's agency in the Global South is often simply seen as problematic 'because it fails to fulfil a normative notion of childhood based on minority world ideals in which children and young people are protected, rather than protectors, and cared for, rather than carers' (Payne, 2012a: 301). Therefore, their behaviour, instead of being acknowledged, is often 'considered to be a social problem in need of fixing by the international development community' (Payne, 2012a: 301; see also Burman, 1996; Guest, 2003).

Accordingly, it can be said that the opposition of 'thick' and 'thin' agency is secretly caught up in a Eurocentric conception of agency, which regards its 'thick' form as the preferred normal case of which the 'thin' unfortunately differs. It also lacks an understanding of the differences in the cultural placement of childhood in communities and in accordance with generational relations, which differ fundamentally from the Western model. This criticism also applies to other occasionally represented concepts such as 'restricted', 'limited' or 'tactical' agency (Honwana, 2005; Robson et al, 2007). Such characterizations go past the complex reality in which children live under the postcolonial constellation. They insinuate that there can be a context-free, absolute standard for real or complete agency. David Oswell (2013: 263) rightly criticizes this notion as an 'ontology of agency' and emphasizes that agency 'is always relational and never a property, it is always in-between and interstitial' (Oswell, 2013: 270). It could also be said to be under the influence of the idea of an autonomous bourgeois subject.

The challenge for researching the agency of children living in precarious conditions is to capture it in a contextualized way. Just as it makes no sense to contrast right and wrong consciousness, agency cannot be measured and evaluated against given criteria, but must be understood from the situation. In this sense, Ruth Edmonds

(2019: 208) pleads for 'situated theories of agency' that do not make normative specifications from outside, but interpret the children's 'agentic practice' from the local context. Agency is not a fact that exists or does not exist, that is perfect or imperfect, right or wrong, but arises and always changes in a concrete context in which it more or less contributes to protecting oneself from risks, enabling the survival and shaping of one's own life. A further differentiation of the different forms of agency could be whether children contribute to reproducing or transforming the living conditions under which they have to assert themselves. One of the characteristics of an 'inventive' (Gallagher, 2019) or 'transformative' form of agency is that the children at their places of living gain ideas of a better life *together* and engage *collectively* for it. This form of agency can be found, for example, in the social movements of working children and is occasionally referred to as 'children's protagonism' (see Liebel et al, 2001; Liebel, 2007a; and Chapter 9). But the judgement in what this better life consists must be left to the acting children.

To understand the forms of agency created in postcolonial constellations, we must treat the concept of the subject carefully. It is stamped by a history that was characterized by the idea of an autonomous, self-governing, nature-subordinating and, finally, world-conquering figure largely identified with the 'white' European man. It was first expressed in pure form in the formula of the French philosopher René Descartes (1596–1650) '*Cogito, ergo sum*' ('I think, therefore I am') and has led to the predominance of a rationality which is superior to all other aspects of human existence. To be freed from this history and the associations it suggests, is occasionally spoken of *social* subjects and the *intersubjective* aspects of human existence, as well as the dialogical and respectful relationships to the non-human nature are emphasized. If, in this context, we speak of *subjectivities* instead of subjects, an understanding of humanity is addressed which does not separate rationality from the body, but links rationality with physical and psychical proportions (see Dreyfus and Taylor, 2015). In South America, for example, this understanding of subjectivity is expressed in the revival of the indigenous cosmovisions of *Sumak Kawsay/Buen Vivir* (good living; see Acosta, 2013) and has also led to debates on a new understanding of 'political subjectivity' (Díaz Gómez, 2005; Alvarado et al, 2008; González Rey, 2012) or 'postcolonial subjectivity' (Rivas, 2010).

When I speak of children as social, political, or postcolonial subjects or actors in the subsequent chapters of the book, I try to take a broad view of their subjectivity. Accordingly, I do not understand their actions as the expression of a consciousness which is fed solely from rationality or even imagined as superior, but consider it an integral part and in the context of the diversity of human and non-human life and its existential foundations.

Notes

[1] 'Subaltern', which goes back to the Italian philosopher and political activist Antonio Gramsci, describes social groups which are subjected to other groups and struggle for their emancipation. In postcolonial discourse, it was taken up by Gayatri Spivak in her famous essay 'Can the subaltern speak?' (Spivak, 1988; see also Chapter 3).

[2] Sharon Stephens (1995; 2012) recalls that since the 1980s there has been an accumulation of publications in the Global North about 'Children without Childhood' (Winn, 1984), 'Stolen Childhood' (Vittachi, 1989), 'Children as Innocent Victims' (Gilmour, 1988) or 'Rise and Fall of Childhood' (Sommerville, 1982). She sees in this signs that the ideas of childhood that had previously been taken for granted have fallen into crisis. This is also expressed in the fears that the dangers for children have increased ('children at risk') or that children have become a risk for societies ('children as risk').

[3] Heidi Morrison (2015: 17) attempts to analyse these processes in a historical study of the changes of childhood in Egypt, which are accompanied by colonialization, in a differentiated way and without a Western bias. For example, she indicates attempts by Egyptian authors to reinterpret Western influence: 'The model of childhood that developed in Egypt had its roots in colonial resistance and Islamic heritage. For example, Egyptian intellectual Muhammad 'Abduh justified his claims for western-style education by saying that western ideas about childhood were Eastern in origin as the East used to be the center of the Enlightenment.' Morrison, however, reverts in the discussion of the colonial influences in a problematic way to the concept of 'colonial modernity'.

[4] The frequently asked question of whether the situation of children in the world is better or worse today, in my opinion, cannot be answered. The attempt at an answer would have to compare apples with pears or create universal criteria that would always have a cultural bias or be historically prejudiced. However, this does not rule out the identification of historical trends, such as demographic changes or the rate of child mortality, which has clearly declined. Some trends and their assessments are highlighted in Grugel and Piper (2007).

[5] Some authors (for example Wagnleitner, 1994) speak of a 'Coca-Colonization', understood here as a propagandist weapon of Western capitalism in the Cold War, or call for a 'De-Coca-Colonization' (Flusty, 2004). The term Coca-Colonization goes back, to my knowledge, to the East German (GDR) writer Alexander Abusch (1950).

[6] However, this also applies to the conditions within the countries and regions of the Global South, which are also characterised by considerable social inequality.

[7] This is the reason why, for years, it has been repeatedly demanded to extend the catalogue of children's rights to include ecological rights and the rights of future generations.

[8] In the case of such global data, it must be noted that there are also very great differences within the mentioned continents.

[9] In this connection, attention should be paid to a problematic and momentous form of 'refugee aid'. Within the framework of a solidarity project, about 430

Namibian children from African refugee camps were taken to the German Democratic Republic (GDR) from 1979 to 1989 to become the elite of a future liberated Namibia. After the end of the GDR, these children and young people were 'transferred' to Namibia, without being asked for their wishes, where only a few of them had lived before. In a study, along the biographical stations, it was examined how the young people were exposed to racist attributions, were looking at their own experiences in the search for affinity, and were looking for specific forms of agency (Schmitt and Witte, 2017).

[10] Anthropologist David Lancy (2012) also takes a critical look at the hegemonic, Western-based use of the agency concept, but pours the baby out with the bath water by rejecting any assumption of agency in children as counterproductive.

[11] Matej Blazek (2016) has impressively investigated in the middle of Europe the example of spatial appropriation as well as intra- and intergenerational relations in a poverty-stricken community of 'post-socialist' Slovakia.

[12] With reference to her studies in India, Sarada Balagopalan (2018: 31) criticises that 'responsibility-based cultures', in which shared responsibility between generations is practiced, are generally devalued as retrograde or unmodern and regarded as contrary to 'rights-based cultures'.

[13] Since 2003 there has been a special journal for this research specialism called *Children's Geographies*.

[14] I cannot go deeper into the actor-network-theory of Latour here, but I would like to say at the very least that in all the merits of its understanding of the complexity and contextual nature of human action, there is the risk of losing sight of the power and domination conditions in society by renouncing the category of social structure.

[15] While there is a differentiated international discussion about agency in working children and children in street situations, children in armed conflicts or 'child soldiers' are presented almost exclusively as victims. Remarkable exceptions, in which attention is also paid to the aspect of agency, can be found in Huynh et al (2015), Fernando and Ferrari (2013); Cook and Wall (2011), and Feinstein et al (2010).

2

Colonialism and the colonization of childhoods

> It is said that the Negro loves to jabber; in my own case, when I think of the word jabber I see a gay group of children calling and shouting for the sake of calling and shouting – children in the midst of play, to the degree to which play can be considered an initiation into life. The Negro loves to jabber, and from this theory, it is not a long road that leads to a new proposition: The Negro is just a child. The psychoanalysts have a fine start here, and the term orality is soon heard. (Frantz Fanon. *Black Skin. White Masks*, [1952]1986: 15–16)

> Although generalizations are of course dangerous, *colonialism* and *colonialization* basically mean organization, arrangement. The two words derive from the Latin word *colĕre*, meaning to cultivate or to design. Indeed, the historical colonial experience does not and obviously cannot reflect the peaceful connotations of these words. But it can be admitted that the colonists (those settling a region), as well as the colonialists (those exploiting a territory by dominating a local majority) have all tended to organize and transform non-European areas into fundamentally European constructs. (V.Y. Mudimbe, *The Invention of Africa*, 1988: 1)

Introduction

In order to develop a concept of childhoods in postcolonial and decolonizing contexts, it is necessary to understand the connections between colonialization and childhood.

Childhood is understood here equally as a form of being a child and a discourse about this form of being (Alderson, 2013). Both dimensions should not be confused, but also should not be separated. The history of childhood is closely intertwined with changes in the modes of production and reproduction of societies, in the modern

European era particularly with the development of the capitalist mode of production and the rise of the bourgeoisie to the ruling class. They have led to a spatial separation of the production and reproduction sphere and the localization of women and children in the small family, which is organized as a private space. In this context, new normative conceptions of a childhood have emerged, which were conceived beyond the production sphere as a 'pedagogical province' (Goethe), 'family childhood' and finally also as 'school childhood' (see Hendricks, 2011). To this extent, the history of childhood is always a history of the ideas and conceptions of childhood. They gain a life of their own and influence the way in which children are treated. They also influence how children perceive themselves, and what opportunities are available to them and are used by them. Here I now argue that childhood, as well as the ideas and conceptions of childhood that have been developed in Europe since the late Middle Age, are closely linked to the colonialization of other continents in many ways.

The concept of childhood, separated from adult life, 'liberated' of productive tasks but also directed to the margin of society, arose almost simultaneously with the 'discovery' and colonialization of the world outside of Europe. The subjugation and exploitation of the colonies, first in America, then in Africa and Asia, formed their material prerequisites by creating a class living in material prosperity in the 'mother countries', which could privatize their children and place them in a reserve of rearing and care. On the other hand, the conquest of the colonies constituted the model for the subjugation and 'education' of the domestic children, whether of the ruling classes, or the subaltern classes, so that we can rightly speak of a colonization of childhood or the modern childhood as a kind of colony. This perspective also served as a model for early childhood science, which was aimed at the control and perfection of childhood. Conversely, the construction of childhood as an immature pre-stage of adulthood constituted the matrix for the degradation of people of any age in the colonies as immature beings, which were still to be developed and civilized, as expressed in Hegel's famous dictum of Africa as a 'land of childhood' (Hegel [1837]2001). Looking at the postcolonial constellation, questions arise around how childhood research can learn from history, how to account for its own entanglement, and how to use critical postcolonial thoughts for the understanding and analysis of today's childhoods.

A few words on the use of the concepts of colonialism, colonialization and colonization, which are here addressed in various contexts and meanings. Under colonialism I follow Osterhammel's (2005: 16–17) understanding. According to him, colonialism is:

> … a relationship of domination between an indigenous
> (or forcibly imported) majority and a minority of foreign
> invaders. The fundamental decisions affecting the lives of
> the colonized people are made and implemented by the
> colonial rulers in pursuit of interests that are often defined
> in distant metropolis. Rejecting cultural compromises with
> the colonized population, the colonizers are convinced of
> their own superiority and of their ordained mandate to rule.

In encyclopaedias or dictionaries, the concepts of colonialization and colonization are mostly understood synonymously, but in two different directions: a) in the sense of the exploration of a natural space not previously used for human purposes; b) in the sense of subjugating a territory, including the population living there, as a colony. The former is identified with the extension of human settlements to virgin forests, deserts, moors, districts, and similar difficult-to-use natural areas within a national territory (sometimes referred to as 'internal colonization'). In contrast, the second sense is identified with the establishment of colonies outside an existing territory ('external colonization') and corresponds to the above-mentioned understanding of colonialism. One problem with this distinction is that in reality it is often not clear (where there are still uninhabited areas in the sense of *Terra Nullius*) and the states themselves can extend their borders, or according to their own (military and economic) power claim spheres of influence and ownership beyond their national borders. I will only use the concepts of colonialization and colonization here in the second meaning. However, I propose an extension by referring the term not only to spaces and areas but also to living persons and their inducement. In the first case, I prefer the concept of colonialization; in the second case, that of colonization. This corresponds to a proposal by Maria do Mar Castro Varela (2015: 23), who distinguishes the terms de-colonialization and decolonization as follows:

> If de-colonialization signifies the formal independence of
> a former colonized country, the concept of decolonization
> aims at the ongoing process of liberation from a rule that
> determines thought and action.

In the first part of this chapter, I shall discuss the mental connections between the emergence of the European-bourgeois childhood pattern and the colonialization of foreign continents. I will then trace the dialectic of education or literacy and power in the colonial and postcolonial relations. In the second part, I will trace how, in the 1960s and 1970s, the discourse on the 'colonization of childhood' arose and finally was linked with postcolonial theories. Finally, I will shed light on some ambivalences of European-bourgeois childhood construction with regard to colonialization and decolonization.

Colonialization as a childhood project

An essential feature of the modern European concept of childhood is the idea of imagining the child as imperfect and in a developing stage before adulthood. This not only justifies the need for strict control and education of children, but also justifies the subjugation of the people in the European colonies. According to the literary scholar Joe-Ann Wallace, the 'idea of "the child"' was a necessary precondition of imperialism – 'that is, that the West had to invent for itself "the child" before it could think a specifically colonialist imperialism' (Wallace, 1994: 176). This connection, however, should not be understood as a one-sided causality, but as a reciprocal relationship, which has intensified over the centuries. As early as in the 'discovery' and conquest of the 'new' continent called America, since the end of the 15th century, when the new concept of childhood was still emerging in Europe, the child metaphor was used to describe the 'primitive peoples' who were perceived as 'wild' and 'uncivilized' (see Chapter 8). We can therefore assume that the ideas and mentalities that shape the conquest and the new experiences have also influenced the development of the new childhood concept.

Bill Ashcroft's *On Postcolonial Futures* (2001) is one of the few contributions of postcolonial theory that has drawn attention to these connections. According to Ashcroft (2001: 37), 'it was the cross-fertilization between the concepts of childhood and primitivism that enabled these terms to emerge as mutually important concepts in imperial discourse'. The Indian psychologist and social theorist Ashis Nandy (1983; 1987) had already previously pointed out that the new concept of childhood, which had emerged in Europe in the 17th century, was associated with the notions of primitivism. The idea of social progress had been transferred to the field of cultural differences in the colonies. Thus, for example, colonized India was located in the infancy of civilizational progress.

Ashcroft also points to the important fact that, at the time when the child emerged as a philosophical concept, 'race' as a category of physical and biological distinction was produced. 'Whereas "race" could not exist without racism, that is, the need to establish a hierarchy of difference, the idea of the child dilutes the hostility inherent in that taxonomy and offers a "natural" justification for imperial dominance over subject peoples' (Ashcroft, 2001: 37). The connection of the child with the savage goes along with the general assumption that the 'races' represent different stages of development in the 19th century. Thus, for example, the French Orientalist Ernest Renan, in his book *The Future of Science*, first published in 1848, argued that the conditions of humanity and human intelligence must be studied in the earliest stages of development. The researcher had to combine the experimental investigation of the child and the exercise of his reason with the experimental investigation of the 'savages' and therefore to deal intensively with travel reports from the newly discovered areas on earth. To him this was urgent, because he expected that the savages would quickly disappear under the influence of their civilization (Renan, 1891: 150).

The moral conflict that results from colonial conquest and occupation for the 'enlightened' Europe is subdued by its naturalization as a parent–child relationship, equated with the contradictory impulses of parents between exploitation and care. The child, at once both other and same, according to Ashcroft (2001: 36–7), 'holds in balance the contradictory tendencies of imperial rhetoric: authority is held in balance with nurture; domination with enlightenment; debasement with idealization; negation with affirmation; exploitation with education; filiation with affiliation. This ability to absorb contradiction gives the binary parent child an inordinately hegemonic potency.'

The interrelations between the new concept of childhood and the colonization of foreigners and continents were already applied in the ideas of the liberal English philosopher John Locke, and the French enlightenment protagonist Jean-Jacques Rousseau, who both influenced childhood history, albeit in various ways. In his *Essay Concerning Human Understanding*, first published in 1690, Locke conceived the child as a 'tabula rasa' or blank page (Locke, [1690]1995). Thus, he gave parents and school masters great responsibility for what is written on this blank page. At the same time, the concept was of great importance to the imperial enterprise, as the idea of an empty space was an important prerequisite for the colonization understood as civilization. While Locke imagined the newborn child as an empty space which had to be filled, Rousseau, just 100 years later, in his novel-essay *Emile, or on education* ([1762]1979), conceived the child as 'pure nature' which represents a worth as such and is ultimately digested by civilization. Following Rousseau, the parallel to colonization consists in the idea of the 'good savage'. According to Ashcroft (2001: 41),

Locke's metaphor of the child as a blank page, an unwritten book, makes the explicit connection between adulthood and print, for civilization and maturity are printed on the tablet of the child's mind. For him the child is an unformed person who, through literacy, education, reason, self-control and shame, may be made into a civilized adult. For Rousseau, the unformed child possesses capacities for candour, understanding, curiosity and spontaneity which must be preserved or rediscovered. In the tension between these two views we find encapsulated the inherent contradiction on imperial representations of the colonial subject.

Both perspectives justify the paternalistic actions of the colonial enterprise, since the innocence of nature, like the blank page of the unformed child, is equivalent to absence and exclusion. According to Uday Singh Mehta (1999: 48), exclusionary strategies involve 'civilizational infantilism'. Neither the child nor the colonial subject has access to meaning outside the processes of colonization and education.

The idea of literacy gained a similar function in the sense of acquiring the ability to read and write, even if it was imposed on an already alphabetized society.[1] It is based on the distinction between civilized and barbarian peoples and nations, and constitutes a hierarchy among them of more or less developed beings. Thus, the discrepancy between childhood and adulthood, caused by the emergence of the need to learn reading and writing, in the late Middle Ages, can be seen in the direct context of the discrepancy between the imperial centre and the unintelligible people in the colonies.

> Just as 'childhood' began in European culture with the task of learning how to read, so education and literacy become crucial in the imperial expansion of Europe, establishing ideological supremacy, inculcating the values of the colonizer, and separating the 'adult' colonizing races from the 'childish' colonized (Ashcroft, 2001: 39).

In this sense, colonialism has always been 'educational colonialism' (Osterhammel, 2005: 110), which pretended to 'free' the colonized from tyranny and spiritual darkness. The equality of the colonized with children provided an opportunity to dismiss this claim even as a moral duty and 'the white man's burden' (Kipling, 1899). 'Colonial rule was glorified as a gift and act of grace of civilization, and was respected as humanitarian intervention' (Osterhammel, 2005: 110). To this end, particularly the schools, which were either run by missions or the state, were used. They have always aimed to convey a certain kind of thought and morality that goes beyond formal reading and writing, a kind of 'moral technology' (Wells, 2009: 111), 'epistemic violence' (Spivak, 1988; Cannella and Viruru, 2004; de Sousa Santos, 2008) or 'colonization of consciousness' (Comaroff and Comaroff, 2008).

One of the most influential consequences of childhood and colonial conquest was the concept of development that emerged in the late 19th century and constituted non-European countries as permanently backward. The meanings of this term result from 'the link between primitivism and infantility and the need for "maturation" and "growth" in both' (Ashcroft, 2001: 38). The equilibrium of childhood and primitiveness was still present in the second half of the 20th century and was regarded as scientifically serious, as can be seen from a chapter on the origin of language in a linguistic textbook published in several editions since 1964:

> In so many languages, the nursery words for mother and father are mama or dada or dada or baba or something similar; there is no magic inner connection between the idea of parenthood and words of this form: these just happen to be the first articulated sounds that the child makes. ... Such words may also have been the first utterances of primitive man. ... The languages of primitive peoples, and the history of languages in literate times, may throw some light on the origin of language by suggesting what elements in it are the most archaic (Barber, 1964: 25).

The question of literacy and education has played a central role in the history of colonialism and still plays it today in the postcolonial constellation. Colonialism used the reference to the lack of education and the idea of childhood as a primitive stage of development in order 'to confirm a binarism between colonizer and colonized; a relationship which induced compliance to the cultural dominance of Europe. Colonizer and colonized were separated by literacy and education' (Ashcroft, 2001: 52). This separation was confirmed by geographic distances, sometimes also by the distinction of nationalities. The question now arises whether these so far clearly visible antitheses exist in the postcolonial present, which is characterized by extensive globalization.

On the dialectic of education and power

In the debate about colonial and postcolonial power relations, it is justified to refer to educational processes. One of the most important insights of postcolonial theory is to understand the relations between the colonizers and the colonized as dialectical (Said, 1978; Bhabha, 1994). While the colonizers themselves are influenced by the colonial relationship, the colonized people can be seen not only as uninvolved and innocent spectators. The colonized are not '"cultural dupes", incapable of interpreting, accommodating, and resisting dominant discourses' (Rizvi, 2007: 261). The same is true of current global relations, which necessarily are accompanied by negotiations on cultural messages, even when they take place in socio-geographic areas characterized by asymmetric power relations. The relationships between the global and local are always complex and ambiguous, and require an accurate ethnographical case-specific analysis.

Ashcroft believes that today 'the gap between colonizing parent and colonized child has been masked by globalization and the indiscriminate, transnational character of neo-colonialism' (Ashcroft 2001: 53). The neo-colonial subject can no longer be fixed by geographical distance and lack of literacy and education. Instead of the colonial subject being placed geographically, according to Ashcroft, the 'subject of global capitalism' (Ashcroft 2001: 53) appears as fluid. To me, this assessment seems to be overstated and inaccurate. The impression aroused by Ashcroft – the separation of colonizers and colonized would be invalidated by globalization, or would be at least no longer visible and perceptible – affects only one of its aspects, namely the unlimited movement of goods and capital. For the people themselves geographic location and politically defined national boundaries remain powerful barriers to one's own physical space of movement; moreover, the barriers become even higher. Even the seeming limitlessness of new communication media remains trapped in private ownership, which make it possible to cut off communications and make someone disappear from the 'net' or remain in it against their own will.

Nevertheless, Ashcroft's consideration that the colonial conquest and domination, legitimized by the childhood metaphor, implies ambivalences and contradictions. The literacy introduced to uphold the up and down is no longer limited to reading and writing, but includes versatile forms of communication that are no longer bound to scriptures. Among the researchers dealing with literacy, especially in so-called development programmes, not only is the limitation of the view on the ability to read and write criticized, but there is also

40

awareness that each form of communication must be considered in the context of the power relations contained therein. They point out that communication and education processes can never be understood merely as technical processes but always include a certain kind of knowledge while excluding other kinds of knowledge. According to Street (2001: 7), 'in developing contexts the issue of literacy is often represented as simply a technical one: that people need to be taught how to decode letters and they can do what they like with their newly acquired literacy after that'. This approach is criticized by Street, who argues that it ignores or conceals the fact that literacy and education can never be neutral or universal. In practice, it goes beyond imposing and over-contributing Western concepts of education to other cultures. Instead, he favours a model that offers a more culture-sensible view of educational practice and recognizes that it is different depending on the context. The model is characterized by the fact that it considers educational processes as a 'social practice', which is

> ... always embedded in socially constructed epistemological principles. It is about knowledge: the ways in which people address reading and writing are themselves rooted in conceptions of knowledge, identity, being. Literacy in this sense is always contested, both in meaning and its practices, hence particular versions of it are always 'ideological', they are always rooted in a particular world-view and a desire for that view of literacy to dominate and to marginalize others. (Street, 2001: 7–8)

Street's model claims not only cultural differences, but also 'the power dimension of these reading and writing processes' (Street, 2001: 9). When the effect is examined, it should be noted that this is always 'part of a power relationship' (Street, 2001: 9).

Another author (Rogers, 2001) notes that literacy in the context of the development of societies can be understood in two ways. On the one hand, education is regarded as a causal condition or a key element for any kind of development ('literacy-leads-to-development equation'), which is typical of educational programmes of the World Bank. On the other hand, education can be seen as a way to promote social transformation or social change, for example in the sense of liberation, for which the so-called *Educación Popular* may serve as an example (see Freire, [1968]2000). In this respect, dominant and non-dominant educational processes should be distinguished. In the interrelations between the various educational contexts, the question arises which is the upper hand, an education that humiliates human beings to 'human capital' and alienates them from their lives, or a formation aimed at the elimination of inequality and oppression which provides tools to people to resist any form of degradation. This also raises questions about how education is institutionalized and who ultimately determines it.

The same is true for the image of the child, which in the colonial relationship was used to legitimize paternalism and the denial of independence. Ashcroft sees the 'allegory of the child' as a 'counter-discourse' of the age because the child is so strongly 'constructed as the ambivalent trope of the colonized' (Ashcroft, 2001: 53): 'The child, invented by imperialism to represent the colonized subject amenable to education and improvement, becomes the allegorical subject of a different trajectory, a site of difference and anti-colonial possibility' (Ashcroft, 2001: 53).

As tempting and promising as this sounds, it must be asked whether a metaphorical view of the child is overstrained. Since being a child always means having a future, the image of the child can become a personification of a better future and gain a mobilizing meaning. This is expressed, for example, in the speech of the 'young nations' emancipated from the colonial rule. In this speech there is still an ambivalence inherited from colonialism, which varies between new beginnings and immaturity. Furthermore, the question arises whether the hopeful metaphorical speech of the child also corresponds to *real* children who do not find themselves in the colonial childhood picture, but represent a new kind of childhood, which also holds its mirror up to postcolonial societies and urges the breaking up the colonial eggshells.[2]

A look at the history of decolonization shows that young people, which we would call children today, have always played a driving role in liberation movements. This can be observed, for instance, from the anticolonial liberation struggles in Latin America at the beginning of the 19th century to the Intifadas in Palestine, or the struggle against apartheid in South Africa at the end of the 20th century. Even today, in the Southern world regions young people are the main players of social movements that push to continue the process of decolonization. They are facing missing life perspectives against corrupt power elites stuck to their chairs, yet also take their lives in their own hands on the path of collective self-help and by producing solidarity forms of subsistence.

In contrast to earlier child and youth movements, these movements are characterized by the fact that they do not turn away from society and are set up in a deprived world of children and adolescents, and they understand themselves as a decisive part of society, which can be transformed in their interest. They represent configurations of childhood (and youth) that go beyond the European-bourgeois pattern of a 'not yet' life phase, and engage in equal participation in all areas and questions relevant to them (see Casas, 1998). For these children and young people, education means more than preparing for predefined functions. They access and make use of the information (including the digital media) accessible to them, as well as the educational elements that are derived from their daily experiences (to which the school belongs today) and mix in their own responses to the problems they face.

Colonization of childhoods

The instrumentalization of the bourgeois concept of childhood for the justification of colonial conquest finds a remarkable correspondence in the consideration of childhood as a colony or as colonized object. Since the 1960s, the concept of colonialization or colonization in a broader sense has referred not only to geographic areas outside Europe and their populations, but also to the internal structure of societies and their people. In the early 1980s, for example, the philosopher Jürgen Habermas introduced the concept of the 'internal colonialization' of the lifeworld (Habermas, [1981]1985: 356). He assumed that, in the late phase of capitalism, the central subsystems economy and the state interpenetrate the 'lifeworld', understood as the independent existence of the members of a society, as 'colonial masters coming into a tribal society' (Habermas, [1981]1985: 355) and seize this life.[3] Thus, he saw the socializing and identity-building functions of the lifeworld in danger. The philosopher Friedrich Tomberg (2003: 315) summarizes the reflections of Habermas as following:

> The term 'colonization' is intended to make it clear that society, as a whole is not a system to which the lifeworld belongs as a sub-area, so that individuals who want to live in this society would be compelled to adapt themselves to the system. … The lifeworld should rather be viewed as an area, which is not under the rule of the system. In its core area the system is not to have anything to look for. However, if it prevails there, the existing society does not realize itself, but there is certainly an occupation by strangers, as if economically leading states, as in the past

centuries, subdue the population of foreign countries by setting up colonies.

The sociologist Stefan Sacchi (1994: 327) interprets the 'social pathology' (Habermas) expressed in the category of colonization of the lifeworld in terms of the political economy:

> Colonization is based on the economic and political subsystem, and is carried out through its specific subsystem media 'money' and 'power'. From the perspective of the lifeworld, the colonization in the case of the economic subsystem is expressed in a subterfuge of ever more social areas under market laws, in the replacement of communicative relations by commodity relations. The interventions of the political system, on the other hand, show themselves above all in a legalization of social relations, as well as their substitution by means of bureaucratically organized, standardized actions.

Here is not the place to discuss the theoretical foundations and basic assumptions of Habermas' time diagnosis and the conclusions drawn from them.[4] It is only a matter of making it clear that in a certain historical period the concept of colonialization or colonization has been extended and applied to new social phenomena. This is also true of the feminist debate on women as a 'last colony', which came up a little later. In a publication that was first published in 1983 and re-published five years later, Claudia von Werlhof, Maria Mies and Veronika Bennholdt-Thomsen (1988) identified the women and the colonized people of the 'Third World' as the last resource to be exploited. They were concerned,

> ... to demonstrate that the subordination and exploitation of women is the foundation and the keystone of all further exploitation conditions, and that the colonization of the world, the plundering of nature, territories and people, as above all capitalism needs as a prerequisite, happens according to this model (von Werlhof et al, 1988: IX).

Similar thoughts were already formulated by the US-American feminist Shulamith Firestone in the early 1970s and transferred from women to children (Firestone, 1970). In this text, the author points to a parallel between the 'myth of childhood' and the 'myth of femininity' (Firestone, 1970: 88–9):

Both women and children were considered asexual and 'purer' than man. Their inferior status was ill-concealed under an elaborate 'respect'. One didn't discuss serious matters nor did one curse in front of women and children; one didn't *openly* degrade them, one did it behind their backs. ... Both were set apart by fancy, and non-functional clothing and were given special tasks (housework and homework respectively); both were considered mentally deficient ("What can one expect from a woman?" – "He's too little to understand."). The pedestal of adoration on which both were set made it hard for them to breathe. Every interaction with the adult world became a tap dance for children. They learned how to use their childhood to get what they wanted indirectly ("He's throwing another tantrum!"), just as women learned how to use their femininity ("There she goes, crying again!"). All excursions into the adult world became terrifying survival expeditions. The difference between the natural behavior of children in their peer group as opposed to their stilted and/or coy behavior with adults bears this out – just as women act differently among themselves than when they are around men. In each case a physical difference had been enlarged culturally with the help of special dress, education, manners, and activity until this cultural reinforcement itself began to appear 'natural', even instinctive, an exaggeration process that enables easy stereotyping: The individual eventually appears to be a different kind of human animal with its own peculiar set of laws and behavior ("I'll never understand women!" ... "You don't know a thing about child psychology!").

Firestone speaks in the past in order to underline the historical genesis of the 'class oppression of women and children' (Firestone, 1970: 89). The text leaves no doubt that she was convinced that it applied to the time in which she wrote it (the readers may judge for themselves whether it has changed significantly to this day).

Firestone's interpretations are unmistakably influenced by the writings of Philippe Ariès on the history of childhood, first published in French and English in the early 1960s (Ariès, 1960, 1962). It would, however, be too easy to trace the work of Firestone and other childhood studies that had arisen during these years back only to the influence of a book. It is to be assumed that their works were also brought about by the new social movements, which had been taking place in the US and other parts of the world since the 1960s. Above all, the movement of civil rights against the racist oppression of the African American population and the movement towards the oppression of other minorities, as well as the movement against the Vietnam War and the closely linked youth movements, which were directed against authoritarian exhortation and structures in schools, universities and other social spheres. Another of the writings, which demanded equal rights for children, expressly speaks of these as the 'last minority', whose emancipation is still outstanding (Farson, 1974).

Some of the writings written during this period understand the suppression of the children as a form of colonization and relate it to colonialism. In an essay first published in French in 1971, Swiss anthropologist and psychoanalyst Gérard Mendel claimed (Mendel, 1971: 7):

> All forms of human exploitation, whether religious or economic in nature – exploitation of colonial peoples, of women, of children – have taken advantage of the phenomenon rooted in the dependent, biological and psychological relationship of infant child to adult. Hence, the destruction of our society, which occurs before our eyes, day by day in a chain of cultural Hiroshimas, goes much deeper than it appears and incorporates various aspects of all societies worldwide.

In the German-speaking world, the writings of the Austrian education scientist Peter Gstettner are particularly worth mentioning; they bear the title *Die Eroberung des Kindes durch die Wissenschaft. Aus der Geschichte der Disziplinierung* ('The conquest of the child by science: From the history of discipline'; Gstettner, 1981). In this nearly forgotten text, Gstettner makes reference to the history of colonialism, and, exemplified in the newly emerging pedagogical and psychological sciences on childhood, he demonstrates a close connection to the ethnology and anthropology arising from colonization. The thesis of his work claims 'that the academic conquest of unknown territories precedes the conquest of the childish soul' (Gstettner, 1981: 15). He demonstrates this especially with the history of developmental psychology, but also in the conceptualization of childhood (and youth) in the corresponding scholarship as a whole (Gstettner, 1981: 8 and 85):

> All dominant models of human 'development' today include territorial associations: populations and individual

people alike are thought of in terms of political regions, as territories to be conquered, occupied, researched and proselytized. Thus, having a look at anthropology, called previously '*Völkerkunde*', can inform us as to why academics consider 'savages' to be primitive, 'primitives' to be naïve, the 'naïve' to be childish, and children, to be naïve, primitive and savage. … From the outset, childhood and youth studies have focused their research interest on the idea that it must be possible to analytically grasp lost 'naturalness' and, in a scholarly manor, to reconstruct it as the 'natural state' of the child (as well as the 'savage'). That's why educational child and youth psychology is connected in a causal relationship with anthropological fields of research, which, despite their different 'research subjects', exhibit the same analytical interests – namely to separate the influences of civilization and culture from inherited predispositions; to separate 'developed' from 'undeveloped'.

At the time that Gérard Mendel and Peter Gstettner formulated their scholarly ideas about the colonization and conquest of children, they could not yet refer to postcolonial theories, as they only emerged in the following years. Thus, they can be credited even more so for drawing parallels and bringing attention to the relationship between colonization and the ideologies stemming from the emerging sciences on childhood.[5]

Twenty years later, similar reflections were also found in a study by the two US-American early childhood educationalists, Gaile Cannella and Radhika Viruru (2004), who have so far received little attention in the field of childhood research. The authors do not limit themselves to challenging childhood studies, but they also make an effort to transfer fundamental ideas from postcolonial studies to childhood studies.

The starting point of Cannella and Viruru's ideas is that, from a postcolonial perspective, Western dominated models of childhood reproduce hierarchies and separations, for which European enlightenment and modernization and the accompanying demand for universality can be blamed. These models of childhood, they claim, are the concurrent product of the same ideologies, which have served as justification for colonial expansion and conquest. This can especially be seen in the parallel application of the idea of the development from a lower to a higher grade of perfection. Childhood, like non-European geographical regions and populations, is classified at the lowest rung of the scale, and colonized people are equated with children, both of whom have yet to be developed. Colonization, they go so far as to say, was even executed in the name of children, whose souls were seen in need of saving and whose parents had the obligation to raise them 'correctly', in terms of modern conceptions of childhood (Cannella and Viruru, 2004: 4).

Similar to the relationship between colonial rulers and the colonized, according to Cannella and Viruru, a strict separation between adults and children is established, and the relationship between both becomes institutionalized as a power structure, based on the force and privilege of the stronger party. This is already expressed, in that the term *child* is associated with a state of incompletion, dependence and subordination, thus means 'a kind of epistemic violence that limits human possibilities' (Cannella and Viruru, 2004: 2). This power structure can also be understood, in that the ability to speak (in the widely recognized form of 'speech') and read written texts are the only form of communications recognized, and in which important ideas can be expressed. Based on their experiences with very young, 'speechless' children, Cannella and Viruru at least attempt, 'a glimpse of the possibilities that the unspoken might offer, that the previously unthought might generate' (Cannella and Viruru, 2004: 8).[6] Their (and others') interest is quintessentially the question: 'What gives some people the right to determine *who* other people are (determinations like the fundamental nature of childhood) and to decide what is right for others?' (Cannella and Viruru, 2004: 7; italics in original).

Modern childhood, seen as separate and opposite from adulthood and which in its institutionalized form isolates children into special reserves, is identified by the authors as a 'colonizing construct' (Cannella and Viruru, 2004: 85). Thereby, 'binary thinking', a pioneering concept of modernity, is reproduced, which can only distinguish between good and evil, superior and inferior, right and wrong, or civilized and savage (Cannella and Viruru, 2004: 88). This division puts adults in a privileged position, since their knowledge is considered superior to that of the child; children may even be denied knowledge under the pretence of protection. This child–adult dichotomy prolongs colonial power, as it is transferred to an entire population group, which is in turn labelled as deficient, needy, slow, lazy or underdeveloped (Cannella and Viruru, 2004: 89). The categories of progress and development, the authors argue, devalue certain population groups, and secure one's own superiority over people from other cultures. The idea of 'childish development' is transferred to adults of other cultures, thereby arguably 'infantilizing' them.

Like colonized people worldwide, children are obliged to see themselves with the eyes of those who have control over them, and they are not allowed to reject the hierarchies of surveillance, of judgement, nor of intervention in their lives. Even at a time when discussions about children's rights are becoming more commonplace, this hierarchical relationship is rarely questioned. Cannella and Viruru argue that the subordination of children remains so steadfast because it is substantiated and objectified by 'the scientific construction of the adult/child dichotomy' (Cannella and Viruru, 2004: 109).

Steps towards the decolonization of childhoods

The thesis of the colonization of childhood has occasionally been called into question because it was precisely in the bourgeois concept of childhood coming up with the Enlightenment that not only the mastery of the children was foreseen by means of disciplinary techniques, but also their autonomy had been sought. For instance, the educationalist Gerold Scholz (1994) argues against Gstettner's view that the discipline of children has been unstoppable since the beginnings of childhood science, with the thesis that 'with the emergence of developmental psychology, also the thought of the child's autonomy arose' (Scholz, 1994: 206). It could not have been a coincidence that at the beginning of the 20th century the 'century of the child'[7] was proclaimed. There must be a relationship between the child's conquest of science and the child's autonomy. This assuming relation compels Scholz in the thesis (Scholz, 1994: 203)

> ... that the childhood constructions are destined from the attempt to remove the contradictions which the distinction between 'child' and 'adult' has brought with. On the basis of this distinction, the adult and the child share a space, and since then the child has called the adult to behave in a manner that takes into account the ambivalence of the child's difference and similarity.

The autonomy mentioned by Scholz has always been imagined in bourgeois childhood construction as a form of education, which is to be generated by education; it was conceived as a task and obligation for adults. It was based not only on the idea that bourgeois society and the labour relations between capitalists and 'free' wage-workers had required a certain degree of individual self-responsibility, but also that it should be granted to children so that the desired norm-adequate behaviour can be produced more effectively and more sustainably. The autonomy granted was always related to this purpose, aiming at self-control and self-discipline (see Elias, 2000; Foucault, [1969]2002). In reform pedagogy, which was conceived as enlightened and directed against the superficial discipline of children, especially in schools, it was called on to respect the 'nature of the child'. But this nature was always regarded as a first to be worked on and developed. In addition, it should be borne in mind that the children of the dominated classes have long been excluded from the bourgeois childhood ideals and left to the mere drill of 'black pedagogy'.[8] That this drift was gradually loosened was itself due to the fact that the new prosperity, which also spread to the subalterns, was largely based on the persistent exploitation of the colonies and is now based on the continuing inequality in the world order. Apart from the exception of the children in privileged classes, in the education institutions of the Global South, the children have had little autonomy.

The construction of a childhood that is strictly differentiated and separated from the adult is necessarily connected with ambivalence. Even though it is intended to provide the children with their 'own space' and to temporarily relieve them of the 'seriousness of life' or to provide them with special protection, it inevitably goes hand in hand with the devaluation of their competencies and their social status. Under these circumstances, the 'privilege' of being spared and protected is at the expense of independence, and the recognition of the peculiarity or difference takes place in inequality. This is shown by the fact that children may sometimes be happy to be overwhelmed by commitments, but they sooner or later perceive childhood as a form of contempt and do not want to be considered as 'children' anymore.[9]

Certainly, human life (as well as animal and plant life) has a beginning and an end, and every society has to find a way how to structure the life course and how to organize the relationship between people of different ages. Nevertheless, the form that has been 'invented' in Western-bourgeois society and which has produced what is now called 'childhood' is not the only possible one. It would also be conceivable and can be found in many non-Western cultures that the relationship of different age groups is not institutionalized and legally regulated as a strict distinction or even as a separation, but as a shared coexistence, which includes different kinds of (co-)responsibility. This also means that people do not have to be distinguished, as is customary in Western societies, primarily according to chronological age, but to tasks, which are more or less vital. The abilities required for this can be distributed very differently and not necessarily lower in younger people than in older adults. Furthermore, it is to be remembered that – according to the saying that each one grows with one's tasks – abilities that are required for such tasks are not given, but rather arise as these tasks are trusted and entrusted to a person.

The strict separation of childhood from adulthood in bourgeois society has to do with the fact that the production and reproduction of life in this society is carried out in forms that make the continuous unfolding of one's own abilities almost impossible. The notion of the 'seriousness of life' is characterized by the fact that it is localized in the 'world of work', which in its turn is separated from the rest of life and follows rules which are not based on human needs, but on the exploitation of human labour power and the maximization of profits. This circumstance makes it difficult to imagine the world of work as a place where children can also have their place and test their abilities. It suggests that childhood should be nailed in places where no important activities are to be done, and where it is only important to 'be prepared'. Thus, children are condemned to a life characterized by lack of independence and passivity or at best by a previously limited and determined autonomy or participation. However, these separations are also questioned in bourgeois-capitalist societies, and there is an increasing search for possible ways of combining abstract learning in educational institutions with life-related or life-relevant tasks. This would be an opportunity to learn from the way children's lives are shaped in some non-Western cultures, rather than to continue setting the childhood pattern as an absolute must and to impose it on the cultures and societies in the Global South.

At the same time, it must be borne in mind that life in such cultures and societies is affected by the postcolonial constellation. This constellation means that not only are the childhoods found here underestimated and made invisible, but they also are damaged and impaired in a very material sense. In order to put an end to the colonization of childhood, which can also be described as postcolonial paternalism, it is particularly urgent to push the decolonization of postcolonial societies further.

Notes

[1] The concept of literacy also includes the ability to communicate as well as the appropriation of ways of thinking and value beyond its written form. To emphasize this is particularly important in the age of digital media.

[2] Erica Burman (2016) has identified metaphorical as well as empirical references to children and childhood in the writings of Frantz Fanon, which were so important for the anticolonial movements, and analyzed them under liberationist pedagogical aspects (see also Dei and Simmons, 2010).

[3] Without using the term 'colonialization', Habermas had formulated this basic idea almost ten years earlier in his work on legitimation problems in late capitalism

(Habermas, [1973]1976). Although Habermas speaks of colonialization, the concept of colonization is most often used in the reception of his works.

4   In the 1980s, in Germany, the theses of Habermas were also taken up in social pedagogy and social work in order to question their legitimizing role. For example, an expert conference focused on the question of 'understanding or colonizing?' (Müller and Otto, 1984). It was also an occasion for the reflection of professional ethics in social pedagogy (Martin, 2001).

5   It should also be pointed out that French sociologist and educationalist Émile Durkheim, one of the fathers of positivist sociology, saw in children 'primitives' and 'savages' who endanger the social order of modern society. They must therefore be educated strictly 'morally' from an early age, especially through school (Durkheim, 1934). With regard to children, the influential US-American sociologist Talcott Parsons spoke of an imminent 'invasion of the barbarians' (Parsons, 1951).

6   Here, it should be remembered that Jean-Jacques Rousseau ([1762]1979), who is considered to be the father of the modern conception of childhood, referred to the alleged speechless utterances of children as a 'universal language', which all children are capable of understanding.

7   Here, Scholz refers to the book of the Swedish women and children's rights activist Ellen Key, which was first published in 1900 and later published in many languages (Key, 1909).

8   The uncritical notion of the 'evil black man', which has been reproduced and reproduced in many popular texts – such as the song of the *Ten Little Negroes* – resonates with this critically-intended designation.

9   This is also reflected in the refusal of many young people who, according to the legal definition of the UNCRC, are still regarded as children until the age of 18 to consider the 'children's rights' relevant to themselves.

3

Postcolonial theories from the Global South

The peculiar object of postcolonial studies is not a natural entity, like an elephant, or even a social subject regarded as sharing the cultural world of the observer, but one formed as a colonial object, an inferior and alien 'Other' to be studied by a superior and central 'Self'. Since the 'elephant' can speak, the problem is not just to represent it but to create conditions that would enable it to represent itself. (Fernando Coronil, 'Elephants in the Americas? Latin American Postcolonial Studies and Global Decolonization', 2008: 413)

Introduction

In order to gain an idea of 'postcolonial childhoods', it is commonplace to resort to thought currents, studies and theories, which, after the end of the colonial rule, deal with its aftermath and the continuing forms of dependence and oppression, and claim alternatives from the perspective of colonial and postcolonial subjects. They are known by multiple names: Subaltern Studies, Postcolonial Studies, Philosophy of Liberation, Ethnophilosophy, Sage Philosophy, Coloniality of Power, Coloniality of Knowledge, De-Coloniality/Decolonization, Epistemology of the South, Southern Theory or Ubuntu, and shall be subsumed here under the term postcolonial theory. Until now, these theories have not extensively taken children and childhoods into consideration. Nevertheless, they can be used and are taken up in this book in order to better understand children in their respective living contexts and their potentials for action, and to place childhoods more precisely in their historical and geopolitical contexts. In this chapter, I will first outline the basic ideas of postcolonial theory and then present some of the most important contributions from Africa and Latin America.

Basic ideas of postcolonial theory

The term *postcolonial* refers to present geopolitical constellations in which former colonies existed and to former colonial states themselves. It even has relevance for states that were never directly involved in colonialism, yet are influenced by the effects of colonial thought and imagination. The cultural theorist Stuart Hall (1992), from the Caribbean, proposes a two dimensional understanding of the term postcolonial. The first, temporary dimension means the time after the formation of the nation states from the colonies, which could thus be regarded as overcoming enduring state of affairs. The second dimension is the critique of a theoretical system, which can also persist in nation states. It is important to note that 'there are long-term effects of colonialism, which still have an effect today, and which must be addressed if one wants to understand the postcolonial present and its corresponding problems' (Kerner, 2012: 9). These problems include poverty and authoritarianism, as well as Eurocentric and racist mentalities, which are found in various facets of politics and society – in the Global South as well as in the Global North.

Aside from rather minor differences in detail, the binding factor of various postcolonial ideas and theories is that they all question the supposed superiority and exemplary character of 'Western' development concepts and strategies. They bring attention to the fact that the supposed achievements of the European modern age are the result of conquest, oppression and exploitation, which have been accompanied by racist devaluation and discrimination of people from different geographical parts of the world (and a different skin colour), which proceed in postcolonial constellations.[1] The widespread claim that the emergence and development of modernity was an autonomous European endeavour is firmly scrutinized.[2] With this in mind, the view stemming from modernization theory, purporting that non-Western societies represent merely the prehistory of Western modernity – and the West represents the model for the development of 'traditional' societies – is also questioned.[3]

The critique on this understanding of modernity relates particularly to the idea that its underlying rationality, and the claim to 'truth' which follows, is somehow the only possible way that human life can proceed and improve. The critique is made that this way of seeing the world – and categorizing societies and modes of life as developed or underdeveloped – is based on abstract distinctions and hierarchies, like the distinction between body and soul, emotion and rationality, or nature and culture (see Prout, 2005: 83–111). Ecuadorian economist

Alberto Acosta (2013: 38) speaks to one of the most momentous distinctions, when he writes:

> Europe consolidated a vision in order to make its aspiration for expansion possible, which, metaphorically speaking, divorced humankind from nature. Without taking humans into account, nature was defined as a fixed component of this vision, and the fact that humans are an integral part of nature was ignored. Hence, the path was opened to controlling, exploiting and manipulation of nature.

It also opened the path for the occupation and exploitation of world regions, which were considered 'bare nature', their members classified as 'wild', often not even recognized as human beings. Today, this exploitation continues in an unequal world order, where, although former colonies have become formally independent states, their dependence has simply taken on new, less obvious forms, or the (usually 'white') former colonial elites continue to oppress and discriminate against the population.[4] Since the mid-20th century the magic word *development* has maintained this status.

Postcolonial approaches oppose persisting worldwide asymmetrical power structures. They are concerned, on the one hand, with material aspects and, on the other, with mental aspects, without completely isolating one from the other. The material aspects focus on unequal economic and political relationships, and how these affect the lives of people in the Global South. The mental aspects can be seen through the dominance of particular ways of thinking and forms of knowledge, which minimize or outshine the already existing wealth of knowledge in the Global South in a form of 'epistemic violence' (Spivak, 1988; de Sousa Santos, 2008; Grosfoguel, 2007b). In other words, postcolonial approaches claim to point out independent and adamant alternatives with respect to knowledge and practical life, based on the recollection of colonialism and the experiences of postcolonial subjects. These suggested alternatives are not limited to the revitalization of cultural traditions, nor the evocation of alleged origins. Rather, they proceed with the hope of demonstrating a 'trans-modern' and 'intercultural' perspective. This perspective attempts to reach beyond the segregating and absolutist thought pattern of Western modernity, without negating it (see Dussel, 1980). Postcolonial approaches are associated with anticolonial resistance but always emphasize 'the diversity and heterogeneity of the "we" and that of the enemy. The postcolonial analysis therefore ranges from multicentrism to the decentering of every center' (Kwan, 2014: 5). If it represents an oppositional position or desire, says Ania Loomba, 'than it has the effect of collapsing various locations so that the specificities of all of them are blurred' (Loomba, 2005: 20).

The book *Orientalism*, first published in 1978, by Palestinian literary scholar Edward W. Said (1978, 1985) is considered one of the fundamental works of postcolonial theory.[5] In the text, Said explains how, through the creation of an entire academic discipline called Orientalism, Europeans create a world of the 'Other'; this 'Orient' becomes the projection screen for the West's own fears, desires, and feelings of superiority. This generated image has little to do with the real-life worlds of the people living in this region; however, it served European colonial powers well, and today provides the US 'imperium' with a means to validate its own superiority and legitimize continued political and military interventions. '*Othering*' is a postcolonial concept introduced by Said, which gained meaning in this context. It implies that people and ways of life which appear to be different to the 'normal', prevailing lifestyle become exoticized and are thereby ostracized. They are made the object of measures seeking normalization and control.[6]

As a follow-up to Edward Said's Orientalism critique, the literary scholar Walter Mignolo, born in Argentina, introduced the term 'postoccidentalism' from the South American perspective, which refers to the fact that the Spanish Kingdom once named its 'American' colonies *Indias Occidentales* (Mignolo, 2000; 2005). In a project that Mignolo calls 'de-colonial', an effort is made to break down discursive forms of postcolonial dependence. Hegemonic, Eurocentric and modernist thought patterns are to be replaced using a critical approach, which takes 'colonial wounds' (for example, the manifold, harmful and destructive effects of colonialism) seriously and, from there, imagines a different, horizontal and diverse world, or 'pluriversum' instead of the Western dominated 'universum'. In the words of the Colombian anthropologist Arturo Escobar (2018: 29): 'a vision of a world where many worlds fit in'.

Yet, in what way are such critical approaches expressed in the form of postcolonial theories connected to social movements, and how can they become a force for movement and change? With her famous question, '*Can the subaltern speak?*', which she formulated as early as the 1980s, Indian literary scholar Gayatri Spivak appealed against the widespread assumption that the living situation and thoughts of postcolonial subjects were brought to light by simply 'giving them a voice' or speaking in their name – as their intellectual or modern advocates (Spivak, 1988).[7] In doing so, her aim was not to doubt that these subjects could express themselves. Rather, she wanted to underline that for the subaltern, as result of being subject to existing power structures and 'epistemic violence', it is not readily possible to make heterogeneous concerns visible or heard. Under the given circumstances, Spivak argues, the subaltern cannot succeed in being heard, nor can they exercise influence as complex people (see also Spivak, 1990; 1999; 2004; Morris, 2010; Smith, 2010).

The problem of the internalization of power structures by the repressed subjects themselves had already been mentioned at the beginning of the 20th century by Afro-American writer and sociologist, W.E.B. Du Bois ([1903]1996). In his work, he referred to the lasting effects of racism in the USA following the abolition of slavery. To illustrate the exclusion of black people from the world of white people, Du Bois imagined a picture of an 'enormous veil', which black people were not permitted to step in front of. He considered the formation of a 'double consciousness', the feeling of, 'only ever seeing oneself through the eyes of others, of measuring one's own soul on a world-scale, left merely with mockery and pity' (DuBois [1903]1996: 194; see Morris, 2015).

A half-century later, Frantz Fanon, a medical practitioner from Martinique, who was active in the 1950s and 1960s in the Algerian struggle for liberation, described quite similarly the mental effects of everyday racism. In his first book, *Black Skins, White Masks* ([1952]1986) first published in 1952, he investigated daily life in the French-Caribbean colonies and the living conditions of black immigrants in France.[8] He characterized the basic situation of black people in the French colonial world as alienated, as blacks being trapped in their own blackness. This became a noteworthy issue, as whites generally saw themselves as superior to blacks and thus based all their interactions and aspirations on this idea. This, in turn, led to the internalization of one's own inferiority. The associated 'division' of consciousness resulted in blacks constantly fighting against their own image and behaving differently towards white people than towards other black people. Based on his own experiences, Fanon spoke of one's self-representation as an object, the feeling of defencelessness and frustration, the feeling of being dissected and fixated, walled-in and loathed. This led to feelings of shame and self-contempt. Blacks and whites alike could only work against this alienation by refusing to allow themselves to be locked in the 'substantialized tower of the past'.

Although Fanon's diagnosis was related to colonial contexts, it nevertheless proved to be relevant for addressing postcolonial self-images and relationships and it has been referred to time and again, for example in Paul Gilroy's equally influential text, *The Black Atlantic* (1993). Gilroy sees the image of the Black Atlantic, which he uses to symbolize the transatlantic slave trade and its aftermath, as characterized by moments of movement, resettlement, repression and helplessness. Accordingly, he characterizes the identities that arise in this environment as fluid and in movement, as opposed to fixed and rigid – called by him *routes*, rather than *roots*. A widespread topos in postcolonial thoughts includes such a rejection of closed, rigid concepts of personal and collective identities that emphasize blending and cultural impurity. Feelings of inner-conflict and alienation, which play an important role in DuBois' and Fanon's works, become, at times, secondary to the emphasis on the potential of cultural hybridization. This is especially true for the works of Indian literary scholar Homi K. Bhabha.

In his book *The Location of Culture*, first published in 1994, Bhabha argues against understanding culture as a unified entity, and therefore cultural borders as something pre-existing or given. Instead, he sees in them fields for negotiating differences. In the act of interpretive appropriation, he claims, displacements and, thus, ambivalences are produced. Bhabha speaks of an 'intervention of the Third Space of enunciation, which makes the structure of meaning and reference an ambivalent process, destroys this mirror of representation in which cultural knowledge is customarily revealed as an integrated, open, expanding code' (Bhabha, 1994: 37). Here, he sees the formation of a new type of '*inter*national culture, based not on the exoticism of multiculturalism or the *diversity* of cultures, but on the inscription and articulation of culture's *hybridity*' (Bhabha, 1994: 38; italics in original). He understands hybridity as an unintended consequence of colonial power, which yields capacity for action and the potential for subversion. Thus, 'the display of hybridity – its peculiar "replication" – terrorizes authority with the *ruse* of recognition, its mimicry, its mockery' (Bhabha, 1994: 115; italics in original). Bhabha's understanding of hybridity is not simply to be understood in terms of cultural intermixture. Rather, he explicitly refers to a hierarchical and asymmetrical power constellation. Nevertheless, how far Bhabha's invoked practices of mimicry and hybridity can succeed in damaging or even overriding postcolonial power constellations? Bhabha is criticized, justifiably so, for a limited understanding of cultural artefacts in terms of human relationships, leaving out the material and structural aspects of postcolonial inequality and class-related power relations, like anticolonial resistance, which is articulated time and again through uprisings and liberation movements (see, for example, Parry, 2004).[9]

In the following sections of this chapter, I will look specifically at Africa and Latin America, and will appreciate some of the contributions to postcolonial theory that have arisen in these continents.

African contributions to postcolonial theory

As in other regions of the Global South, there have also been several strands of thought in Africa that deal with colonialism, its aftermath and today's postcolonial constellation. They usually reflect the specific situation on this continent, but also have numerous links to the debates on the aftermath of slavery and its overcoming in the Caribbean and the United States. This connection has prompted the Cameroonian philosopher Emmanuel Chukwudi Eze (1997a) to draw attention to the early interactions and to point out that postcolonial African philosophy is not confined to those authors who are at home in Africa.[10]

A striking example of the period between the Second World War and the beginning of decolonization in the 1950s is the intellectual exchange between the poets and philosophers Aimé Césaire, who came from the Caribbean, and Léopold Senghor, who led Senegal into independence and in 1960 became its first president. To both of them the anticolonial current of the *Négritude*, which was first understood as a cultural-political response to racism in the metropolis of Paris and the French colonies (Senghor, 1964; Césaire [1950]2000), has a long history. According to them, the blacks are distinguished by their integrative spiritual qualities, which were opposed to the rational features of Western populations, and were regarded as equal or superior. The representatives of the Négritude confronted the Eurocentric legitimations of white domination with the violent and destructive regime of their actual practice. Senghor, in particular, emphasized the practice of Africa's own cultures with its firm social network and the communitarian way of life and production as sources of its own strength. This still happened in an idealizing and homogenizing manner. Instead of referring to Greek antiquity as in the case of Western philosophy, the representatives of the Négritude purposefully went back to African knowledge archives, especially the high civilization of Egypt, as well as the legends, myths and proverbs of African peoples.[11] The movement of the Négritude, which had its place in the French colonies, corresponded to the so-called Pan-Africanism in the British colonies (see Geiss, 1974).

Another early example, drawn directly from African archives of knowledge, is the *Ubuntu's* current of thought, which is prevalent mainly in southern Africa (see Ndaba, 1994; Gade, 2011; Kuwali, 2014). It was a spiritual source of the struggle against apartheid in South Africa and was incorporated into the transitional constitution of South Africa after apartheid had been ended. Ubuntu can be interpreted similarly to the Négritude in response to the dehumanizing experiences during the colonial period. According to Ubuntu, humanity is a quality that manifests itself in virtues such as hospitality, care, respect and community orientation. In addition, according to Ubuntu, people are not only linked to each other, but also to non-human beings. It requires the help of the ancestors to restore a lost balance in the world of being, in order to achieve justice, understood as harmony and order. At the centre of the thought current of Ubuntu there is a social practice oriented towards community and harmony, as such it can also be understood as communitarian ethics (see Metz, 2007).

Négritude and Ubuntu are different parts of thought currents that the Kenyan philosopher Henry Odera Oruka (1981; 1988; 1990) critically called *ethnophilosophy*. Though he saw in ethnophilosophy an attempt to oppose the racist stereotypes by the ethnographic reconstruction of traditional belief systems and forms of culture and to offer them a positive alternative, it seemed to him as a naïve escape into an idealized precolonial past. He regarded the idea of closed African thought systems, their communality and their radical demarcation from Western rational thought as the mirror image of a racist-colonial tradition. On Négritude, and ethnophilosophy in general, Odera Oruka criticizes the fact that the people living in Africa supposedly attribute homogeneous African personality characteristics on a racial and tribal basis.[12] Cameroonian writer Achille Mbembe, in his work *Critique de la Raison Nègre* (Mbembe, 2013), also warns about giving the supposedly black skin the status of a biologically based fiction in the fight against the racism of whites, and takes it as the basis of a specific kind of African reason.

In an earlier piece, which is now seen as one of the classical writings of postcolonial theory, Mbembe (2001) had already intensively discussed racism as an enduring basis for postcolonial rule. Shortly afterwards, with critical reference to the French philosopher Michel Foucault ([1969]2002), he emphasized that the European project of modernity is to be seen in a constitutive context with slavery and colonization, civilization and barbarism. According to him, the counterpart to modernity is the lack of rights of the colonized, whose life in the eyes of the conquerors was nothing but a form of animal life. It was a kind of 'necropolitics' aimed at 'the generalized instrumentalization of human existence and the material destruction of human bodies and populations' (Mbembe, 2003: 14). In the postcolonial present, this constellation continues in a modified form. The postcolonial discourse in Africa – according to Mbembe in a later published book in reference to the legacy of slavery – 'arises from the darkness, from the depths of the hold in which Negro humanity has previously been confined to Western discourse' (Mbembe, 2010: 79).

It is typical for Africa that leaders of the liberation movements understood themselves also as political philosophers or writers, and that their political programmes, similar to Senghor, have been laid down in writings for the period after independence. In this context, mention may be made of Amilcar Cabral (Cape Verde), Kwame Nkrumah (Ghana), Ahmed Sékou Touré (Guinea), Julius Nyerere (Tanzania) or Nelson Mandela (South Africa). Most of them were influenced at times by Marxist ideas, but they always sought to establish a form of 'African socialism' in their own way, which takes up African traditions and connects them with forms of state and society that are understood as modern. In the Pan-African movement, with Nkrumah as main protagonist (see Nkrumah, 1964; Lundt and Marx, 2016), the national boundaries that the colonial powers had left had been struggled. Today the efforts for an African socialism have been almost entirely replaced by the orientation of the African power elites to the capitalist world market.[13]

The first anticolonial concepts and theories were passed on in various aspects by authors who were not satisfied with the revival of the precolonial past, but who also attempted to decipher the current situation in the African countries as a conglomerate of colonial and precolonial influences. After independence, postcolonial thinking in Africa developed mainly in the context of political philosophy, supported by thinkers who were temporarily employed at European or North American universities, but eventually went back to the universities of their African homelands. They represent different positions, but agree that the decolonization must include a decolonization of mentality and thought, also called 'conceptual decolonization' by the Ghanaian philosopher Kwasi Wiredu (1996). In the introduction to a critical reader on Postcolonial African Philosophy, Emmanuel Chukwudi Eze (1997b: 4) characterizes this challenge by saying:

> The simple and important factor that drives the field and the contemporary practice of African/a Philosophy has to do with the brutal encounter of the African world with European modernity – an encounter epitomized in the colonial phenomena.

Insofar as political philosophy is postcolonial, it attempts to arrive at normative positions without surrendering to Eurocentrically impregnated universalism. The Cameroonian philosopher Fabien

61

Eboussi Boulaga (2015: 121–2) emphasizes the need to deconstruct the development ideology of the West:

> We have adopted the term 'development'. If we accept this concept, we are lost. It is a substitute for other concepts such as 'civilization' and 'progress'. The underlying philosophy of 'development' is that of the superiority of modern Western civilization. Development is the successor to those ideologies that define the ultimate truth of humanity in their lifestyle – whether it be religion, culture, science or technology. As such, it also has the right, indeed the duty, to spread, if necessary by force. It is a conversion mission.[14]

Kwasi Wiredu (1996: 5) is somewhat more reserved. He distinguishes 'cultural universals' from 'cultural particulars', which can apply only within a (local-speaking) context, as they are language dependent. The task of conceptual decolonization is to examine colonial ways of thinking critically and thus to override reflexively the consequences of the mental domination of colonialism. The decolonization of thought is also the concern of some African writers, such as the Kenyan theatrical author Ngũgĩ wa Thiong'o (1986), who oppose the dominance of the colonial languages by writing their works in African languages.

Wiredu also points out that the reference to African knowledge archives, such as consented practices of political decision making, was collapsed, delegitimized or modified according to the interests of the colonizers during the colonial period. One can therefore not simply return to the 'origins'. According to him, their critical reconstruction is inherent in the potential for self-assurance and the historization of political thought. At the same time, however, they are at risk of ignoring the traditional hierarchies, exclusions and forms of oppression, and of legitimating their influence in actual African societies as an *African way of life*. Such a variant of self-assertion is often based on a dichotomy between Africa and Europe. To overcome this, the philosopher Paulin Hountondji (1994), from Benin, considers it important to distinguish between 'endogenous' and 'indigenous' knowledge. According to him, *indigenous* knowledge is, first of all, unchecked, traditional knowledge, which often contradicts the knowledge of modern sciences. As *endogenous* knowledge, on the other hand, he describes the practices, concepts and experiences that can be used to solve contemporary problems.

Most philosophers who want to postulate their thinking in the postcolonial context and contribute to conceptual decolonization assume that political decision making in African cultures has been dialogue- and consensus-oriented and that these have been asserted in the everyday practice of the people, but are in competition with imported ideas and practices of state organization.[15] It is therefore no coincidence that attempts have recently been made by African law scholars to establish a specific African legal theory that questions the legal systems imported in the colonial era and emancipates itself from them (see Onazi, 2014).

The vast majority of African thinkers who have discussed in their own writings questions of colonialism and postcolonialism are males. This is due in part to the fact that women in Africa still have fewer opportunities than those in the Global North, or they may be less interested in establishing themselves in academic institutions or expressing their thoughts in a scientific way. In the writings of female African scientists I know, the central issue is gender justice, and the postcolonial criticism is expressed above all in the struggle against so-called white feminism. The contributions of African authors (for example, Okonyo, 1976; Ogunyemi, 1985; Nzegwu, 1994; Ogundipe-Leslie, 1994; Oyèwùmi, 1997; Nnaemeka, 1998), of which some were formulated decades ago, are often based 'on a relational ontology, according to which the struggle of individual women must always be related to their community. ... This idea is partly based on the idea of the complementarity of the sexes in the sense of a cosmological equilibrium based on animism' (Dübgen and Skupien, 2015: 39). Similar beliefs also form the background of the philosophical ethics of Ubuntu.[16]

Latin American contributions to postcolonial theory

The dominance of English language literature has led to contributions of Latin American authors on questions of decolonization and, ultimately, on postcolonial theory outside the subcontinent being hardly perceived for a long time.[17] They became known outside Latin America only through their association with Latin American studies based in the US.[18] In the early 1990s, the so-called Latin American Subaltern Studies Group emerged as a critical current from Latin American studies with the participation of some Latin American authors. The self-set task was to revise Latin American studies by including a postcolonial perspective. The group was inspired by the work of the South Asian Subaltern Studies Group, which had been founded around the Indian historian Ranajit Guha in the 1970s (see Guha, 1997). The members of the group wondered how the concept of 'subalternity' could be applied to the Latin American situation (see Rodríguez, 2001). They were looking, in particular, at the subaltern resistance practices of the indigenous peoples, which had already begun immediately after the colonization of the continent had commenced in the 16th century, and has recently been revived by, among others, the neo-Zapatist movement in Mexico.

One of the members of the group was the semiotician Walter Mignolo from Argentina. He reclaimed 'local sensibilities' and described the postcolonial constellation of Latin America in paraphrasing Edward Said's critique on Orientalism as 'post-Occidentalism'. Mignolo traced the beginnings of postcolonial theory back to the Peruvian José Carlos Mariátegui (1894–1930), the Brazilian Darcy Ribeiro (1922–97) and the Cuban Roberto Fernandez Retamar (born 1930). In these authors' writings, he found critical answers to the social and scientific project of modernity linked to colonialization and imperialist globalization. He defined the fact that Latin Americans had formulated ideas for Latin Americans in Latin America, which broke through the Eurocentric thinking and language forms imported by colonialism (Mignolo, 1993, 2000). Latin American representatives of post- and decolonial theory are convinced that 'every statement is committed to its place of origin' (Costa, 2005: 283; see also Costa, 2013) and thus is always part of a 'geopolitics of knowledge' (Mignolo, 2001).[19]

Concerning the Latin American perspective, it should be kept in mind that the colonialization process initiated by European powers in this subcontinent began much earlier than in other continents of the South: the so-called discovery of America by Christopher Columbus and other emissaries of the Spanish crown since 1492.[20] Here, the postcolonial period began earlier as well; with the declarations of independence of Latin American and Caribbean republics, of which Haiti – which is often overlooked – was first as early as 1804 as the result of a slave revolt (see James, [1938]1980; Trouillot, 1995). The Uruguayan publicist Eduardo Galeano described the colonialization process and the insurrection movements impressively in many episodes within his epochal work *Open Veins of Latin America* (Galeano, 1971). Since the emerging postcolonial republics were dominated by the white descendants of the conquerors, demands for a second independence emerged in the first decades of the 19th century, which is understood as an early articulation of postcolonial critique of the internal survival of the inherited domination. Similar attempts have been made since the 1960s in the so-called liberation theology (Dussel, 2011) and popular education (Freire, [1968]2000), and are still reflected in the ever-renewed attempts to separate from the economic and political predominance of the USA and the international institutions dominated by it (International Monetary Fund, World Bank, World Trade Organization).[21]

Soon after the Latin American Subaltern Studies Group was founded in 1992 (it dissolved in the year 2000) and partly with personnel overlaps, the research project 'Modernity/Coloniality' (*modernidad/colonialidad*) was developed with the participation of humanities and social scientists from different Latin American countries. This project was inspired by the Peruvian sociologist Aníbal Quijano. Since 1998, symposia and conferences were held with varying participation, where questions of Eurocentrism and postcolonial theory were discussed. A first joint publication was issued in 2000 by the Venezuelan sociologist Edgardo Lander. It bore the title of the group: *The Coloniality of Knowledge. Eurocentrism and Social Sciences. Latin American Perspectives* (Lander, 2000). Another important publication of the group, which appeared in 2007 and provides a good overview of the discussions held up to that time, is *The Decolonial Turn. Reflections on an Epistemic Diversity beyond Global Capitalism* (Castro-Gómez and Grosfoguel, 2007). With the reference to 'de-coloniality' (*decolonialidad*), an expression was introduced to the debate, which remains a specific characteristic of postcolonial theory in Latin America.

Criticism of the exclusive universal claim of modern Western rationality, which had been developed with the European Enlightenment, was at the centre of the group's first work. It is accused of having emasculated the military, political and economic conquest of the subcontinent beyond religious indoctrination with the semblance of a supposedly superior knowledge and made precolonial ways of thinking and knowledge marginalized and invisible.[22] This 'coloniality of knowledge' has been boundlessly connected with the 'coloniality of power', an expression that Aníbal Quijano (2000, 2008) had coined. Quijano sees it as based on an ethnic classification of the world's population, which, since the conquest of the continent, has been the hub of the organization of capitalist rule. To both manifestations of coloniality were countered the ways of thinking, the knowledge and the resistance practices of the indigenous peoples and various social movements of the oppressed and marginalized groups of the population, often with forms of a non-capitalist social or solidarity economy and new 'plurinational' and 'communitarian' forms of statehood (see Grosfoguel, 2007a).

Coloniality is understood as the structural continuation of a colonial pattern of domination that ensures the Spanish, Portuguese, Dutch, British, and ultimately US-American control over the subcontinent and the Caribbean. This structure comprises four different societal and experimental areas:

- the economy characterized by land occupancy, exploitation and financial control;
- the politics, which manifests itself as centralized institutionalized political control;
- the sphere of the social, which stems mainly from the control of sex and sexuality; and
- the sphere of culture, in which knowledge and subjectivities are subjected to given norms.

The modernity/coloniality group dates the emergence of this power matrix to the 16th century and in particular to the European Renaissance and the 'discovery' or invention of America. Ina Kerner (2012: 92) summarizes this idea as follows:

> Enlightenment and industrial revolution, which in the mid-European and Anglo-Saxon traditions are generally regarded as a prelude to modernity, appear from this perspective as a subordinate historical development resulting from a transformation of the colonial power matrix.

The group dates a second such transformation to the post-Second World War era, when the US took over the imperial leadership role that had once been exercised by Spain and then by Britain. Capitalism, and the economic globalization under its 'maxims' with 'free trade' and other forms of 'unequal exchange', the group attributes a constitutive role for all phases of modernity and coloniality.

Mignolo (2005) sees this power structure as paradigmatic for the 'idea of Latin America', which emerged in two steps. The first step was the 'invention' – and not simply a finding in the sense of a discovery – of America in the centuries after 1492, the high phase of Spanish and Portuguese colonialism. In order to justify the conquest, the local population was given an inferior status based on racism. This was accompanied by the colonization of knowledge in the sense of the establishment of a certain hegemonic worldview, which was also expressed in naming the 'new' continent 'America, the New World'. The second step took place in the second half of the 19th century, when the Creole (the descendants of the European conquerors) in the now independent states drew on the conceptions of 'Latinity' to establish an independent postcolonial identity. The reclusive Latinity, which was based on Western European models, updated the patterns of colonization of knowledge and helped to hide internal colonial borders under the cover of an inclusive historical and cultural identity. The original population and the descendants of African slaves were thus, in some cases, even more cruelly excluded than under the colonial regime and making invisible their forms of thought and knowledge.

In the project of de-coloniality, the aim is to deconstruct the dominant Eurocentric and modernistic patterns of thought and make their injurious and destructive effects visible. Here, another, diverse world is to be imagined, which recognizes and communicates all traditions of knowledge and existence in the same way. Terms are to be interpreted in order to counteract epistemic violence. Interculturality in the sense of epistemic plurality is to be encouraged, which in many Latin American countries includes the recognition of indigenous and African American knowledge systems. The 'knowledge of the people', which has so far been dismissed as irrational and backward, is to become the basis of a locally anchored, new form of social criticism. In this sense, Catherine Walsh (2007, 2010) speaks of 'critical interculturality' as opposed to 'functional interculturality', which is aimed only at cementing the unequal power relations through tolerance towards minority cultures. The Portuguese sociologist Boaventura de Sousa Santos (2008, 2009, 2016) supplements this programme by reflecting on an 'epistemology of the South', also called 'ecology of knowledge' (*ecología de saberes*), which is also centred on a critical reconstruction of suppressed knowledge and thought. Referring to the suppression and destruction of these modes of knowledge and thought, Sousa Santos speaks of an 'epistemicide'. For him, the struggle for global social justice necessarily implies global cognitive justice. He extends the pluralism of suppressed knowledge, emphasized by him, in an anthology of authors from Asia and Africa, as well as from Brazil, to the prospective search for different epistemologies of the South and their manifold potential for a 'geopolitical subversion' (de Sousa Santos and Meneses, 2014).[23]

In his *Philosophy of Liberation* (Dussel 1980, 1994, 2007), the Argentinean philosopher Enrique Dussel, who had been living in Mexico since the 1970s, also reflected the ideas of decolonial practice, which counteracts the coloniality of power and knowledge. At its centre is the concept of trans-modernity. By this, Dussel does not understand neither the rejection nor the fulfilment of modernity, but its transcendence into a historically new sociality in which people and cultures are connected in mutual respect. According to Dussel, the construction of trans-modernity begins by affirming the value of the cultures and knowledge that have been degraded and made invisible by modernity as 'waste' and to reconstruct them critically. He sees this process as a result of the experience of social exclusion and alienation, which he calls 'exteriority' in the words of the French philosopher Emmanuel Levinas (1968). Dussel understands this primarily as an ethical relationship (Dussel, 1980: 64): 'The ethos of liberation is other-directed impetus or metaphysical justice; it is love of the other as other, as exteriority; love of the oppressed, not, however, as oppressed but as subject of exteriority.'

Dussel's understanding of exteriority is not about – yet can be easily misunderstood as – an ontological exterior, not a purity unaffected by modernity, but about difference and dissent to hegemonic discourse, which absolutizes the forms of existence and thinking attributed to modernity. Instead, it devaluates, oppresses and negates the ways of existence and different ways of thinking. Dussel expressly emphasizes that 'one should not only take into account the discursive formal exclusion, but must also include the material (ecological, economic, cultural) exclusion' (Dussel, 2013: 123). According to him, injustice is 'experienced as pain' (Dussel, 2013: 114) and must therefore always be perceived in its physical dimension, too. With his concept of trans-modernity, Dussel sets a counterpoint not only to nostalgic aspirations that seek their salvation in the allegedly original precolonial cultures of the indigenous peoples, but also to the Eurocentric modernization and developmental ideologies which justify the unequal postcolonial power constellation.

To achieve enduring change, Dussel attaches great importance to social movements that have a positive notion to political power. At the same time, however, according to him, they must be aware of the permanent danger of power fetishism. He sees the benchmark for the legitimacy of political institutions in their 'ability to respond to the actual needs of social movements, the poor, the oppressed, and the excluded' (Dittrich, 2013: 17). How difficult it is to win and maintain this ability can recently be seen in the crisis and loss of power of the leftist governments of several Latin American countries. The crises are based not only on the continuing imbalance of power between the Global North and the Global South, but also on the difficulty of the political leaders to overcome the authoritarian mental heritage of colonial rule. This shows again the great importance of the 'de-coloniality of knowledge' (Lander, 2000) and 'epistemic disobedience' (Mignolo, 2009) attributed to postcolonial theory by the Latin American contributions.

Conclusion and outlook

The question posed by Gayatri Spivak (1985, 1988, 2008), whether literate persons and privileged social groups can represent the subaltern classes and speak for them, is a permanent challenge especially for postcolonial and decolonial thought. It covers any kind of research or social action that claims to meet the perspective of other people and to provide them social and political attention. This contradiction, which also applies to childhood research conducted by adults, can never be completely dissolved. Nevertheless, research and theories with an emancipatory claim are not only legitimate, but also necessary. In the case of postcolonial theory, at least one element of its legitimacy can be seen in the fact that its authors are (mostly) from world regions and countries that have emerged from colonies, that is to say, they are (most) affected by postcolonial power and injustice. This is especially true for those who have experienced racism and other forms of discrimination due to their origin and skin colour. This building block, however, only comes into play when it is supplemented with permanent self-critical reflection on the contradictions and dilemmas associated with one's own knowledge production. I would like to mention some that are partly reflected in the writings presented here.

One of these contradictions, which the Indian historian Dipesh Chakrabarty (2000) describes as a 'postcolonial dilemma', is that postcolonial thinking is not viable without recourse to categories such as justice and freedom that have emerged with European Enlightenment, but at the same time are connected with European expansion and colonial rule. In order to counteract this indissoluble dilemma at least, it is obvious to re-conceptualize and re-interpret the concepts. It is also important not to 'essentialize' them and to escape the claim to absoluteness, which can only distinguish in a binary way between true and false, or rational and irrational (see Bhambra, 2007; Connell, 2007; Go, 2016; 2017). The considerations on 'trans-modernity' emphasized by Enrique Dussel (2013), and the need for a practice of 'inter-culturality', as emphasized by him and other authors (for example, Walsh, 2007), are examples of how the dilemma can be circumvented.[24]

A further contradiction is that the theories are formulated almost exclusively in the former colonial languages, whereas the people in whose names the theories are spoken often cannot express themselves in these languages. The dilemma is difficult to avoid because the colonial languages have become world languages, without which it becomes increasingly impossible to communicate 'internationally'. But the dilemma must remain conscious and, if possible, at least be relativized by the fact that the knowledge contained in the local languages and the ways of thinking associated with these languages are actually taken up. It will also be necessary to think about the problems in any translation. Attempts should also be made to translate ideas formulated in the former colonial languages into the invisible made 'local' languages wherever and whenever possible, and to communicate directly with the people who are at home mainly in these languages. The methodology of 'sage philosophy' designed by Henry Odera Oruka (1988, 1990) is a successful example.

Exposed to a comparable dilemma is also any kind of pedagogy that is conceived with an emancipatory claim and tries to be transformed into practice. In the liberation pedagogy designed by Paulo Freire ([1968]2000) and others, this problem is attempted to be solved by clearing and 'deciphering' the disregarded knowledge of the oppressed and breaking up the hierarchical relationship between teachers and learners, and the respective roles being exchanged. Similar thoughts are found in the 'pedagogy of tenderness' conceived by Alejandro Cussiánovich (2007) in the context of the social movements of children, and the deliberations formulated by Giangi Schibotto (2015) on the 'decolonization of the pedagogical space', whereby he refers explicitly to reflections by Boaventura de Sousa Santos (2009) and Hugo Zemelman (2007, 2009). Meanwhile, there are pedagogical concepts that expressly understand themselves in a critical sense as postcolonial (Rizvi, 2007; Coloma, 2009; Andreotti, 2011; Bristol, 2012), but it is not always clear to what extent they are aware of the dilemma mentioned and how they deal with it.

Finally, an immanent dilemma of postcolonial theory that itself is responsible for this consists of the fact that the claim to formulate alternatives from the perspective of the colonial and postcolonial subjects does not have all the same subjects in mind. In relation to Africa, I have already mentioned that only a few of the writings on postcolonial theory are formulated by women, or that their contributions are less respected. The same is true for Latin America and other regions of the world. It is just as important that children and childhoods are an almost complete vacuum in postcolonial theory. With the exception of one reference by Gayatri Spivak (1999: 415) to working children, and the notable reflection of Bill Ashcroft (2001: 36) on the 'colonial subject as a child', children are not present in the writings of postcolonial theory.[25] Conversely, at least references to postcolonial theory are made by a few childhood researchers, such as Gaile Cannella and Radhiku Viruru (2004), who deconstruct childhood as a colonization project, Sarada

Balagopalan (2014), who traces the after-effects of colonialism in the educational system of India and its destructive consequences for the children of the subalterns, or Giangi Schibotto (2015), who analyses Latin American childhoods from the perspective of critical decolonial thinking. In the following chapters, I intend to use post- and decolonial thinking for the study of children and childhoods in an emancipatory way. In doing so, the question is how to situate and study the life of children and the constructions of childhood in postcolonial contexts.

Notes

[1] Based on experiences with German Fascism, this 'dark side' of modernity was formulated in 1944 by Max Horkheimer and Theodor W. Adorno (2002) in their philosophical study *Dialectic of the Enlightenment* (see also Dhawan, 2014).

[2] For this reason, Indian historian Dipesh Chakrabarty (2000) pleaded for the 'provincialisation of Europe'.

[3] Here, the term 'West' refers not to the geographical, but rather the geopolitical understanding of the word. The same can be said for the terms 'Global North' and 'Global South'.

[4] In the first case, this means 'exploitation colonies' (most common in Africa, South and Central America or parts of Asia), and in the second case, 'settlement' or 'settler colonies' (for example, Australia, New Zealand, Canada or the United States) (see Osterhammel, 2005; Ashcroft et al, 2013: 236–8).

[5] Julian Go (2016) points out that postcolonial theory did not begin with Edward Said. He sees his work starting a 'second wave' based on the 'first wave' of activists and thinkers rooted in the anti-colonial and anti-racist liberation movements.

[6] Here, Said refers to ideas and concepts of French philosopher Michel Foucault (as an example, see Foucault, [1969]2002). An earlier conception of *othering* dates back to the French writer Simone de Beauvoir ([1949]1997), and was systemized in the framework of Postcolonial Studies by Gayatri Spivak (1985; see Jensen, 2011).

[7] Spivak borrows the term 'subaltern' from Marxist Italian political activist and philosopher Antonio Gramsci (see Forgacs, 2000; Smith, 2010), who uses it to identify the population groups that are subject to the hegemony of a ruling class or elite. Gramsci sought a term that could expand the ideas associated with the working class onto other population groups and to make mechanisms of rules visible, which were not solely based on economic exploitation and political-military violence, but were also based on cultural dominance.

[8] Here, the terms 'black' and 'white' are not used to label skin colour, but rather they describe a superior and subordinate relationship, a visible reference point to racism.

[9] For an overview of different approaches of postcolonial thinking, see Young (2003); Childs et al (2006) and Ashcroft et al (2013).

[10] In a similar way, Fairchild (2017) drew attention to the intercontinental references in the development of so-called Africana psychology.

[11] This is especially true for the historian Cheikh Anta Diop (1959; 1960), who, like Senghor, comes from Senegal. By emphasizing the 'black' origin of the Egyptian high culture, he drew an antithesis to the alleged lack of history and culture in Africa and stressed the need to use the African languages. The fact that he had to use French in order to gain international attention is one of the postcolonial paradoxes (see also Sarr, 2016).

[12] Odera Oruka (1988: 36) opposed against ethnophilosophy the so-called sage philosophy: 'Sage Philosophy is a way of thinking and explaining the world between folk wisdom (old maxims, aphorisms, common sense) and didactic wisdom. It is the wisdom and the rationalized thinking of individual, specific individuals within a society. While the national wisdom is frequently conformist, the didactic wisdom is often critical of the general social rules and the national wisdom.' Odera Oruka attempted to reconstruct 'didactic wisdom' through interviews with revered persons of African communities, for which he developed and used certain methods (Odera Oruka, 1990).

[13] Their involvement in global corruption networks is occasionally a reason to speak of 'third colonialism'; which follows the second colonialism founded on the domination of global financial institutions, which in turn replaced the first colonialism based on conquest and settlement (Inosemzew and Lebedew, 2016). However, this is by no means restricted to the African power elites (see Cockcroft, 2014).

[14] For related discussions in Latin America, see Lang and Mokrani (2013).

[15] The Ghanaian philosophers Wiredu (1996) and Gyekye (1995, 1997) therefore put the idea of plurinationality within the national state into play. In South America today, Bolivia and Ecuador define themselves as plurinational states by recognizing the different indigenous and African descent groups as nations with their constitutions, which in the meantime, however, have received little attention in government policy.

[16] For a further overview of anticolonial and postcolonial thoughts and the attempts to establish an independent social theory in Africa, see Connell (2007: 89–110).

[17] The reasons for this are presented by Fernando Coronil (2008), who also explains the different perspectives of Anglo-Saxon and Latin American postcolonial studies.

[18] In the US, Latin American Studies have a long tradition, which goes back to the years immediately after the Second World War. They were particularly and strongly promoted by the US government during the Cold War, and they were partly manifested in research projects carried out jointly with government departments (see Delpar, 2008).

[19] Ramón Grosfoguel (2016) draws attention to the fact that some Latin American representatives of postcolonial theory – such as Walter Mignolo or Anibal Quijano – have built their theories on the thoughts of indigenous thinkers without mentioning them by name, among them Silvia Rivera Cusicanqui in Bolivia and Leanne Betasamosake Simpson in Canada. Grosfoguel sees in this intellectual practice a form of 'epistemical extractivism' or 'ontological extractivism' (see also Klein, 2012; Lajo, 2010; Rivera Cusicanqui, 2010).

[20] For Africa and Asia, however, it must also be borne in mind that colonialization did not begin in the 19th century, but centuries before by means of trade undertakings, as well as by Islamic and Christian missions. Also, trade with African slaves had already begun in the 15th century.

[21] Important here are the efforts to transform international law in a way that the influence of multinational corporations and international institutions that are democratically unauthorized is pushed back and the influence of grassroots social movements and local economics is strengthened. These attempts, expressed in Social World Forums and other initiatives, are sometimes expressed in the formula of replacing 'globalization from above' with 'globalization from below' (de Sousa Santos and Rodríguez-Garavito, 2005).

[22] Gayatri Spivak (1985) describes Latin America as the 'first-born child of modernity', which was 'secularized' by Europe and at the same time pushed into the world. Europe had emphasized itself being 'modern' and devaluated non-European societies as 'traditional', 'static', 'prehistoric' and denied their own dynamics and capacities (see also Ashcroft, 2001: 26–35).

[23] Margaret Kovach, a social scientist of indigenous origin in Canada, represents similar ideas under the heading 'Indigenous methodologies', which she sees as closely linked to a 'decolonizing theoretical lens' (Kovach, 2010: 80).

[24] Under the influence of indigenous social movements, interculturality has become part of the official discourse and specific laws in several Latin American and Caribbean countries, for example as intercultural education or intercultural health. However, this understanding of interculturality is usually limited to tolerating other languages and cultural practices, without shaking the dominance of languages and cultural practices inherited from colonial rule (see e.g. Bolados García, 2017; Clavería Cruz, 2019).

[25] Another exception: inspired by the social upheavals during the short reign of Salvador Allende in Chile, two cultural scientists made the remarkable attempt to analyze 100 editions of Disney's comic books for children on their colonialist messages (Dorfman and Mattelart, [1971]1975).

PART II

Children under colonial and postcolonial rule

4

State violence against children in British Empire and former settler colonies

> The Council is fully persuaded of the importance of prompt action in order to prevent the growth of a race that would rapidly increase in numbers, attain a maturity without education or religion, and become a menace to the morals and health of the community. (State's Children Council, Australia, 1911, cited in Smallwood, 2015: 68)

Introduction

Generally speaking, a state is considered the guarantor of protection and safety for the people living within its borders or subjected to its sovereignty. Yet history is full of examples in which state authorities not only neglect their responsibility toward at-risk people, but also actively contribute to threatening and endangering the lives of these individuals. This can be observed especially within state policies towards people considered 'foreign', or whose benefit towards society is questioned. In this chapter, some historical examples will be reviewed in which children have been affected by such marginalizing state policies, the consequences of which can still be felt today.

Since the emergence of nation states in the 18th century, children have been attributed a special significance for the future of societies. States recognize their need for protection, and measures are taken to provide for their education and learning. However, the notion that nation state formation is often accompanied by processes of marginalization, on the one hand, and violent assimilation practices, on the other, is often overlooked (Anderson, 2006; Douglas, 2002). This occurs especially in instances where 'national identity' is ambiguous (Appadurai, 2006). In such cases, children may experience systematic persecution, abuse and denial of citizenship. Here, the question emerges whether the state 'merely' neglects its obligation to protect children, or actively contributes to their abuse and endangerment.

There is a fine line between the two. The cases of state violence discussed here can be understood as a form of colonization of children (Ashcroft, 2001; Cannella and Viruru, 2004; Liebel, 2017). They are not limited to the ideological upbringing of children (assimilation), but rather extend to forms of disciplining, exclusion, oppression and even genocide, or 'ideocide'.[1]

Systematic violence against children was undertaken in two particular ways in the British Empire and in the USA, Canada, Australia and New Zealand. In the British Empire, children of the lower classes who were considered useless and unwanted were deported to British colonies, where they were supposed to equilibrate the labour shortage and contribute to the growth of the white population. In the USA, Canada, Australia and New Zealand, the violence was directed primarily towards black and indigenous children, to hinder their reproduction and destroy their collective identity. This was done most commonly through kidnapping and assimilation.[2]

The deportation of children as a contribution to colonial conquest

A neglected side of British imperialism and colonialism was the violent deportation of children to the colonies and former colonies. The British state initiated this measure to rid itself of children whose parents could not care for them, or who were attempting to survive, homeless on the streets of the metropolitan cities. These children were considered an eyesore and threat to public order. They were not even regarded as fit to function as cheap labourers inside the country's borders. The first children's transport is dated to the year 1618, when approximately 100 children were shipped from London to Richmond, Virginia. In the following years, tens of thousands of children, between 3 and 14 years old, were deported to New England (today the north eastern region of the US), Canada, Australia, New Zealand, South Africa and Rhodesia (present day Zimbabwe). This practice was justified as a social measure, in which children were saved from negligence and death, and were given the chance for a better life. In reality, they were forced to work as farm and domestic labourers whose status resembled that of slaves. They were at the complete and utter mercy of their masters' control, were not compensated for their work and had no opportunity whatsoever to escape the situation, nor make own decisions for their lives (Bean and Melville, 1990; Kershaw and Sacks, 2008; Darian Smith, 2013).

From the second half of the 19th century onwards, non-governmental children's relief organizations also began to play a significant role in the deportation of children. Organizations such as the Fairbridge Society and Barnardo's Believe in Children as well as various Christian churches established labour farms in the colonies, in which a great number of deported children were subjected to a strict labour and education regime. Dr Thomas Barnardo, the founder of one such farm, described the deportation of children as laying the 'bricks for empire building'. William Fairbridge, a founder of similar labour farms in Canada, South Africa, Rhodesia and Australia, romanticized deportation as a pathway toward a better life for these children: 'Train these children to be farmers! Not in England … Shift the orphanages of England to where farmers and farmers' wives are needed, and where no man with strong arms and a willing heart would ever want for his daily bread' (quoted in Kershaw and Sachs, 2008: 142; see also Corbett, 2002; Skidmore, 2012).

Following the victory in the American War of Independence and the constitution of the United States of America, the forceful transport of children within the newly established nation state continued. So-called 'abandoned' and 'useless' children were picked up from the streets of New York, Boston and other cities and transported by railway, the new means of transport at the time, to settlements in the Western region of the US. Like slaves, these children were put on display at train stations in the arrival towns, where settlers could take possession of them. This practice was presented as 'orphan trains', although only in rare cases were these children in fact orphans, without living relatives. Between 1854 and 1930 an estimated 200,000 children were affected by this practice (Warren, 1998).

Those children, who could not defend themselves or claim their rights at the time, were instrumentalized by their countries' governments for the interests of the British Empire and its colonization practices. They served the purpose of replenishing the shortage of labourers in the colonies and former colonies, and of increasing the proportion of 'white' people in the local populations. In many cases, parents were not informed as to what was being done with their children, and children were led to believe that their parents had died or sought to abandon them (Cregan and Cuthbert, 2014: 124). It is stated that there were at least 150,000 children who were sent by the British government primarily to Canada and Australia without the permission or knowledge of their parents (Darian Smith, 2013).

It took 300 years until the imperial practice of deporting children was brought to an end. The last mass transport from Great Britain took place in 1967 at the port of Liverpool, Australia being the final destination (Cregan and Cuthbert, 2014: 123). It took another 43 years before the then British Prime Minister Gordon Brown (2010) apologized on behalf of the government for this practice, calling the deported children 'migrants':

> To all those former child migrants and their families ... we are truly sorry. They were let down. We are sorry they were allowed to be sent away at the time when they were most vulnerable. We are sorry that instead of caring for them, this country turned its back. And we are sorry that the voices of these children were not always heard, their cries for help not always heeded. And we are sorry that it has taken so long for this important day to come and for the full and unconditional apology that is justly deserved.

Removal and assimilation of indigenous children in former settler colonies

Many states including the USA, Canada, Australia and New Zealand emerged from so-called settler colonies. Official accounts of the history of the origins of these states, namely the accounts commonly taught in schools, often speak of peaceful settlers who cultivated unpopulated or sparsely populated territories, thereby resisting and defending themselves from hostile and violent native tribes. After conquering these tribes, so the story goes, the founding fathers of the new states, who were now free from colonial rule, took it on themselves to begin integrating or civilizing the indigenous populations, the so-called 'Indians' (US) or 'Aborigines' (Australia).

This account of what happened has nothing to do with reality. In truth, the settlers violently drove the indigenous people and communities from their land, claiming it for themselves. They stripped them of their means of livelihood and condemned them to a life of poverty and dependence. If the indigenous people were not violently brought to their death, they were isolated in reservations and kept alive in meagre conditions, marketed subsequently, and until today, as folklore. This practice was justified with the claim that the suffering, miserable indigenous population needed to be 'civilized' and 'protected' from their own demise. Another component of the accurate historical account is that – similar to the exploitation colonies – women in the indigenous populations were degraded, reduced to sexual objects, robbed and raped.[3]

Another part of this history is how children of indigenous populations, as well as children of indigenous women, fathered by white soldiers or settlers, were treated. From the end of the 19th century onwards, children from indigenous communities in the USA, in Canada and Australia were systematically taken away from their parents with the goal of turning them 'white'.[4] They were adopted into white foster families and/or were forced into special boarding or residential schools where they were barracked and ideologically indoctrinated (Milloy, 1999; Churchill, 2004; Cassidy, 2006; Blackstock, 2007). In doing so, the indigenous cultures, languages and communities were to be gradually extinguished. State authorities, Christian organizations and other involved institutions presented this practice as a good deed, which represented the best interests of the children as well as the state. By these means, children, according to the official explanation, could be 'civilized' and 'saved' from a life of backwardness and poverty and made 'useful' for modern society. 'Policy makers regarded the surviving indigenous populations as standing in the way of national unity, modernity and progress and envisioned child removal as a means to complete the colonization of indigenous peoples' (Jacobs, 2009: 26).

Whether to populate the territories with 'white' settlers or to remove indigenous children from their families, the goal of such procedures was to control the identities as well as the social and economic practices in these territories. According to Kate Darian Smith (2013: 161), 'within the white settler colonies of the British Empire, white children were seen to be symbolically, socially and economically tied to the success of the colonial project'. While in the United States and Canada, *cultural assimilation* was favoured, in Australia, *biological absorption* (sometimes referred to as 'breeding out the colour'), was the preferred practice. Child removal was cynically justified and glossed as a measure of 'protecting' these children. This practice, which had been exercised in Canada since 1876 and in the US since 1880, was presented as a humane alternative to warlike and hostile combat against the indigenous population. Educational influence and cultural assimilation were supposedly the alternative to militaristic violence. In Australia, a distinction was made in the policy, which also began in the 1880s, between 'full-bloods' and 'half-castes'. Children of the former were strictly separated and forced to live in conditions, which would accelerate their extinction, whereas the latter were to be distributed and absorbed into the white population. Talking about the practice of the Australian government which removed Aboriginal children from their families 'subjecting them to civilizing regimes in institutions or white homes', Anna Haebich (2011: 1036) explains how most white

Australians saw it as a fair and even responsible action of a 'just society' caring of its 'indigenous charges' (see also Haebich, 2002).

In New Zealand, there was no overt policy prescribing the mass removal of indigenous children, but racist and Eurocentric attitudes undoubtedly drove the disproportionate removal of Māori children under the Child Welfare Act 1925. It is estimated that between the 1950s and 1990s 100,000 children and adults were removed by the state and placed in children's homes or psychiatric institutions, the overwhelming majority of children in institutions being Māori (Human Rights Commission, 2017). This continued even after the enactment of the Children and Young Persons Act 1974, which stated that in the exercise of such powers the interests of the child should be treated as 'the first and paramount consideration'. Although New Zealand also operated under assimilation policies at the time (Metge and Ruru, 2002: 55) its history differs somewhat from that of Canada and Australia in that placement of Māori children in white families or institutions was not the absolute rule. It appears that in New Zealand one may have depended more on the beliefs of the social workers involved, but recurring concerns were poorly considered placement decisions and consequent abuse, lack of oversight and follow-up, the sudden removal of children without explanation, and absolute disregard for children's voices and opinions (CLAS, 2015: 32).

In all countries, child removal was usually justified with the assertion that these children were being neglected by their families or did not have any living relatives. Yet the criteria for this alleged neglect were arbitrary and often limited to the claim that indigenous parents were generally incapable of providing for and raising their children. Many children who were labelled as orphans did in fact have families who cared for them. Even in the case of the death or disappearance of parents, in indigenous communities, it was not customary to leave the children to care for themselves – they would be cared for by the extended family.

Through the removal of their descendants, indigenous populations with their own language, culture, lifestyle and economic practices were supposed to be wiped out. In doing so, the 'white' settlers sought to ensure that the land they had acquired or claimed to be theirs, could not be reclaimed. This was a manifestation of racially motivated genocide.

It was no coincidence that the practice of child removal in the USA and Australia began at a time in which these countries were preparing to become modern, industrialized nation states. The dominant groups strived to create a unified national sentiment, in which European heritage and the dominance of the 'white' immigrants could be ensured. This was inevitably tied to the marginalization of the segment of the population, which did not correspond to this image and these imaginations. Just like the descendants of black slaves, the indigenous population stood in stark contrast to the now dominant population. Racist ideologies underscored their foreignness, incapability and inferiority and justified the special treatment of indigenous and black children. In Canada, similar procedures were forced on indigenous children under a policy openly aiming 'to kill the Indian in the child' (Darian Smith, 2013: 171).

The 'white' population was considered to have the highest rank in a 'cultural evolution' and was a synonym for modernity and progress. In contrast, the 'non-white' population was considered regressive and uncivilized, not only in a racist sense (as dark-skinned people) or in a religious sense (practising pagan customs), but also in an economic sense (as non-capitalist and old-fashioned). Notably, the indigenous population was accused of clinging to modes of tenure and economic practices which contradicted the idea of private property and were branded as irrational. Individuals were only considered useful if they were prepared and mentally in a position to work for a white employer. Consequently, indigenous child removal appeared to be 'necessary to properly integrate indigenous people into the modern nation, albeit in the lowest, most marginalized positions' (Jacobs, 2009: 82; 2013). With regard to the indigenous children in Australia, British administrative officials stated, according to Dirk Moses (2004), that they did not need education, because the Aborigines would eventually 'become an extinct race'.

In the US, the removal of indigenous children was practised until the Second World War and occasionally after the war. Mary Crow Dog, a woman from the Sioux tribe, recalls her experiences and those of other indigenous children in the 1950s and 1960s (Crow Dog, 1991: 16):

> Many Indian children [are] placed in foster homes. This happens also in some cases where parents or grandparents are willing and able to take care of them, but where the social workers say their homes are substandard, or where there are outhouses instead of flush toilets, or where the family is simply 'too poor'. A flush toilet to a white social worker is more important than a good grandmother.

During the 1970s, many mothers, primarily of black or indigenous descent living in poverty, faced having their children taken away from them, to 'free them up' for adoption, admit them to orphanages or give them to 'white' foster families. In 1978, LeRoy Wilder, a member of the indigenous Karuk community in California and lawyer in the Association on American Indian Affairs reported about a 'frightening, pervasive pattern of the destruction of Indian families in every part of this country' (cited in Solinger, 2002: 21). Available figures at the time documented, for instance, that one in eight Indian children in Minnesota was adopted. In the State of Washington, the adoption rate for Indians was 19 times higher than the rate for 'white' children. The pattern can be found across the country. Indian families continued to encounter disrespect, especially the practice of non-Indian social agencies to challenge their 'parental capacities' (Solinger, 2002: 21). Children who were removed to foster parents by the state due to 'abuse and neglect' by their parents, and who were allocated to adoption were disproportionately children of 'poor black women. A number of scholars and policy experts, using cross-class data about parental behavior and other variables, assess the policy practice as racist' (Solinger, 2013: 116, with reference to Roberts, 2002, and National Foster Care Coalition, 2007).

After the Second World War, in the USA indigenous activists began to demand the protection of their rights. Indigenous women in particular organized themselves to act against the continued practice of indigenous child removal, their placement in homes and boarding schools and their adoption by white families. Thanks to their struggle, in 1978 with the Indian Child Welfare Act, this practice was at least made more difficult. However, despite well documented research (see Jacobs, 2009), an official recognition of this dark chapter in the US is outstanding to this day.

In Australia, the state first admitted to its longstanding removal practice of Aboriginal children from their homes in an official so-called *Bringing Them Home Report*, which was released at the end of the 20th century (HREOC, 1997), and only several years later did the government issue apologies (Rudd, 2008; 2009; Gillard, 2013). Since then, the affected children have been coined the 'stolen generations'.[5] Whether and in what form the individuals who were forcefully deported as children as well as the families and communities of origin deserve reparations, is still a matter of debate today.[6]

At the same time, Canadian Prime Minister Stephen Harper did issue a national apology for the suffering experienced by 150,000 indigenous children forced into residential schools, calling this practice 'a sad chapter in our history' (Harper, 2008). The compensation since offered to those affected has been accompanied by the establishment of a Truth and Reconciliation Commission, with the aim to provide Canadians with greater knowledge about the history of the residential schools as part of a national healing process (TRCC, 2012). Nevertheless, current research suggests that indigenous children in the care of child welfare services further on experience physical, sexual and emotional abuse, as well as higher death rates than non-indigenous children in care (TRCC, 2015). Indigenous communities always face the highest levels of poverty and have inequitable access to housing and other resources.

In New Zealand, under pressure from the Human Rights Commission in particular, a revision of the policy towards children of indigenous minorities was initiated. It led to the Children and Young Persons Amendment Act in 1983. Although the Act does not mention the Māori and other indigenous minorities by name, it is the first attempt to specifically identify the wellbeing needs of the children of these minorities. This is done in particular by recognizing indigenous forms of family and upbringing as 'normal' and 'equal'. Thus the law represents a paradigmatic shift towards what Avril Bell (2017) calls 'bi-cultural imperative'. It calls into question the previous policy of assimilation, but has not yet led to an end of the discrimination and disadvantage of Māori children. Critical reviews such as the *Report of the Ministerial Committee on a Māori Perspective of the Department of Social Welfare* (Puao-te-Ata-tu, 1988), and more recently the Final Report of the Modernising Child, Youth and Family Panel (Ministry of Social Development, 2015) and the *Our Schooling Futures: Stronger Together* Report (Ministry of Education, 2018), show that in New Zealand an intensive discussion on a reorientation in the way Māori minority children are treated is under way.

Conclusion

These collective examples from various continents and eras of despotic acts at the hands of the state against children illustrate that the violence that accompanied the colonization of 'foreign' territories spared no one, not even children. The fundamental basis for this can be traced to the arrogance of developmentalism by the colonial elites and the accompanying imagined superiority of the social classes and 'ethnic' groups who profited from colonization. Children were affected in at least two respects. On the one hand, the ideology of childhood developed in modern Europe stylized children into primitive, not yet developed beings, and this was utilized to legitimize rule over the colonized population. On the other hand, the children were classified into a matrix of command, in which people were judged and treated according to their presumed racial characteristics and their economic utility. When individuals did not correspond to predominant expectations and moral beliefs, they were condemned to a life in the shadow of society, or even driven to 'disappear' from society. Although in contemporary postcolonial societies this practice has shifted from direct violence and discrimination to scientifically veiled forms of pity and commiseration, there is a long road ahead until the recognition of human dignity and children's rights will have been achieved. Confrontation with the history of violence against 'foreign' children is well under way, and the young people affected are searching for their roots.

Notes

1. I support the claim by Rashed and Short (2014) that the notion of genocide encompasses the case in which ethnically defined population groups are systematically annihilated, not only directly through militaristic violence, but also indirectly through the destruction of their basic necessities and collective identities. Appadurai (2006) describes 'ideocide' as when entire groups of people, states or ways of life are deemed harmful, when they are not considered members of the circle of humanity and no longer deserve to be treated with moral dignity. This can be compared to a 'social death' (Patterson, 1982).

2. Only a portion of the colonial and postcolonial forms of destructive violence against children, enacted, supported or tolerated by states, is mentioned here.

3. For more on the distinction between 'settler colonies', 'exploitation colonies' and other forms of colonialism, see Osterhammel (2005).

4. In Australia, between approximately 1900 and 1969, this practice applied to around one third of aboriginal children (Darian Smith, 2013: 163).

5. Australian historian Peter Read coined the expression 'stolen generations' in a text first published in 1981 (Read, 1998; see also Read, 2002).

6. Beyond the issue of 'compensation', Chris Sarra (2011a; 2011b; 2014) and Gracelyn Smallwood (2015), both Aborigines, develop the concepts of emancipatory pedagogy and human rights policy, in which the 'otherness' imposed on Aborigines by the dominant white thinking becomes the basis of a new self-image.

5

Racist civilization of children in Latin America

The discovery of gold and silver in America, the extirpation, enslavement and entombment in mines of the aboriginal population, the beginning of the conquest and looting of the East Indies, the turning of Africa into a warren for the commercial hunting of black-skins, signaled the rosy dawn of the era of capitalist production. (Karl Marx, *Das Kapital*, Vol. I, Chapter 24, p 790)

Introduction

The colonization of the subcontinent that is now called Latin America first took the form of exploitation colonies. It was aimed at the exploitation of natural resources in favour of the European colonial powers, especially Spain and Portugal. With the massive immigration of European migrants and the recruitment of slaves from Africa, the colonies in this subcontinent gradually changed to settler colonies.[1] They were at first dominated by the minority of invaders and colonists who saw themselves as 'whites', and took the right to exploit the indigenous so-called Indian and black populations at their own expense. In contrast to North America, Australia and New Zealand, where separation prevailed, the conquest of the southern subcontinent from the beginning went hand in hand with an extensive biological intermarriage between the colonists on the one hand and the indigenous and African populations, predominantly their women, on the other (Spanish *mestizaje*, Portuguese *mestiçagem*). This mixing continued after the formation of independent Latin American republics from the beginning of the 19th century, but without first changing the supremacy of the descendants of the 'white' conquerors (*criollos*). This fact has led critics to emphasize that the 'first' must be followed by a 'second' independence, in which their racist legitimacy is ended.[2]

Similar to the colonization of Africa, the European conquerors have equated the colonized population with children (see Ashcroft, 2001: 36–53). In the Viceroyalty of Peru, for example, the Spanish authorities – the state as well as the ecclesiastical – have often characterized the indigenous peoples of the Andes as childish. The cultural historian Carolyn Dean (2002: 21) describes this as follows:

> Infantilizing analogies not only justified paternalistic attitudes on the part of the colonizers but also legitimized political domination; children, after all, do not have the same social rights as grown-ups and can (and frequently ought to) be controlled by adults. Thus, the often-alleged arrested intellect and childlike behavior of the colonized shifted the focus from the initial relationship of European to Andean to the secondary, less problematic, relationship of parent to child.

The subjugated populations were neither trusted nor allowed to raise their own children. The colonizers had difficulties understanding accepting the independent treatment of the colonized children. In particular, it pained them that the children were not classified according to the European pattern of childhood as irrational beings with little intellectual ability, which had to be developed into the supposedly rational adult having been previously separated from adults and subordinated to them (Dean, 2002: 46). The children were also not differentiated according to their chronological age, but according to their physical powers; according to their physical size and other physical properties, they already performed certain tasks within the community (Dean, 2002: 44). However, the conquerors also took advantage of this kind of childhood by degrading the children, as well as their adult contemporaries, to workers to be exploited. The children and adults were regarded as objects that could be dealt with as desired.

In the territory of today's Chile, for example, at the end of the 16th century some indigenous people were captured and dragged to Europe to show them as exotic creatures like animals in special shows. In 1599, for instance, the Dutchman Olivier van Noort kidnapped four boys and two girls to bring them to Holland. All died during the crossing. At the same time, Sebald de Weert, another Dutch navigator, had taken a six-month-old child from his mother and brought him to Amsterdam where he died shortly afterwards (Rojas Flores, 2010: 97; see also Báez and Mason, 2006: 21).

In the same territory, the case of a boy and a girl from the peoples of the Yagán and Kawésqar is best documented. At the beginning of the 19th century, both children were taken by Captain Robert Fitz-Roy on board of his ship, the *Beagle*, to test the extent to which they could become 'civilized'. They were given English names (Jemmy Button and Fueguia Basket) and they were taught English. Fitz-Roy (1839) portrays the children and their 'civilization process' in detail and with obvious satisfaction; there are doubts, however, that this was more than the shining description of an ambitious seaman filled with a mission spirit (see Rojas Flores, 2010: 100).

The case of the two children has also attracted particular attention, as one of the *Beagle*'s passengers was Charles Darwin, who was still young, but soon to become famous. He recorded what he felt when he landed in the south of today's Argentina (Darwin, 1845: 205):

> When we were on the shore the party [of the natives] looked rather alarmed, but continued talking and making gestures with great rapidity. It was without exception the most curious and interesting spectacle I ever beheld: I could not have believed how wide was the difference between savage and civilized man: it is greater than between a wild and domesticated animal, inasmuch as in man there is a greater power of improvement.

In the following paragraphs, I will present a number of different practices which can be traced back to similar causes: first, the racist violence against so-called illegitimate children; and second, the treatment of children of indigenous and African descendant populations in order to 'civilize' them. These practices are based in part on the racist convictions of the colonial potentates and continue in the Latin American societies.

Racist arbitrariness against 'illegitimate' children

An innovation introduced by colonial rule, which has had a significant impact on the lives of children in Latin America, is the hierarchical distinction between legitimate and illegitimate birth. In the colonial era, illegitimacy was referred to as an 'infamy', a 'stain' or 'indecent and shameful mark' (Konetzke, 1958–1962: 473–4 and 335). Such views were particularly promoted by the Catholic Church, which condemned any sexual relationship outside marriage as immoral. They were also associated with certain ideas of honour, derived from the Iberian 'mother countries'. The Chilean historian Nara Milanich (2002: 75 and 79, italics in original) notes:

Attitudes toward illegitimacy were also intertwined with beliefs about race and ethnicity. One important component of the early modern Iberian worldview was the notion of *limpieza de sangre*, or purity of blood. To have 'pure' blood meant that one's lineage with free of 'contamination' by Jews, Moors, people of illegitimate birth, and – in the new-world context – Africans or Indians. ... Thus, in the colonial imagination, illegitimacy became inseparably identified with miscegenation – so much so that illegitimates and people of mixed race were often considered two virtually interchangeable categories.

So-called wild marriages between white men and women of indigenous or African origin were widespread, especially in slavery societies, as studies from colonial Brazil, Saint Domingue (from which the two states Haiti and Santo Domingo arose) or Cuba demonstrate (Martínez-Alier, 1989; Nazzari, 1996; Collins, 2006; Weaver, 2006). 'White' fathers in colonial Brazil rarely recognized illegitimate coloured children as their own, and even if they did, the courts were seldom willing to recognize the legacy of such descendants (Nizza da Silva, 1993: 184).

Nevertheless, these practices were by no means restricted to slavery societies and continued after the end of slavery. The Mexican social historian Francesca Gargallo (2007: 539–40) draws from her research the conclusions that the *mestizo* children who emerged from the often violently enforced relationship of white men to indigenous women had stood before a relentless alternative:

The mestizo children became children, or Spanishized, by the recognition of the father, or children of nobody, also called children of an Indian (*hijos de india*). The mother kept them close, fed them and sought work in the new society – whose values were being reconfigured – but if she committed a crime and was arrested, if she became ill or died, her children did not have the protection of the patriarchal Spanish family or that of the indigenous community. They had to live in the streets, in abandoned fields, or to be picked up by some convent. ... The colonial violation perpetrated by the white gentlemen to black, mestizo, indigenous women and the resulting mixture is at the origin of all constructions on national 'identities', structuring the decanted myth of Latin American racial democracy.

Referring to the Brazilian historians Sueli Carneiro (2005) and Ángela Gilliam (1996), Gargallo describes the colonial sexual violence as the foundation of all religious and racial hierarchies, which are omnipresent in the societies of Latin America. According to them, they have led to reject the role of the black and indigenous women in the development of national culture, eroticizing the inequality between men and women and making the sexual violence against black and indigenous women appear as a 'romance'. For the children who emerged from such 'romances', this meant, and to a large extent still means today, that – like their mothers – they were excluded from society and the structures of protection. Their so-called defencelessness and neediness were even instrumental in legitimating the alleged superiority of the ruling class. Francesca Gargallo (2007: 540–41) writes:

> It seems that childhood, being viewed as weak physically and morally, and therefore in need of some kind of protection, does not deserve the recognition of a full humanity: it is fresh and unfinished, it represents a hope and a burden.

Under these circumstances, children of single mothers or households run by women were predestined to become the object of discrimination. The colonial and postcolonial elites liked and still like to link such family constellations and the children's education with disorder, laziness and crime. Nara Milanich (2002: 87) comments:

> At the same time that single mothers were deemed an immoral influence on their children, there existed a parallel belief that illegitimate children were somehow bad for their mothers. Some charitable societies who worked for the moralization of the poor, for example, even thought to remove the fruits of sinful relations in order to rehabilitate fallen mothers.

Since the 17th century, the abolition of illegitimate children has been a widespread practice throughout Latin America. After many of the traditional rules from the colonial era had disappeared, the new family laws adopted by the independent states led even to intensify the discrimination against illegitimate children. In addition to the discrimination suffered, the children were regarded as a latent danger to the social order.

Children who were considered to be 'orphans', 'exposed children', or 'children of the Church' (children whose father was a priest or another religious functionary) were treated similarly. Usually, they were born out of wedlock, which, as shown above, was viewed as illegitimate. Such children were a constant issue in the colonial era, especially when they were the result of relations between Spaniards and black slaves. They were partly kept in special houses and raised under strict, often violent, regulations. With reference to a contemporary *Dictionary of Authorities* (*Diccionario de Autoridades*), edited by the Royal Spanish Academy between 1726 and 1739 (Real Academia Española, [1726–1739]1987), the Mexican social historian Cristina Masferrer León (2010: 309, italics in original) writes as follows:

> In any case, we may suppose that being a child of a family was better than being an orphan or an inmate, but then one had to be careful not to be a *son of a bitch*, for it meant that he was not born of a legitimate marriage. Being a *son of his mother* was not very good either, in that case it was better to be *his father's son*, because the first was a bastard or a son of a bitch, while the second was said '*he is entirely equal to his father in actions and customs*' (Dictionary: 156). While there was a difference between being the son of his mother or the son of his father, there was also a difference between being a son or being a daughter. So the phrase '*do we have a son or daughter?*' was used to ask if a business was going well or was going wrong (ibid.). Or, the phrase '*bad night and there will be born a daughter*' meant that in spite of having '*applied all the greater work and care to get something, finally were poor results*' (Dictionary: 157).

During the early 20th century, the attitude towards illegitimate children changed from direct discrimination to scientifically gilded compassion and corresponding institutional arrangements by the state. Illegitimacy became mainly a question of public health. State officials and a new corps of professional physicians increasingly devoted themselves to illegitimacy, believing that illegitimate children were more susceptible to illness and showed higher mortality rates – twice as high as with legitimate children. Moreover, according to an Argentinean commentator in 1927, they transmit 'infections that devastate the population' (Nelson, 1927: 220, cited by Milanich, 2002: 92). In this way, 'a traditional moral preoccupation with out-of-wedlock birth was assimilated into a new, positivist worldview, and illegitimacy came to be seen as a public health problem and social crisis' (Milanich, 2002: 92).

A growing number of contemporary commentators questioned the traditional stigma associated with illegitimacy. Instead of a 'stain' or an 'infamy', illegitimate children were increasingly viewed as innocent victims of the circumstances. Thus, the illegitimate child could be characterized, so the Argentine author quoted above, as 'the scapegoat of others' vices, of seduction, inexperience, ignorance, superstition, individual and social egoism' and even as 'a tender victim … a silent social reformer' (Nelson, 1927: 221, cited by Milanich, 2002: 92). Equally, illegitimacy was still heavily loaded with negative associations. In the positivist discourse of the time, it was connected with delinquency, crime, illness, and, above all, child mortality. Illegitimacy rates were even understood as indicators for the rank of a country on a given civilization scale. Nara Milanich (2002: 93) cites as evidence a Chilean politician from the late 1920s (Rubio, 1928): 'In the most civilized countries of Europe more than 90 percent of births are legitimate, [which] shows that … the legally constituted family is the basis of … the progress of peoples.' Milanich's conclusion (2002: 93) is the following:

> Like the categories of race, ethnicity, and gender, filiation is a socially constructed designation that has been fundamental to the production of social hierarchy since the beginning of the colonial enterprise in Latin America. Illegitimacy has endured as culturally significant category because, historically, family order has been perceived as essential to social order, and filiation has been perceived as integral to the very existence of the family.

The aforementioned Argentine author from the 1920s assumed that 'undoubtedly the complete equalization of the illegitimate child with the legitimate one … would lead to the beginning of the dissolution of the family as we know it' (Nelson, 1927: 227, cited by Milanich, 2002: 93). His commentary summarizes a conviction that has been repeatedly confirmed by many political, religious, and social authorities from colonial times to the present. Birth status not only had far-reaching consequences for later life, but the children were also directly affected by prejudices and destructive practices. 'Illegitimates faced the very real possibilities of subordination, downward mobility, enslavement, and, in the context of the foundling home, premature death' (Milanich, 2002: 94).

Today, many of the life situations associated with illegitimacy continue. Households led by women, in which many illegitimate children grow up, continue to be the most widespread family form in

Latin American societies. The practices of taking children from such families of their mothers and handing them to strangers, neighbours or special institutions are still on the agenda in many countries. A Brazilian author is of the opinion that today's international adoption practice still largely corresponds to the pattern handed down from the colonial era (Fonseca, 1998). It is true that, since the 1990s, the laws governing the family, children and young people in most Latin American countries have legally equated children out-of-wedlock with those of married parents, but the discrimination and common special treatment of the children who were labelled illegitimate for a long time is still culturally deeply rooted throughout Latin America.[3]

'Civilization' of indigenous and 'irregular' children

After the independence of the Latin American States in the first half of the 19th century, the new potentates were faced with the question of how to deal with the indigenous populations who had survived the colonial genocide. Instead of military extinction, attempts were made to adapt the remnants of indigenous peoples to the agenda of the white upper class, a process known as 'civilization'. I will first briefly refer to the example of Chile, then to Mexico.

During the Spanish colonial period, the indigenous peoples, especially the Mapuche in southern Chile, were able to maintain a relative cultural and political autonomy. The old colonial authorities had enforcedly accepted the territorial borders and the self-government of the Mapuche, and occasionally even made arrangements with them for trading. Since the Spanish colonial power had never been able to gain possession of the territories of the Mapuche, these did not consider interfering in the struggle for independence. They regarded this as a matter of the white settlers, whose economic and political interests were quite different from their own. After a long struggle for independence in 1813 and then finally in power in 1826, the white upper class came close to the Mapuche with mistrust. On the other hand, the new republican authorities had a patriotic discourse, in which the indigenous peoples were formally declared citizens of the new state and even their 'precious blood' was praised, but in reality the signs of hostility, discrimination and conflicts increased. While in the centre of Chile, all indigenous peoples were practically extinguished or compulsorily assimilated in the first decades of the Republic, the Mapuche south of the Bio-Bio River could preserve a certain independence almost throughout the 19th century despite the colonial wars against them (Bengoa, 2014: 44–51).[4]

Even during the colonial period, it was initially the Catholic missions that pushed into the regions of indigenous peoples to convert them to the Christian faith and to impose on them the 'achievements of civilization'. From the mid-19th century onwards, the new Chilean state largely undertook this task, with increasing emphasis on the education of children. One of the main criticisms of the indigenous peoples was that they gave their children too much freedom. Their generous educational practices should be replaced by discipline and obedience to the adult persons and authorities. 'Gradually, it was thought that the "civilization" of the Mapuche was best achieved through a modernized primary school' (Rojas Flores, 2010: 199). The postcolonial 'civilization process' followed a similar procedure and the treatment of the indigenous children and – not to be forgotten – those of the black ex-slaves in all parts of Latin America and the Caribbean as well. Having said this, I will now turn to Mexico and have a closer look at the situation there.

While in the colonial era the children of the indigenous and poverty-stricken population groups were met with an attitude of charity, after independence, which had been achieved in the year 1810 the tendency to 'improve' the children gradually increased. In particular, children were fought, who 'roamed' the streets of the fast-growing cities, where they pursued a wide range of activities to support their livelihood, and often that of their families, as long as they had one. For the children who were picked up on the streets, a new kind of 'reformatory' was created with the aim 'to eradicate vagrancy and the forms of life that it entailed (robbery, begging, etc.), as well as instil in them work discipline and respect for authority' (Sánchez Santoyo, 2003: 43). In 1926, a special court for minors was established in the city of Mexico, which implied imprisonment for the 'delict of vagrancy'. Girls were condemned in particular, when they went out alone to relax by dancing or in the cinema, instead of devoting themselves to domestic duties. The presumed intention of meeting a man was regarded as an offence. The most suspicious were single mothers, who were denied any moral quality for the education of their children. A woman who did not get married was regarded 'very harmful' to society (Sánchez Santoyo, 2003: 53).

Juvenile offenders were perceived as 'abnormal' individuals who 'had received from their parents the natural tendency to crime and would inevitably inherit it as their offspring' (Sánchez Santoyo, 2003: 55). Consequently, it was surely less of a coincidence that in the 1920s sterilization programs of condemned children emerged to prevent further propagation of what used to be called 'bad racial qualities'.

Beyond Mexico, in the *Pan-American Child Congresses* held since 1916, the following trends were generated (Corona Caraveo, 2003: 14–15):

> During the period from 1916 to 1935, the discussion was characterized by an emphasis on the concern to improve the race. The phrases that refer to an ideal child were: 'healthy, clean, preserved by science, the child with a mother capable of nourishing and defending him with her love and knowledge, the child educated to be the heir of a great culture'. However, this approach contrasted with the reality of the majority of American children, who by large were children of indigenous, mestizo or black descent or impoverished Creoles. The intention was to improve their racial features using science and a positive application of knowledge.

This openly racist view was based on the positivist discourse that interpreted misery and poverty in society as the result of 'genetic' differences between classes. According to Mexican social scientist Yolanda Corona Caraveo, in her country, poor childhood was seen as a latent danger to society and as an obstacle to progress. Their 'bad nature' was justified even by the labour activity that children performed to earn their daily bread (Corona Caraveo, 2003: 16). In the Pan-American Congresses, a racist discourse was used with the pretension of 'combating and correcting the defects inherent to the "nature" of children through eugenics, hygienic discipline through medicine and biology, as well as the sciences of the personality' (Corona Caraveo, 2003: 16). For obvious reasons, after the Nazi experience in Germany, a programme that spoke of the 'superiority of the race' could not be upheld. Thus, from 1942 it was replaced by the notion of the dangerous or antisocial child and focused on the need to establish programs to correct antisocial behaviour. 'The term "minors" arises at this time to refer to children living in an irregular situation or poverty, who only belonged to marginalized social sectors or migrants were considered prone to different criminal behaviour' (Corona Caraveo, 2003: 17).

Conclusion

In Latin America, throughout history since colonization until today, a trace of violence has been spreading. It does not always refer directly or specifically to children, but children are nearly always affected and are particularly vulnerable to violence. The phenomena described in this chapter can be found in many parts of the world (also in Europe), but they were first 'invented' in Latin America and 'cultivated' to perfection there.

It is true that since the 1990s, owing to the UN Convention on the Rights of the Child, this pattern of child neglect and discrimination has begun to be seen as problematic. However, there is still a long way to go until all children, regardless of their social position, their social background, their appearance, their gender and their age, can grow up under equitable conditions and lead a life in which their human dignity and their rights are preserved. It is important to note that these basic human rights, their human dignity, are to be understood in a way which takes account of the subjectivity of the children and the cultural peculiarities and cosmovisions of the original peoples of Latin America. In Part III of this book, I will elaborate on the possible perspectives for action.

Notes

[1] On this process in Mexico and Peru, see Guttiérrez (1995) and Radcliffe (1995).
[2] One of the first who thought it necessary was Simón Rodríguez (1769–1854), the teacher of Simón Bolívar (Rodríguez, [1828]1990).
[3] On the ambivalence of postcolonial Latin American legislation on child protection, see Milanich (2007).
[4] The conflicts continue to this day. For years, Mapuche has been calling for land that was stolen by the Chilean state at the beginning of the 20th century and that was handed over to colonialists from Europe. In this context, police actions are commonplace, where Mapuche people are abused, arrested and subsequently sentenced to imprisonment.

6

Pitfalls of postcolonial education and child policies in Africa

Africa proper, as far as History goes back, has remained – for all purposes of connection with the rest of the World – shut up; it is the Gold-land compressed within itself – the land of childhood, which lying beyond the day of self-conscious history, is enveloped in the dark mantle of Night. (G.W.F. Hegel, *The Philosophy of History*, [1837]2001: 109)

'Did not the great thinker Hegel call Africa a land of childhood?' Professor Ezeka asked, in an affected tone. – 'Maybe the people who put up those NO CHILDREN AND AFRICANS signs in the cinemas of Mombasa had read Hegel, then,' Doctor Patel said, and chuckled. – 'Nobody can take Hegel seriously. Have you read him closely? He's funny, very funny. But Hume and Voltaire and Locke felt the same way about Africa,' Odenigbo said. 'Greatness depends on where you are coming from…' (Chimamanda Ngozi Adichie, *Half of a Yellow Sun*, 2007: 50)

Introduction

With 70 percent of people under the age of 30, more than 450 million children and adolescents under the age of 18, including approximately 150 million children under the age of five (UNICEF, 2014: 190), Africa is the continent with the youngest population. However, there are only a few social studies that deal comprehensively with children and childhood in Africa. Childhood research is even less likely to address postcolonial issues. It usually refers to specific issues such as child labour, child trafficking, street children, children in armed conflicts or child orphans as result of the HIV/AIDS pandemic and wars. These accents fit into 'a completely outdated blanket presentation of Africa as a horror continent of backwardness and disasters in the public and media' (Lundt, 2016: 33).

In this chapter, I want to give an impression of how the situation of children and the characteristics of childhood in Africa are influenced by postcolonial power and childhood politics. I want to concentrate on three aspects. First, on the changes that follow with the establishment of schools according to Western patterns. Second, the debate on the appropriateness and implementation of children's rights, especially with regard to particularly marginalized and precarious groups of children. Third, the relationship between children and adults, and the limitations and opportunities for them to play an equal and active role in their societies.

Children, childcare and school

> One of the greatest fallacies of developmentalism in Africa is the equation of education to Western education. ... The total and un-calibrated embrace of the Western paradigm of socialization will only yield to one outcome: a nation of confused people totally alienated from their primordial and time-tested productive cultural practices of economic sustenance, thrown into the uncertain world of Western global cash economy. ... The African worldview does not in any way subsume the personhood of the individual in a deterministic manner under the will of the collective. Rather the African worldview underscores the reciprocity in the mutual dependency of the individual and community for purposes of sustenance and the continuity of all. (Arewa, 2014: 250–51)

In postcolonial Africa, childhood has been shaped to a great extent by the schools introduced during the colonial period, which were considered integral part of 'modern' development. In the sub-Saharan countries, these were predominantly Christian missionary schools and colonial schools established by European colonial powers. Although in some states Islamic influences on schooling can also be found, they seldom became a part of official school systems and have almost exclusively continued extracurricularly, as specific institutions for religious education (as Madrassas or Koran schools) (Nsamenang, 2010; Adick, 2013).

Cameroonian psychologist and educationalist Bame Nsamenang (2008; 2010) is one of the few African scholars who has explicitly focused on childhood in the context of postcolonial power relations. He examines the various influences of childcare in different parts of Africa, which have been influential since Arabic-Islamic and, subsequently, European colonization. According to him, precolonial childhood patterns do not exist any longer in their original forms, but they have not disappeared entirely and continue to influence contemporary perceptions. The question is how, and to what extent they do and may do so in the near future. What are their main characteristics, at least in the sense of their pretensions? According to Nsamenang (2010: 42–3),

> ... in its holistic, pronatalist, and theocentric outlook, an African worldview imputes a sacred value to childbearing and childrearing. Religious ideas such as the theocentric origin of children, are explicit or implicit in and central to every aspect of childbearing, childcare, and education in African family traditions. Indeed, kinship is the nucleus from which social networks ramify, moral behaviour is initiated and prosocial values, productive skills and the mother tongue are learned. The family is central to all this, because it is the acceptable institution for 'the supply' of new members and their care, such that childcare is a collective enterprise rather than a parental prerogative.

A review of traditional, precolonial childcare in Africa, at least in West Africa, reveals a landscape in which particularly mothers maintained a delicate balance between caregiving, self-subsistent production and homemaking, while the bulk of the day care and security of children after they had been weaned was left to older siblings in neighbourhood peer groups (Nsamenang, 2008). A comparative explanation for this childcare setting is that Euro-Western cultures often privilege adults with childcare, while African cultures tend to separate childcare skills from the life period of parenthood and position childcare training as a familial commitment for children to learn as part of a 'shared management, caretaking and socially distributed support' (Weisner, 1997: 23) of the family. That means, according to Nsamenang (2010: 43) that

> ... childcare was a social enterprise, in which parents and kin, including sibs, were active participants. ... From an early age, children observed and participated in family tasks as well as in caregiving to younger siblings with little or no instruction, but with guidance and encouragement of parents and peer mentors. This pattern of early learning

through caregiving is rooted in African perceptions of children as social agents in their own 'becoming'.

As a rule, the children had a particularly close, but not exclusive, relationship with their mother until the end of breastfeeding. Nevertheless, they were not primarily assigned to the parents, but understood as part of the village community, which saw itself as responsible for them. The legal scholar and sociologist Gerhard Grohs (1967: 32) describes the role of the mother on the basis of autobiographical records of Africans who were active in anticolonial movements:

> The most important feature of the first two to three years of the African child is the fact that the mother not only carries the child with her constantly, with a cloth tied to her back. She also nourishes the child, who sleeps with her at night, whenever the child asks, whether it is at night or during the day, whether the mother has milk or not. Sometimes she entrusts the child to an older sister of the newborn or to a younger relative, but she too immediately returns the child to the mother when it starts to cry. This mother's exclusive dedication to the child is based on the notion deeply rooted in all African tribes that the mother has a duty to protect and nurture the child for the tribe, for the extended family, to increase the fame and fortune of the community and the obligation to comply with the ancestors.

The form of the family for long time prevalent in Africa was characterized by the fact that it was embedded in far-reaching kinship relations. The family form that had long prevailed in Africa was characterized by being embedded in far-reaching kinship relationships. While the mother was primarily responsible for the newborn, the child was largely handed over to other members of the extended family after the end of lactation and 'joined in the crowd of his peers' (Grohs, 1967: 32). The author presents the relationships as follows: 'The one-sided bond with the mother is replaced by a variety of relationships with the aunts, uncles, grandparents, siblings, and cousins living in a farmstead, expressed in European terminology' (Grohs, 1967: 33).

According to the matrilineal succession, the woman had a strong position in the community. It was accompanied by an open gender concept, in which the gender roles were not subordinate, but were defined as being complementary. The children were not primarily assigned to their parents, but were understood as part of the wider community, which shared responsibility for them. The European colonial powers tried to eliminate all these cultural forms partly by introducing the school as a new, individualizing and separating form of education, and partly by bringing in the capitalist mode of production and cash economy, which forced women out of their central role as producers of vital goods and degraded them to 'housewives'.[1] Although traditional forms of family and community life have only been partially preserved, they continue to play a basic role in social relations and the socialization of children (see Miescher, 2009; Ampofo, 2013; Kam Kah, 2015).[2]

Looking at the present, Bame Nsamenang (2010) sees schisms and challenges in the childcare landscape emerging from the scarcity of traditional support by the community and especially by siblings, because most of the children now spend a great deal of time in school. According to him, schooling has not eliminated peer group activities, but modified them somehow, as pupils and students of all ages and at different levels of education can be observed functioning in the reciprocal sociability of peer networks for various purposes in educational institutions and non-school settings. According to him, these informal networks can be linked in order to fulfil vital tasks in family and community.

Finally, Nsamenang states that also nowadays, for African parents, children are 'better together' in the 'school of life' (Moumouni, 1968: 29), an environment imbued with invisible cultural scripts that foster the individuation of relational interconnectedness, such as 'a person is only a person with other people' (Zimba, 2002: 98). In contrast to Euro-Western cultures with their emphasis on self-centred attitudes and behaviour, 'African sociogenic orientations bind and mutually oblige individuals to promote a sense of relatedness' (Nsamenang, 2010: 46). The cultural anthropologist Alma Gottlieb (2004) also points out in her study on child rearing in West Africa that children were not seen as separate, existing beings, but as part of a network of reciprocity. With their holistic and integrated perspective on the family and the universe, state Gottlieb and Nsamenang, African cultures could deal with everyday things differently than the Euro-Western influences so far suggested.

The introduction of the school by the colonial powers constituted a sharp break with traditional education and training practices. In contrast to learning by the model of the elders, the telling of stories and the participation in the everyday work of the adults, in the school verbal commands, drill and punishment practices came into the foreground. Even if the children's life in the community was strongly regulated by the elders, the children also had many free spaces to explore their environment, and physical punishment was very rare. At school, on the other hand, these were now becoming an essential means of educating children to discipline and obedience (see Grohs, 1967: 33–5).

Similar to school education elsewhere, that dominant in Africa today is completely disconnected from the daily lives of children. In this context, children's experiences count just as little as the knowledge they have acquired through their contribution to daily work within and outside of their families (Katz, 2004: 59–122; Katz, 2012). The content taught in schools is far removed from the lived realities of children and ignore the manifold African cultures and knowledges (see Shizha, 2014; Ngalim, 2014). In the primary schools of Kenya, for example, 'the biological, nuclear and monogamous family model is by far the most popular textbook representation of family life' (Archambault, 2010: 230). The families represented emulate a European middle class ideal, and in an African context, they at most represent the privileged populations, which were beneficiaries of colonial rule.

Textbooks largely continue to be imported from Europe and come from large publishers, whose headquarters used to be based in the former colonizing countries. 'So while the African educationists were busy fulfilling the promise of schooling for the masses of Africans, the curricula and textbooks along with the methods of teaching were in the hands of the educational industry and publishers of the North' (Brock-Utne, 2000: 116). Until recent times, '(t)he powerful money-lenders and donors to education in Africa have the power to define not only the type of schooling they see fit for African children but also the concept of "education" itself' (Brock-Utne, 2000: 276). It is widely identified with classroom education. Consequently, some African authors, such as Joseph Ki-Zerbo (1990: 12), an educationist from Burkina Faso, criticize that 'the formal system of classroom education looks like a foreign cyst in the social body, a malignant tumor'.

The current approach to schooling in Africa is seen by some scholars 'as part of the problem rather than a solution to the continent's numerous problems' (Dei et al, 2006: 11). Particular attention is drawn to the 'marketization of education'; it intensified the class divisions in Africa by bringing with it unaffordable costs, while at the same time becoming an inevitable tool for the hoped-for social mobility (Dei et al, 2006: 10). It also threatens the cultural and linguistic diversity of African societies as it is instrumentalized for national integration within the boundaries of the state pre-constructed by the colonial powers (Dei et al, 2006: 7; see also Dei and Opini, 2007).

Due to the institutional conditions of classroom education, children and their families have no influence whatsoever on school curriculum.

As in other parts of the world, children are mainly treated as 'funnels' for predefined knowledge and potential 'human capital'. They are subject not only to the repercussions of colonial rule, but also the subordination of African states under the guiding principles of the globalized capitalistic economy and the accompanying instrumentalization of education for the purpose of economic exploitation. However, a mere imitation of education is entrenched in subordinated status of African societies in the hierarchical structure of the capitalist world order. Beyond the transmission of learning content, schools can be understood as a vehicle of 'moral technology', in that they promote a 'specific kind of subjectivity of moral character in the child' (Wells, 2009: 111). This subjectivity aims at a particular habitus, one in which subordination and individual concurrence are internalized as natural ways of life.

How such a habitus is produced in school is expressed very vividly in the autobiographically inspired novel *Purple Hibiscus* by the Nigerian writer Chimanda Ngozi Adichie. She let the daughter of a privileged Christian-oriented family describe her experiences in an officially recognized private school (Adichie, 2004: 38–9):

> I took … my report card tightly pressed to my chest. The Reverend Sisters gave us our cards unsealed. I came second in my class. It was written in figures: "2/25." My form mistress, Sister Clara, had written, "Kambili is intelligent beyond her years, quiet and responsible." The principle, Mother Lucy, wrote: "A brilliant, obedient student and a daughter to be proud of." But I knew Papa would not be proud. He had often told Jaja [Kambili's brother; ML] and me that he did not spend so much money on Daughters of the Immaculate Heart and St. Nicholas to have us let other children come first. Nobody had spent money on his own schooling, especially not his Godless father, our Papa-Nnukwu, yet he had always come first. I wanted to make Papa proud, to do as well as he had done. I needed him to touch the back of my neck and tell me that I was fulfilling God's purpose. I needed him to hug me close and say that to whom much is given, much is also expected. I needed him to smile at me, in that way that lit up his face that warmed something inside me. But I had come second. I was stained by failure.

The isolation of school curriculum from the daily lives of children as well as frontal, teacher-centred methods of education are only strengthened by the fact that the main language of instruction in primary schools and sole language of instruction in secondary schools are the (former) colonial languages. 'Where a colonial language becomes the language of instruction, with all knowledge and education fed into the people in the language of the former colonial overlord, this removes and negates the development of confidence in home or original cultures' (Prah, 2005: 28), and 'entrenches the schism between the elite and the masses' (2005: 32).[3] The same author, in reference to a study from the Centre for Advanced Studies of African Society (CASAS) points out, in contrast to the argument that the use of native languages would lead to a splintering, that 12 to 15 'core languages' could be identified in Africa (Prah, 2005: 40). In an overview article about education in sub-Saharan Africa, Adick (2013: 130) notes, in response to another frequently raised argument, namely that African languages do not exist in written form, that the process of Islamisation was accompanied by the 'application of writing and numbers'. As a result, 'a number of African languages, even prior to European colonial rule, had been transcribed into written form using the Arabic alphabet. Thus, Islamic African populations were able to make use of a new method of communication in their own language, which could also be used for secular purposes'.

In order to bring learning closer to children's lived realities and their experiences outside the school setting, a logical conclusion would be to offer instruction in multiple languages in schools in multilingual African countries. In the initial years following colonial independence, this practice could be found in some states, but did not last (see Brock-Utne and Holmarsdottir, 2004). According to the authors, it is not a matter of replacing the former colonial languages but of assigning them a complementary function to the mother tongues. Multilingual teaching would therefore not restrict the children and devalue their knowledge in an international context, but *expand* and *enrich* it. Moreover, lessons could be learned from precolonial forms of education, which were most often transmitted by parents, grandparents or within the scope of village communities or peer groups.

Numerous traditional child rearing and educational methods remain prevalent in rural regions of African countries. Basically, the aims of education and child rearing practices have followed rather functional objectives in African tradition:

> Education was generally for an immediate induction into society and a preparation for adulthood. In particular, African education emphasized social responsibility, job

orientation, political participation and spiritual and moral values. Children learnt by doing, that is to say, children and adolescents were engaged in participatory education through ceremonies, rituals, imitation, recitation and demonstration. ... Education in Old Africa was an integrated experience (Fafunwa, 1974: 15–16).

Despite cultural heterogeneity and differences between regions, there were certain commonalities in educational practices and objectives. The aim of traditional African education in general was based on collectivism and responsibility training and thus had a strong integrative function in contrast to the dominating Euro-Western educational values, which are based on individualism. According to educationist Ina Gankam Tambo (2014: 127), the development of children's character, their sense of belonging and active participation in community and family life, respect for the elders and obedience, understanding and appreciation of the cultural heritage of the community, and the development of physical, intellectual and vocational skills as well as to be hardworking and honest counted as the main educational objectives. Children's education and childrearing, however, were not the responsibility of the parents alone, but of the extended family as well as the community (Fafunwa, 1974: 21). According to educationist Renate Nestvogel (1996: 15), this collective and social learning was expressed in the way that learners and educators of all age groups usually were involved in the learning process, which took place in public and everyday life and only on special occasions was part of institutionalized processes. Thus, traditional African life promoted 'a sense of community' (Nsamenang and Lamb, 1994: 136), which strengthened collective responsibility as well as the social network.

Ina Gankam Tambo (2013: 282–3) describes this education practice using the example of the Igbo and Yorùbá cultures in contemporary Nigeria:

Tradition and culture of the Igbo ... were based on 'community based education'. Child education and child rearing were the responsibility of the extended family as well as the community. The children and youth were sensitized to social responsibility and solidarity with their community. The curriculum consisted of six major parts which were interwoven and in contrast to the western education system, not to be understood as separate categories. Next to music, physical education, moral and religious education as well as social learning the children also acquired competencies in agriculture and fishing. This happened through learning by doing, i.e. learning as a process. Children learnt participatory through imitation and observation as well as through interaction in ceremonies and rituals. Education was thus a holistic process comprising intellectual, manufactural and physical activities. ... The Yorùbá followed education with the aim of developing personalities integrated in the society. Hence, education is a lifelong process, in which values as for example honesty, generosity, courage and above all diligence are trained together with a mentor or a teacher.

Although I do not argue that such an educational practice should be entirely replicated in contemporary African societies, it does include many elements that could contribute to the emancipation of African children from the constraints and one-sidedness of education in the postcolonial classroom. Educationist Ute Brock-Utne (2000: 111–12) describes these elements, which she sees rooted in many African regions,

> as a system of linkages between: [a] general knowledge and practical life; [b] education and production; [c] education and social life; [and d] education and culture (through the use of the mother tongue; the incorporation of cultural practices like games, dancing, music and sports; and the teaching of ethical values).

Such elements, to which may be added the aim of gender equity, could be easily extended to a dialogical, intercultural and community-related education that respects children's agency, strengthens their sense of justice and self-confidence, and encourages their resilience and participation (see Ensor, 2012; Shizha, 2014; Ngalim, 2014; Dei, 2016).[4]

Dogmatic implementation of children's rights

> Juxtaposing children's narratives to the global discourses of rights reveals important dissonances between their lives on the one hand and, on the other, the rhetoric that sadly discounts their capacities and contributions. (Abebe, 2013: 86)

As is the case in other continents of the Global South, a great number of children in Africa live in very precarious conditions. This can, to a large extent, be considered a result of postcolonial power structures. These structures are founded on expanding a means of production, which serves the capitalist world market and largely makes the production of essential goods within postcolonial countries themselves impossible. Large landowners and multinational corporations agree, at times violently, and at times with the support of corrupt regimes, to hand over locally-owned farmland, also known as 'land grabbing', for the widespread cultivation of cash crops or for tourism projects, thereby destroying the self-sufficient, local, small-scale farming forms of production. The competition over scarce resources at times result in violent conflicts. These initiatives are often led by powerful groups, which take advantage of religious identities and competition, thereby seeking to gain additional economic profit and political power for themselves. One result of this is that young people, especially, are urged to migrate to cities and other countries. The number of children who must support themselves is increasing. As a result of forced undernourishment, illnesses spread, which, once again, because of a missing or inaccessible healthcare system and medical treatment, may go untreated and often have the potential to be deadly. The longstanding tradition of support by extended family members in Africa is also threatened, with the result that children and youth, to a larger extent than in the past, must rely on their own strategies for survival.[5]

Through these processes occurring in the postcolonial realm, children's rights are without a doubt being violated.[6] This is especially true for those children who are forced to live in extreme poverty, whose health, or lives, are threatened and who are torn out of their living contexts, being forced to survive on their own, without familial support. Yet the way in which international relief organizations and even UN agencies deal with children's rights, and translate them into campaigns, projects or measures, often overlooks the reality of these children and tends to harm them, rather than support them. This practice is based on an image of childhood stemming from Western ideals, but has nothing to do with the real-life circumstances on the ground and fails to take social and cultural contexts into consideration. Rather than adjusting to local circumstances, children's rights are understood as eternal, ahistorical rules, which supposedly 'speak for themselves'.[7] As a result, the intervening organizations appear first and foremost to be 'moral watchdogs' (Valentine and Meinert, 2009). Children are viewed as helpless victims and, in a paternalistic manner, are made the objects of institutional supervision. In this process, on a mental level, the unequal postcolonial power constellation is habitually strengthened rather than challenged.

I would like to draw attention to the literature surrounding several campaigns and relief programmes, which fight against child trafficking and intend to benefit so-called street children and orphan children.[8] In doing so, I will also attempt, at least briefly, to spell out some possible alternatives. In examining the campaigns against child trafficking in Africa, which have been carried in connection with the UN Convention on the Rights of the Child and the International Labour Organization (ILO) conventions on child labour, British childhood researchers Jo Boyden and Neil Howard (2013) have criticized them for being based on a Eurocentric image of childhood. They accuse the campaigns of scandalizing child movement in a sweeping manner as abuse and exploitation of children, without taking the specific circumstances into consideration.

> Institutions across a variety of contexts have come to understand a child's departure from the parental home (whether for care, learning, or labour) as a child protection violation, seemingly representing an involuntary act that stems from adult negligence and exploitation, and leading inexorably to harm for children, their families and their communities. Child movement has thus increasingly become conflated with trafficking, a conceptual confusion that has significant consequences for policy. (Boyden and Howard, 2013: 354)

Such a policy construction, called by Howard (2012: 557) 'child exceptionalism' in the frame of a 'globalized childhood', asserts that migrant children are driven from their homes through 'poverty, harmful social practices, or the breakdown of societal values' (Heissler, 2010). In this way, mobile, homeless and nomadic children had become a site of widespread institutional moral panics. Instead, Boyden and Howard (2013: 365) suggest understanding children's movement in the 'historical and economic-moral contexts in which households have always depended on the work of all active members, and childhoods were never fixed spatially within stable, nucleated family structures'. Referring to his own research in a rural region of Benin, Howard (2012: 566) asserts, 'children work in this region because they need to and their work is individually and collectively valued, with the tipping point between "work" and "exploitation" significantly more finely nuanced than in the rigid, aged-based binary structure of policy-maker norms'. With regard to the moral aspects of an adequate child rights-oriented policy, Boyden and Howard (2013: 365) say:

> Rather than attack the moral integrity of families and essentialise children as victims, policy that wishes to promote the well-being of migrant and potentially migrant young people should reconfigure itself along lines that take into account children's socio-cultural and economic realities, including their gendered roles and responsibilities.

Similar questions arise with regard to policies, which try to improve the situation of children living in urban streets. Like 'trafficked children', these children are often seen purely as passive and helpless victims. British sociologist Matthew Davies (2008: 327), based on his research in a small town of northwest Kenya, questions expressively the assumption that such children are 'in dire need of help'. He does not deny that they are victims of violence, but emphasizes the need to recognize the relevance and support the creation of the children's own networks, here called 'subcultures':

> Recognition of street children's subcultures necessitates that policy be based on dialogue and asks adult society to fundamentally reform its philosophy. It asks us to provide opportunities unconditionally to both those who will and will not make use of them. It asks us to view street children not as children out of place but as competent agents who, given greater access to information and a broader range of choices, are able to make life-changing decisions. ... We have the time (if not the resources) to work *with*, rather than *for* these children. Our aim should be to help these street children to improve their lives through their own 'child cultures' rather than by imposing aspects of our own. (Davies, 2008: 327)[9]

Ghanaian educationist Yaw Ofosu-Kusi and British sociologist Phillip Mizen (2010), based on research with street children in central Accra, the capital of Ghana, have arrived at similar conclusions. A notable aspect of this study is that the researchers interpret the social bonds they perceive between children to be 'new ways of living' and 'new modes of childhood'. They do not describe how these bonds came to be, but it can be assumed that memory or experience with traditional cultural forms of reciprocity are reflected within these children and in the face of the new challenges of urban street life, they are reactivated. The forms these traditions take on may be contradictory, and their scope limited, as far as overcoming daily deprivations, risks and discriminations. However, they clearly contain a resistant potential, in that a societal form is able to emerge, in which people are not judged by their outward appearance or their purchasing power, and their human dignity is unconditionally respected (see also Ofosu-Kusi and Mizen, 2012; Mizen and Ofosu-Kusi, 2013).[10]

One challenge in working with children who are forced to live in very precarious situations is to handle their undeniable vulnerability in such a way, which does not withhold their ability to independently problem solve. In the case of migrating children, as well as children who have lost or have been separated from their parents and relatives, the question must be raised around what kind of support they actually need.

Patricia Henderson (2006, 2013), collaborator of HIVAN – Centre for HIV/AIDS Networking in South Africa, examines some assumptions circulating in development or interventionist discourse concerning the vulnerabilities of HIV/AIDS orphans in her country. In an ethnographic research with rural children and youth between the ages of 14 and 22, she points to the ways in which global terms may fail to describe local particularities. Based on her research, she argues that a 'too narrow focus on the vulnerabilities of AIDS orphans' implies the risk to obscure 'the ways in which they share similar circumstances with other poor children, as well as the strengths they bring to bear on their circumstances' (Henderson, 2006: 303). Her findings show the varying circumstances in which the orphans live; the degrees to which they have been accommodated within wider kin groups; their dexterity, knowledge and skill in navigating local environments; and a reiteration of rich sets of cultural understandings and local performance repertoires in holding experience and loss. She feels induced to challenge some of the implicit meanings in children's rights discourse as filtered through interventionist programmes aimed at HIV/AIDS orphans, namely, what it is to be a child, and the social placement of children in relation to caregivers.

> It is within the space of the insistence upon a patronizing form of vulnerability that assumptions to do with 'appropriate childhoods', implicit within child rights discourse, become intertwined with intervention projects. The result is frequently a crude insistence on the promulgation of presumed ideals of childhood within particular localities. In many cases, imported knowledge utilized to shape

an intervention is taken for granted, and may block any appreciation of local understandings. The ways in which imported assumptions may be inappropriate are therefore submerged (Henderson, 2006: 304–05).

In another text, Henderson (2013: 45) concludes:

> The result is a shallow engagement with young people in relation to rights as promulgated in the CRC [Convention on the Rights of the Child] and a complete avoidance of the way in which local forms of sociality may begin to fulfil some of the aspirational demands contained in the document. In some respects this renders NGOs 'blind' to lessons they could learn through paying attention to the local.[11]

Likewise, Helen Meintjes and Sonja Giese, two other South African researchers, with regard to 'the tireless advocates, researchers and activists in HIV/AIDS work', call for reflection on the effectiveness of 'their orphan-centred, rhetorically charged appeals to mobilize interventions in a disastrous epidemic compromise' (Meintjes and Giese, 2006: 425). The authors illustrate how the global focus on orphans leads us to consolidate stereotypes of children's experiences, and they argue that more careful attention should be paid to conceptual and representational issues by those writing about and responding to childhoods in the context of HIV/AIDS. They warn against the assumption that children are helpless victims due to their 'orphanhood' and call to pay more attention to their similarities with other children living in poverty. When poor children are characterized as passive victims, negative stereotypes adhere to them. For example, Nancy Scheper-Hughes and Carolyn Sargent (1998: 3) show how poor children, through being delegated to a place of marginality and hence cast as passive recipients of national or global policies, come to be described as the 'quintessential supernumery other'.

Looking for alternatives in this context, it is of great importance to value the experiences of child-headed households that came into being mainly in Southern and Eastern Africa as a consequence of the HIV/AIDS pandemic and war conflicts. Contrary to mainstream research focused on the children's risks and vulnerabilities, Maureen Kendrick and Doris Kakuru (2012), two researchers from Uganda and Canada, look at child-headed households in Uganda as places of 'funds of knowledge'. Using ethnographic methods, they document the experiences and activities of children in five rural home contexts.

They advance the view of children as resourceful, competent and knowledgeable, highlighting their ability to build on, utilize and acquire new funds of knowledge while simultaneously recognizing their conditions of extreme adversity. The authors' aim is to expand and strengthen the current knowledge base on children living in child-headed households by providing a more nuanced understanding of the relationship between children's risks and capabilities. In a research realized in Zambia, Ruth Payne (2012a; 2012b) comes to similar conclusions.

Taking the example of children who take on the full responsibility of leading households, I want to depict to what extent only a contextualized understanding of children's rights can do the children justice and support them. Child-headed households are often criticized and refused, as some believe that children are not supposed to take on parental responsibilities. Ignoring the particular situation, and the capacities and the will of the children, they are obliged to live in institutionalized settings under the supervision of adults. Any living arrangement that deviates from this norm has the tendency to be seen as a source of misdevelopment. Instead of recognizing a justified interest and innovative survival strategy of children, officials and NGOs who dedicate themselves to orphans tend to discriminate and marginalize these children further (for more details, see Ennew, 2005; Cheney, 2012; 2013; Colonna, 2012).

Hereby, no consideration is made of the fact that in African countries children are involved in taking care of younger siblings, many of whom are still very small. They learn this alongside their parents and disburden them by caring for the physical and psychological needs of their younger brothers and sisters and taking on household chores. For many families, looking after siblings is seen as part of a normal development and as an essential step in preparing for adult life.

The gathering of children on their own authority has a long tradition in African societies. Sometimes, it is part of some sort of rite of passage, in which children are left to themselves for a period of time, in order to prove themselves in autonomous child groups and to make themselves fit for life together (see Liebel, 2004: 93–6). In many parts of Africa, groups of children take on very clearly defined social functions, for instance the maintenance of wells or mosques (in Muslim communities), keeping villages clean, helping the sick and handicapped or supporting of victims of hard rainfalls or fires (Sall, 2002: 89).

However, the widespread use of child-headed households is now mainly due to an emergency situation. A particularly large number of such households are found in countries that are severely affected by the HIV/AIDS pandemic, for instance in South Africa, Zimbabwe, Malawi, Swaziland, Uganda or Tanzania (Germann, 2005, 2010; Penn, 2005: 104–11; van Breda, 2010; Wolf, 2010; Tolfree, 2004). In southern Africa, it is estimated that 15 per cent of all households are run by children (Penn, 2005: 181). In Rwanda, an estimated 60,000 child-headed households arose as a result of the genocide (Tolfree, 2004: 163).

Children who live in child-headed households must face many difficulties. As they experience little recognition for their way of living and are hardly supported, they often have difficulties earning their living. Sometimes they lack needed experience to direct their day-to-day life and to solve problems that arise on their own. When these children find neither protection nor support, they are in particular danger of being abused and exploited (see van Breda, 2010: 269–71; Germann, 2010: 290). The children themselves complain very often that they do not have anyone who speaks for them and defends them against accusations. They frequently feel left alone and claim for example: "If you are alone, you are discouraged" (quoted in Tolfree, 2004: 166). Children who care for their own survival and that of their siblings may lack opportunities to be with other children and, when they grow older, to find a possible partner for life. The following statements of children from Rwanda and Tanzania who lived in such households illustrate well what affects these children (quoted by Tolfree, 2004: 162):

> I am 14 years old and I am a child. But if I ever get married, I know I will always continue to take care of my children. How could a family abandon its children? To me, a family is a group of people who care for each other when they are hungry or sick. I have a family, I just need a home.

> I am too young to be a mother, but I am a mother and I would never leave my brother and sister alone.

> I am 12 years old and came here with my parents who all passed away one year ago and I don't like to be separated from my young sisters and brothers, we stay together, I take care for them especially the young one who is 1 year old … In order to care for him I have been compelled to drop from school … But we enjoy when we are together without being interfered by anybody outside our family.

Such preferences are usually not respected by organizations who, in the name of children's rights, promote the protection of and provision for abandoned children and children living separated from adults. David Tolfree (2004: 161) reports that, for instance, children living in such households in Tanzania were hard to convince to confide in a substitutive family despite enormous difficulties encountered in their own house. In Malawi, child-headed households are principally viewed as inappropriate by other members of the communities, even if the oldest 'child' is already 18 or older.

Children who live in child-headed households encounter many difficulties. As they experience little recognition for their way of living and are hardly supported, they often have difficulties earning their living. A 15-year-old boy uses these words (quoted by Tolfree 2004: 165):

> What choice do I have? I am 15 years old. I do not know how to raise these girls. I do not know how to look after them. I can take care of myself but I cannot take care of them. Sometimes I do not know what to do. Without me, they would have no food to eat, no place to sleep. But what can I do?

Insofar as they have to provide their own livelihood and the state authorities do not pay attention to their particular situation, they often cannot attend school (van Breda, 2010: 272–4). The children, who have to take care of their survival and their siblings around the clock, are under heavy social and emotional stress (van Breda, 2010: 266–68). The children's problems result not least from the fact that they are deprived of acceptance, recognition and respect for the unconventional ways of life they have developed (Germann, 2010: 294).

Nonetheless, child-headed households can be more than an emergency solution and can bring some advantages for the children. They enable siblings to stay together and strengthen mutual relations that are also important later in life. David Tolfree (2004: 163–4) reports, that some children particularly mentioned the fear of being separated from their siblings and to be maltreated when living in care families or homes. This is partly based on their own experiences. Sometimes, living together can also be a way of not losing the house or to continue work and practices established there that are indispensable for survival. Older children emphasize that it is especially important to them not to lose economic independence in order to have a better start to adult life.

The children show a strong sense of togetherness and develop skills to deal with even the most difficult situations (Germann, 2010: 293; Kendrick and Kakuru, 2012). Angelika Wolf (2010: 189) quotes a boy from a child-headed household in Malawi:

> What I see that enables us to live together, is the spirit of unity that is among us. We do not argue about certain issues... – for example, when our father died, there were conflicts over property – and one wants to go his own way. But we, we sit together and consult each other or tell each other how we should do things, we exchange ideas. We do not care about age, one listens to the other. We do things like a single person.

The difficult life situation rarely allows consistent solutions. The children are usually forced to find compromises in which some have to forego wishes in favour of others. For example, in two child-headed households studied in Malawi, 'the eldest sisters took over the household and care of the younger siblings. They did not go back to school to find work and earn money. They attached great importance to enabling younger siblings to attend school' (Wolf, 2010: 199). The children were not content with this situation, but tried to 'be heard by neighbours and other villagers, to persuade others or to move them to act in their favour' (Wolf, 2010: 197).

For the children, much depends on the recognition and support by adults in their unusual, need-born way of life in order to solve their problems. In some African countries, the need has now also been seen by governments to provide support to children's budgets and to create a legal framework for them. South Africa is the first country where child-headed households have gained legal recognition as a new form of family and have been included in the state welfare system (see Couzens and Noel Zaal, 2009; van Breda, 2010). However, there has been much debate in South Africa and other African countries over the years, as to whether children are only considered as care subjects or are included as partners in their search for possible solutions and accepted in their own individuality and with their own ideas.

When children are reliant on helping themselves, as in the cases of migrant, street or orphaned children, their interests are met best if they find recognition and support for the form of living they feel appropriate. Only then will the children be able to see the value in children's rights and perhaps use them to their advantage.

Paternalism and children's participation

> The modern concept of childhood, which in Europe dates from the sixteenth century and stresses the innocence, frailty and dependence of children, forcefully ejected children

> from the worlds of work, sexuality and politics – in which previously they were active participants – and designed the classroom as the major focus for their lives. Children were no longer allowed to earn money or to decide how to spend their time; they were forced into dependency on adults and obliged to study and play. (Franklin, 2002: 17)

This model of childhood is based on a strict separation between adults and children. As opposed to traditional forms of paternalism, which assumes the unquestioning subordination of children under the power of adults, the modern model of childhood provides children with spaces, in which they, within a limited framework, can learn and develop freely. Yet this independence is limited by the spatial and time constraints of childhood and does not allow children to interfere with the adult world. Thus, the paternalism of society has not been overcome, it has simply been made less visible. The providing of protection and care for children went hand in hand with their loss of independence, a historical process, which is sometimes also referred to as 'infantilization'.[12]

At the time of European colonization, the Western model of childhood was gradually propagandized in Africa and an attempt was made to implement it, as can be seen especially in the institutionalization of classroom education. The accompanying freedoms, however, were granted to children in the colonies in an inconsistent, unequal manner, or were limited to privileged minorities.[13] The modern concept of childhood, until today, often discredits certain life practices as backwards or outdated. These include circumstances in which children take on responsibilities in a completely independent way, thereby learning essential capabilities at an earlier age than is expected by the European model of childhood, and assume an active role in their living environment. In looking at the contemporary postcolonial situation in Africa, questions must be asked about which model of childhood has emerged out of the encounter of European influences and African traditions, and how, therein, the relationship between children and adults is structured.

In African societies, the child is usually viewed as an integral member of the community, perhaps endowed with specific capabilities, and not rigidly separated from the adult members, their activities and practices. Depending on their capacities (which are not necessarily assessed by chronological age), children are expected to take over specific tasks which are important for the community.[14] These tasks can be social, economic or political in nature, as, for example, taking part in fieldwork, carrying out household chores or assuming political responsibility in and for the larger community. Concurrently, specific arrangements can be observed (for instance in Western and Eastern Africa), through which children are granted specific goods and resources such as arable land or animals. This may occur in the form of early inheritances during the lifetime of the parents or as a collective contribution of the community. These inheritances do not have the quality of 'private property', but are expected to be used to serve the whole community (Liebel, 2004: 77–111). These expectations and arrangements can be interpreted both as prerequisites for participation and forms of it (without explicitly being called that way or being individually obtainable rights). In terms of the social position and influence of children, these arrangements can go well beyond Western concepts and practices of children's participation, since these children are thought of as full and responsible members in their respective communities or societies.

A different but relatively common conception in African cultures requires children to be unreservedly obedient towards and at the disposal of elder members of the community (above all, in relation to their 'providers'), and to absolutely respect and follow their elders' decisions. For example, Tanzanian jurist Bart Rwezaura (1998: 59) describes the intergenerational relations in Eastern and Southern Africa as characterized by an ethic of dominance, through which children's social and economic contributions are determined:

> [The bond between children and elders] is contained in the notion of filial respect and is in turn reinforced by the ethic of dominance. … Every child was born and raised into this system in which his or her social and economic roles and duties were more or less predetermined.

The situation in parts of Western Africa is depicted in similar terms by Ghanaian sociologist Afua Twum-Danso (2005), who also emphasizes children's risk to be castigated violently. In such cases, children are not entitled to question elder persons or to demand explanations or reasons for their behaviour and decisions. Such a pattern of generational relations could be described as paternalistic in a traditional sense. That means, children participate in the doings of society, while being excluded from the talking and deciding about the contents and terms of their doing. It is not only difficult to conceive how such a situation could be conciliated with children's participation based on their own will, but it also violates their dignity and possibly endangers their life.

Ghanaian philosopher Kwasi Wiredu (1996: 158) emphasizes, here with regard to the beliefs of the Akan people in Ghana, that all human beings from birth on are valued as *social* beings qualified to 'human dignity', and therefore must be treated with a 'certain basic respect'. According to him, the Akan have a strong sense that children, due to their biologically conditioned dependency, have the right to be lovingly protected, nurtured and educated. He sees a problem, however, in the Akan attitude that children do not have the right to their own opinion, especially if it differs from that of the older people.

> It is easy to understand that in a traditional society both knowledge and wisdom would tend to correspond with age. Hence, the deliverances of the old would command virtually automatic respect. But an unhappy consequence of this was the self-expression of minors was apt to be rigorously circumscribed. Dissent on the part of a minor in the face of adult pronouncements was almost equated with disrespect or obstinacy. ... Indeed, given the traditional ethos, minors usually came to internalize the imperative of acquiescence. But in the modern context such an ethos must take on an aspect distinctly inconsonant with the rights of nonadults in the matter of freedom of expression (Wiredu, 1996: 170).

Nevertheless, the *respect* often emphasized and demanded of the young towards senior persons in African societies can have significations that might elude such a verdict. Respect does not necessarily mean subordination under others, but can also allude to the recognition of expertise and traditional knowledge represented by these persons. Respect in this sense is not only directed towards persons, but includes a thoughtful approach towards the natural environment and livelihood. It could be interpreted as aiming at a more 'harmonic' coexistence characterized by solidarity, attention and mutual esteem, also practised in relation to children.

These, at times contradictory, norms and practices described in the preceding paragraphs can coexist within the social reality of a community or society, overlap, only be valid for select spheres or levels of the social (for instance the family, the 'public' sphere)[15] and be applied differently depending on the child's gender. We also have to distinguish between the norms and pretences of a society and the actual practices, with the latter possibly being much more fluid than the former would suggest. Additionally, the question arises as to what extent specific ideas of participation or its contrary are intertwined with power structures and aspire to change or preserve them. Participation is not transformative per se, but can also be put to manipulatively integrative uses or maintain power relations.

To demonstrate how diverse and, in part, contradictory both the relations between elder and the young and the social position of children in African societies and communities can be understood, I finally turn towards an example from Eritrea. Among the two Eritrean ethnic groups the Tigrinya and Saho, the rule applies to always keep children away from important, especially complicated matters.

> The Tigrinya and Saho informants stated that the participation of the child in family and community issues depends on whether the child could be bothered or mentally disturbed after hearing the conversation. ... The informants believe that if a child listens to family or neighbourhood disputes it could develop feelings of resentment or hostility against one of the parents or neighbours. ... A child can attend discussions in the local assembly upon reaching adolescence. (Woldeslase et al, 2002: 30, quoted in Fleischhauer, 2008: 77)

In sharp contrast, in the same country, among the ethnical groups Tigre and Hedareb, a child has

> ... maximum opportunity to participate in family and community affairs. A child is permitted to listen and contribute ideas in family discussion held between a mother and a father. A child is welcome to suggest choices of pasture and render an opinion which of the livestock could be sold or exchanged. ... A male child is welcome to attend any discussion held in a local assembly. The purpose is ... to educate and inform the child in all family and community affairs (Woldeslase et al, 2002: 30, quoted in Fleischhauer, 2008: 77).

In dealing with such stark differences in the social position of children (also keeping in mind the differing social position between boys and girls), it is urgent not to conventionalize Africa, or individual African countries, as culturally homogenous. The same can be said for the way in which colonial heritage and present day Western influences are reconciled. Apart from subservient imitation, which can especially be found in African 'elites' and state authorities, many people try to arrive at quite independent, and at times also resistant answers to the aforementioned opposing influences and challenges. This applies especially to young people. Just as much or perhaps even more so than adults, they do not live isolated from what is happening in other countries and other parts of the world. For the future, much will depend on how they can make use of the information available today, including children's rights, for their own position in society and the world.

Conclusion

The postcolonial constellation is an unequal material and ideological, or rather epistemological, power relation, which leaves little room for childhoods that do not represent the dominant model of childhood in the Global North. On a material level, the lives of most children in Africa are defined by the notion that they are cut off from essential resources and must grow up in precarious circumstances. These circumstances are a result of lasting economic and political dominance of the Global North and the corresponding dependencies, disadvantages and forms of multiple discrimination. On the epistemological level, children's lifestyles that represent the cultural traditions passed down in African societies are made invisible. Furthermore, in dominant discourses, Africans children's lifestyles are not only denied recognition, they are mocked, pitied and considered 'children without childhood' at best. The postcolonial exercise of power, however, does not simply replace 'old' childhoods with 'new' childhoods, it creates rather a hybrid entity, with a masked potential for subversiveness. This potential for subversiveness cannot merely be lifted, by making an inquiry into original African childhoods. Such an inquiry will necessarily be entangled with myths and idealisms, yet, denial also not the solution. On these grounds, it was not my intention in this chapter to search for a so-called 'lost childhood', but rather to look into the positioning of new childhoods, which have arisen and continue to arise from the postcolonial constellation.

If we look at African children, particularly those living in precarious conditions, from a critical postcolonial perspective, we may become aware that many of them are on the move to new horizons. They cannot be perceived only as victims but rather as social subjects with own ideas and strategies for a better life. Many of them are aware that their future neither can be found in an idealized past nor in imitating Western life models. Rather, they feel obliged to invent solutions for their day-by-day problems by mixing own answers from the information and knowledge they are able to access. Surely, being aware of their right to live in dignity and to be respected may be a strong motive for their agency. Nevertheless, they cannot realize such a life without the support of others.

Ways must be found to strengthen the social position of children in African societies in order to work against the pressure and marginalization they face. Advocating for one's own rights, such as those embedded in the UNCRC or the African Charter of the Rights and Welfare of the Child, may be helpful if the children can utilize these rights in their particular circumstances. It is equally important that children find the opportunity to join forces and form organizations where they can discuss their mutual interests and provide support for one another and together with adults. When this occurs, as for instance in the case of working children's movements (see Liebel, 2012b) or child-headed households, it can be observed that children take a stand for their interests and rights with confidence, and that they attach great importance to playing an active role in their associations, communities and societies. The scope of participation claimed and practised by these children goes beyond the forms of participation usually allowed to children in the Global North.

To these children who organize themselves, it is not about conserving traditional customs, but rather picking up on experiences and knowledge which grow out of international interdependence and postcolonial constellations. Their movements embody a perspective of *liberation* from below, which reaches beyond the *emancipation* from a determined generational relationship. Within these movements, a concrete, 'exteriorised' corporeality is articulated (Dussel, 1980). One could argue that social movements of children in the Global South are marked by the creativity of a renewed, not only de-colonized, but also unique, novel culture, based on equitable, intercultural dialogue and mutual recognition.

Notes

[1] Dorothy Munyakho (1992: 10) also points to the fact that the British colonial power hindered women from continuing to use the land and forced them to migrate to the cities through a new regulation of ownership. 'The official registration of land that begun under the colonial era meant that farms were almost always registered in the name of individuals, invariably men. This put an end to the group ownership systems that used to pertain, where a village might own land communality and plots were then allocated to families according to their need. ... For women whose husbands had migrated to cities this was a double blow. Forbidden [in colonial times] to accompany their husbands to the towns, they then found their access to land was forfeit because their husbands were not there to register the land in their names. [In the slums] of Nairobi, an in-depth study [in 1990] revealed that only 20 per cent of the parents had been born in the area. The rest had all come in from

the surrounding countryside. … The reasons they gave for migrating illustrate the problems women in rural areas have in maintaining their access to land.'

[2] In the Islamic African societies, polygamy was widespread and legally permissible, but it is largely rejected by today's young generation, especially women. On the debates of women with polygamy, see the impressive novels of Mariama Bâ (1979; 1981) and Sembène Ousmane (1995).

[3] Brock-Utne (2000: 126) also points out that African elites support the use of colonial languages, as they do the privatisation of the education system, first and foremost because of the advantage it provides for their own children. See also Myers-Scotton (1993) on elite closure by language strategies.

[4] In Africa, I have repeatedly met children and adolescents who were at home in several African languages, without always governing the respective state language (English, French or Portuguese).

[5] Ina Gankam Tambo (2014) examines this for Nigeria with the example of children migrating to the cities to find a job as domestic workers. In doing so, she also pursues the restructuring of family relations forced by the capitalist mode of production and the changing division of labor between men, women and children (for similar processes in the Ivory Coast, see Jacquemin, 2006).

[6] In the Global North and in China, the fact that trade policy and the development policies of European nations, the European Union, the United States and now China play a part in these violations is often overlooked.

[7] For a critique of this understanding of children's rights and possible alternatives, see Liebel (2012a); Hanson and Nieuwenhuys (2013); Vandenhole et al (2015).

[8] These are ILO Convention 138 of 1973, which sets minimum ages for work, and ILO Convention 182 of 1999, which defines the 'worst form of child labour'.

[9] On the problem of the term 'street children' and the research approaches associated with the term 'children out of place', see Invernizzi et al (2017).

[10] An ethnographic study with street children in Dar es Salaam, the capital of Tanzania, came up with similar results (Wagner et al, 2012).

[11] On the importance of local orientations in the practice of children's rights, also with reference to examples in Africa, see Vandenhole (2012).

[12] On the distinction of 'traditional' and 'modern' forms of paternalism in the relations between adults and children, see Liebel (2007a).

[13] It should also be noted that during colonial rule many children were denied a childhood status at all with the purpose of exploiting them more easily (see Nieuwenhuys, 2007).

[14] This is reflected in the African Charter on the Rights and Welfare of the Child (1990) where is stated in art. 31, among other things, that 'the child … shall have a duty to work for the cohesion of the family, to respect his parents, superiors and elders at all times and to assist them in case of need'. This duty mirrors that proclaimed by the American Convention on Human Rights (1969), where it provides in art. 32(1) that 'every person has responsibilities to his family, his community, and mankind' (on the African Charter, see Olowu, 2002; Lloyd, 2002; 2008; Kaime, 2009; Ekundayo, 2015).

[15] For instance, see the differentiation of social 'levels' and correspondingly different extents of economic participation within a society or community in Girling's (1960) description of the Acholi of Northern Uganda.

PART III

Children's rights and
the decolonization of childhoods

7

Postcolonial dilemmas
of children's rights

The fact that there is no guaranteed universality of human rights but only a process of their universalization, has consequences for how every conception of human rights must understand itself and must act towards itself: it must undergo a permanent self-criticism. (Christoph Menke and Arnd Pollmann, *Philosophie der Menschenrechte*, 2007: 85)

White people think of themselves as white and without a race, just as men (and often women) consider gender to be an issue for women. The claim of unsituatedness is made by and on behalf of those with power. To the extent the Convention [on the Rights of the Child] deals with children as unspecified, unsituated people, it tends in fact to deal with white, male, and relatively privileged children. (Frances Olsen, 'Children's Rights: Some feminist approaches to the United Nations Convention on the Rights of the Child', 1995: 195)

Introduction

Whoever wants to deal with children and childhoods in the world today and wants to be clear about their universal rights must refer to the UN Convention on the Rights of the Child (UNCRC, the Convention). This international convention unanimously ratified by the United Nations General Assembly in 1989 and ratified by almost all states (with the exception of the US) is the culmination of a process that is based on the postulation of human rights in the European Enlightenment. It has also strongly influenced worldwide debates about what is suitable for children and what children are to be entitled to. In these debates, the Convention is by no means unanimously welcomed. In addition to those who question children's rights in general, reasoning that children are not capable of rational thinking, even children's rights advocates stand hold at least two opposing positions. While some consider the

Convention as a 'milestone' on the way to a better childhood and only complain about its lacking implementation, the others see it as an imperial Eurocentric project that globalizes the Western notions of childhood despite cultural diversity and imposes it on the 'rest of the world'.

This chapter is an attempt to go beyond these controversial positions and to arrive at a more differentiated assessment of children's rights. The construction of childhood, which is transported with the Convention, is undoubtedly of Western origin and can lead to ignore and misinterpret childhoods that do not correspond with this construction. However, it is important to acknowledge that the Convention has sensitized for the needs and interests of children who have so far received little attention and who have been given little consideration. Presumably, the existence of an international treaty on children's rights has not prevented the abominations and crimes committed against children, but the Convention has created a legal instrument to accuse (and prosecute) and combat such atrocities and crimes more effectively. Not least by children themselves, who can now rely on rights of their own, which are guaranteed internationally.

In recent years, research approaches have emerged which can be helpful for a differentiated evaluation of children's rights – also in postcolonial contexts. These include concepts like 'children's rights from below' (Liebel, 2012a), 'living rights' (Hanson and Nieuwenhuys, 2013) or 'critical children's rights studies' (Vandenhole et al, 2015). They have in common that they comprehend children's rights not only as a legal construct that speaks for itself and needs only to be implemented, but also as a historically developed specific result of social disputes, which is understood in a process-oriented and contextualized manner and must be further developed. In their understanding, 'children's rights are not only about rules, but also about structures, relationships and processes' (Reynaert et al, 2015: 5; see also Morrow and Pells, 2012; Mayall, 2015; Cordero Arce, 2015). These new approaches do not doubt that children's rights as stated in the UNCRC are the most important legal basis for all children in the world. However, they also draw attention to the fact that children's rights can have a different relevance and significance for children depending on their life situation and that they must be critically questioned again and again regarding their appropriateness and claim to universality.

To avoid the dilemma of a Eurocentric understanding and use of children's rights, Roy Huijsmans (2016) proposed to 'de-centre' the idea of children's rights, based on a review of two studies on the importance and use of children's rights in India (Balagopalan, 2014) and Egypt (Morrison, 2015). This proposal does not reject children's rights because of their European prehistory, but rather tries to re-conceptualize them from the perspective of children in postcolonial world regions. It resembles earlier proposals to theorize and implement a subaltern strategy for human rights (Spivak, 2008: 14–57) or to historicize their origins through 'provincializing Europe' (Chakrabarty, 2000), and re-establishing them in non-European contexts.[1] In this chapter, I will discuss some of the issues raised in this context.

Since children's rights are to be understood as human rights (Freeman, 2009; Invernizzi and Williams, 2011), the question is first of all about how the claim for universality of human rights is to be understood and assessed. I will then discuss this issue with a view to children's rights and, with reference to concrete cases, highlight their relevance for the children of the Global South, and the possible ways to decolonize them.

Ambivalences of human rights

Human rights are not free from ambivalence. They are, on the one hand, associated with their European or liberal origin, in which a human ideal prevails which emphasizes the self-responsibility of individuals. On the other hand, they revert to the circumstance that they can be instrumentalized by certain groups of people or power elites in their particular interest and have been used in this sense again and again. The universal claim of human rights is therefore also related to the concrete interest context in which they are brought into play and applied.

Against this background, for instance, Immanuel Wallerstein (2006) distinguishes, with a view to human rights, a 'European universalism' and a 'universal universalism'. He tries to show 'that the universalism of the powerful has been a partial and distorted universalism' (Wallerstein, 2006: XIV). He calls it a European universalism 'because it has been put forward by pan-European leaders and intellectuals in their quest to pursue the interests of the dominant strata of the modern world system' (2006: XIV). In the struggle between European and universal universalism, Wallerstein sees 'the central ideological struggle of the contemporary world' (2006: XIV). He describes European universalism as a 'morally ambiguous doctrine', as justifying 'simultaneously the defence of the human rights of so-called innocent and the material exploitation engaged in by the strong' (2006: 28). It attacks the crimes of some and disregards the crimes of others. Wallerstein does not deny that global universal values exist and must exist, but they only gain meaning for all if they cannot be monopolized by the fittest. This requires a worldwide 'structure that is far more egalitarian than any we have constructed up to now' (Wallerstein, 2006: 28).[2]

Also Edward Said (1978) expressly warns of alleged universalisms in his seminal work *Orientalism*; they not only conceal power structures and their inequalities, but also decisively promote and preserve the existing immoral polarizations. He sees an expression of 'doctrines of European superiority' (Said, 1978: 8) in them, which are embedded in a 'formidable structure of cultural domination' (1978: 25). It is certainly not coincidental that criticism of human rights discourse dominated by states and NGOs from the Global North is expressed by representatives of postcolonial theory. It is striking that many double standards are applied to human rights again and again, and the Global North stylizes itself as the guardian of human rights, while the Global South is subject to a backlog of demand in human rights.

The legal scholar Makau Mutua (2016), from Kenya, criticizes human rights discourse as only seeing deficits in the Global South. This results from the shortcomings of an international order that is characterized by multiple asymmetries and, in setting standards, produces a cultural bias in favour of the North. In an earlier work, Mutua (2002) had criticized the human rights movement of being interested in proving that the Global South is barbaric and cannot bring about any functioning state structures. According to this, the saviours from the civilized nations pretend to stand by the victims against the savages:

> The human rights movement is marked by a damning metaphor. The grand narrative of human rights contains a subtext which depicts an epochal contest pitting savages, on the one hand, against victims and saviours, on the other. (Mutua, 2002: 10)

Human rights policy is criticized by Mutua as a victimizing tool. He sees the action and power in the governments of the Global North and the International Non-Governmental Organizations (INGO), which also reside in the North. According to him, their gesture toward the Global South stands in a line of continuity with the former colonial officials and missionaries. Human rights would often be instrumentalized for pushing liberal ideologies of government and trade, for example through so-called free trade-agreements (see also Mutua, 2009). As an alternative, Mutua calls for an inclusive and participatory standardization process on a global scale, and devises a 'multicultural' concept of human rights that recognizes and takes up human rights traditions from non-Western cultures (Mutua, 2002).

This includes an understanding of human rights that does not see them as a licence to control and exploit non-human nature and does not contrast the dignity and rights of non-human beings (see also Borg, 2015; Scheid, 2016; Rües and Jones, 2016).

Mutua's considerations revolve around the conceptions of the state and the individual. He doubts that the modern-day national state can be the impartial (or even committed) body that monitors the observance of human rights. At least in Africa, according to him, the state is a colonial construct imposed on the people, and is not suitable as an entity that guarantees human dignity. Instead, instances that are closer to and committed to the people and that could actually represent them would have to be revived or created. Regarding the individual, he criticizes the idea that people exist self-perpetually as 'atomistic units'. Instead, he recommends recalling the conceptions of humanity, common in Africa, which understand people as dependent on each other and committed to one another. This also requires reaffirming the dialectic of rights and duties (see also Wohlgemuth and Sall, 2006).

Indisputably, human rights in their dominant form date back to the European Enlightenment since the 17th century. They found their most comprehensive legal expression in the Universal Declaration of Human Rights (UDHR) of 1948 and in the following both Covenants on Civil and Political (1966), and Economic, Social and Cultural Rights (1966). All people, according to the basic postulate of the UDHR, are endowed with equal rights. These are universally valid, indelible and indivisible. 'The idea of universal human rights was unquestionably shaped by the European philosophers of the Enlightenment, which is why the reproach of Eurocentrism is as important and just as banal at the same time' (Castro Varela, 2011: 46). A problem arises not from the idea and its European origin, but from the assertion that the history of human rights embodies a linear and unbridled progress of the Enlightenment, and is a sole achievement of Europe, a mission which the people outside of Europe would only have to copy.

Nevertheless, the UDHR is not the result of a smooth progress, but the response to the barbarism which became materialized within Europe with fascism and outside with colonialism, which, paradoxically was applied during the Enlightenment itself (see Horkheimer and Adorno, [1947]2002). It is also not free of ambiguity, as it was adopted by a minority of nation states and at a time when large parts of the world were still in a state of colonial dependency. The claim to universality was first neglected in the face of the colonies, whose desire to relate the idea of human rights to themselves was combatted with brute force by the European powers. This became clearly visible in Napoleon's campaign against the Haitian revolution at the beginning of the 19th century, and later in the colonial wars, for example, in Vietnam and Algeria. To this day, the imperial claim and the corresponding instrumental use of human rights in the 'development message' show that the Western 'democratic' powers had to teach the 'underdeveloped' nations what in their eyes are human rights.

According to Gayatri Spivak (2008), it is not a matter of condemning the idea of human rights because of its European origin, rather it is about the development of a reading of human rights from the perspective of the Global South which corresponds to the local conditions. In this way, the imperial message would also be denied that Europe as a whole was the model to be imitated. In view of the barbaric European history, which is also manifested in colonialism, and which is still present in the postcolonial world order, this would be unbelievable. It is therefore necessary to look for another way of dealing with the ideas and writings of the Enlightenment, which, according to Spivak (2008: 181), might be to 'ab-use' them by the subalterns themselves. Referring to the dictum of Horkheimer and Adorno ([1947]2002: 1), the Enlightenment programme was 'the disenchantment of the world', it could be said that this programme will be completed only when the Enlightenment itself is disenchanted.

Human rights cannot be derived solely from the 'human nature'. Hannah Arendt ([1955]1994) had already criticized this idea, which also goes back to the European Enlightenment, with reference to the 'aporias of human rights'. It meant that human rights could ultimately only be claimed by those who are recognized as part of a political community – what does not apply to the many 'stateless persons' or 'expatriates' who wander about the world. The 'right to have rights', proclaimed by Arendt, can only be solved by the political guarantee of rights and the legal recognition of all people as citizens. Consequently, the idea of human rights would have to be materialized by a 'universal citizenship', which is not linked only to national affiliation.

The legitimacy of human rights and handling them are closely linked to the issue of global justice. The universality of human rights is only credible when it goes hand in hand with efforts to achieve global justice, and when these have practical results. To this day, there is a serious social inequality in the world between the prosperous countries of the North, especially the former colonial powers, and the former colonies in the South. This inequality is based on unequally distributed economic power and is reflected by the unequal trade relations between the states and the influence of the international financial institutions dominated by the North, such as the International Monetary Fund (IMF), the

World Bank and the World Trade Organization (WTO), which nail the former colonies to the status of raw-material suppliers. A partial aspect is the 'debt trap', in which the former colonies are captured by states of the Global North and the international financial institutions. From the point of view of the Global South, the global injustice is reluctantly related to the moral guilt and the economic debts that the colonial powers have accumulated through the long-term economic exploitation of their colonies.

This inequality in the relationship between states and their populations cannot be compensated by means of benevolent aid measures, which may be seen as development aid or development cooperation, called 'international charity' by the Kenyan philosopher Henry Odera Oruka ([1989]1997: 48). The same applies to humanitarian interventions which Michael Barnett (2017) calls 'paternalism beyond borders' or David Chandler (2017) 'new international paternalism'. Instead, the moral responsibility of the wealthy states and their populations must be emphasized to recognize the fundamental right to self-preservation and to live a life of dignity, and to fulfil it with a policy, which ensures such a life for all people living on earth. It is a shortened and historically doubtful point of view that such a policy can only be understood as a 'fight against causes of flight', especially as this is the result of the interest of excluding people from the former colonies from their own territory and their own prosperity in the North.

Global justice, as understood here, goes beyond *international* justice, insofar as it transcends the national state as the horizon of possible solutions. Felix Heidenreich (2011: 207) formulates this as follows:

> While international justice means the interstate relationship, the concept of global justice involves a greater claim. It addresses the question of a fair world order, which is neither spatially nor temporally limited, takes into account all living and future people.

It is controversial to discuss how such a world order, which still exists in modest approximations to this day, could be characterized and realized. Heidenreich (2011) distinguishes three streams of thought. First, theories that are cosmopolitan: they advocate the establishment of a world order that should take over the role of the national states as a guarantor of fundamental rights. Second, theories that hold onto the role of the nation state: they conceive the future world order as a cooperation project between principally sovereign nation states (the United Nations is constructed according to this pattern). Third, mediating positions: they design models of a federal order in which (as in the case of the European Union) different bodies are to share the tasks in a multilevel system, and where there is a network of tiered liabilities between the citizens of the various states in this system.

Cosmopolitan theories, which I will discuss here, advocate

> think[ing] of justice as a value that must be realized globally and cannot be implemented on the national level alone. We are committed to justice as a person or as a citizen of the world (not only as a citizen of a particular community) (Heidenreich, 2011: 208).

If the idea of global justice is taken seriously in this sense, a global redistribution of the resources on earth must be undertaken, and all human beings would have to equally commit themselves to a lifestyle and consumption style that deals very gently with these resources and by this guarantees their existence also for future generations. Since it is not to be expected that people who have so far benefitted from the unequal world order would not relinquish privileges, the necessary redistribution would have to be ensured by a kind of global government with comprehensive competences. This also applies to people who have suffered under the unequal world order for centuries and are hoping for a better life in economic prosperity leading to attempts to escape misery through migration. They will only agree to a careful handling of natural resources if their material needs are fulfilled, as for them to be able to lead a life free of hunger and in dignity.

How complex the tasks that are to be solved are, but also the possible ways of doing so, are highlighted by the Agenda 2030 debates and negotiations by the United Nations on the Sustainable Development Goals (UN, 2015). In them, questions of global social justice are closely linked to questions of ecological and climatic justice. A just world order, which combines both dimensions, must be constituted democratically and be accountable to all people. The question arises whether the attempts to 'international' agreements between the national states made so far are the appropriate way. From a pragmatic point of view there is no other alternative to national states; however, prospectively, solutions must be envisaged and strived for in which people themselves approach each other and generate the necessary pressure to create a more just and equal world order in mutual recognition. Basic categories that can be the basis of such agreements are human dignity and the recognition of human beings as *social subjects* who are linked to, dependent on, and committed to other people.[3]

Universality claim and cultural reference of children's rights

Like all human rights codified in United Nations treaties, children's rights enshrined in the UNCRC apply worldwide. However, in Southern regions of the world, they are often criticized as being the expression of Western dominance or even arrogance and are not compatible with certain cultural traditions. The question is whether and to what extent this criticism is justified and how the universal claim of children's rights can go with cultural diversity and how the material inequalities of the present world order can be taken account of. In particular, the question of how the further development of children's rights can promote cultural specific ways of life for children as well as their equality and recognition as social subjects with their own views and how their interests can be examined.

In (academic) literature and reports, various positions are represented. Some authors, and in particular the UN Committee on the Rights of the Child,[4] stress that the CRC is open to different cultures and point out that cultures are not static, self-contained structures, but 'learning systems' (Alston, 1994; Brems, 2007). In this sense, the Convention and the UN system of human rights are generally understood as a permanently changing learning system. However, the cultures, too, are often expected to 'open up to' the idea of human and children's rights, implying an approach in which they evolve, so to speak, to become more human rights-friendly. This perspective is expressed particularly clearly by representatives of development cooperation, focusing on raising awareness and capacity building on human rights in general and on children's rights in particular.

On the other hand, some childhood researchers (Boyden, [1990]1997; Burman, 1994) noticed shortly after the adoption of the Convention that it is based on a concept of childhood that follows the dominating understanding of childhood of the Global North.[5] This concept is characterized primarily by the fact that childhood is understood 'as a time of innocence and vulnerability' (Cregan and Cuthbert, 2014: 32), in which children are dependent on protection and care by adults. The implicit reference point is a society that harms the child if they are not protected against it. This is supplemented by the idea that, as first premise, the child must be supplied with all it needs, that is, the relationship to adults or the state is not presented as interdependent but as dependent.

It is true that this concept has been expanded in comparison with the Declaration on the Rights of the Child of the League of Nations of 1924 and the UN Children's Rights Declaration of 1959. Children are identified now as legal entities capable of action and participation, but the paternalistic basic pattern is preserved. According to the UNCRC, the participation of children is limited to the promise that adults and adult-led institutions fulfil their obligations to listen to them and take the children's views into account in their decision making. In the background, it is assumed that the children would have to acquire the necessary maturity for their own decisions. The implicit point of reference here are the adults, who are presented as perfect or at least superior, not least by including the rationality embodied by them. Such assumptions confuse a paternalistic or adultist order of power with personal properties.[6]

While other authors assume that the UNCRC and the concept of human rights are open to different cultures, they also take a critical look at the ways in which human rights and, in particular children's rights are interpreted. Among other things, they criticize the fact that the discourse of human rights and children's rights is instrumentalized by certain power groups and that these act as 'moral watch dogs' in order to 'modernize' and 'civilize' backward cultures and ways of life (Pupavac, 1998; Bentley, 2005; Burr, 2004, 2006; Valentine and Meinert, 2009; Montgomery, 2001, 2017). A 'colonialist paternalism' would be encouraged 'where Northern "child experts" offer their help and knowledge to the "infantilized-South"' (Cockburn, 2006: 84). The objections to this intercourse with human and children's rights are not necessarily guided by cultural relativist considerations, but expressly distinguish between 'real culture' and the 'culture presented to outsiders by governments and intellectuals' (Freeman, 2002: 30; similar Harris-Short, 2003). Their objections are, above all, that human rights and children's rights are ordained from above by state orders and by power elites, and they argue for a 'localization' of the understanding of the law and 'dialogical' procedures (Vandenhole, 2012). In this way, lifestyles and cultures are not to be depreciated as fundamentally backward, but their diversity and their particular meaning are to be recognized and promoted. This assumes, however, that the concept of childhood, on which the UNCRC is based, is not understood as the historically most advanced stage of childhood ('childhood of modernity'; criticized by Alanen, 1992) and as the absolute norm for supposedly left-back societies and cultures (critically, Bentley, 2005).

The UNCRC is based on a seemingly simple formal definition of the child by naming an age range within which young people are considered to be children (up to the age of 18). Such a definition may be difficult to avoid in a legal document, but it does not necessarily correspond to what is understood in a specific society or culture as a 'child' or 'childhood'. The age range is very broad and can therefore only be comprehended in a relatively abstract manner, according to the specific interests and self-understanding of young people in this age group. The subjective interests of a 16-year old have little in common with the subjective interests of a toddler; a child who lives in absolute poverty will set different priorities from a child living in prosperity. Likewise, the children's and young people's agency competences differ and demand for specific concepts and arrangements for protection and participation. Children who take responsibility for others at an early age often feel 'infantilized' by being called a child.

In most cultures of the Global South, a distinction is made between children and adults, but this is usually not achieved by marking the chronological age, but by recognizing their competences that are expressed in transmitting tasks and the assumption of responsibility. In such cultures and societies, the date of birth is often not regarded as important, and hardly anyone knows in years or is interested in how old someone is 'exactly'. The sharp separation between childhood and awakening-sense, marked by chronological age indications, inevitably leads to misunderstandings, 'wrong' attributions or discriminations. This also applies if the children's concrete living conditions and the cultural context are not sufficiently taken into account, as the following example from South America demonstrates.

In contributions to a comparative study between the UNCRC and childhood representations in the Andean and Amazonian cultures of South America, fundamental differences are indicated. The preamble to the Convention stresses that 'the child, by reason of his physical and mental immaturity, needs special safeguards and care'. Differently, in the mode of life and cosmovisions of the Andean and Amazonian peoples, the child is not considered as 'a person in evolution', but the children are seen as 'persons with attributes and responsibilities in their family, as well as in their community and the natural environment' (ABA, 2011, cited in terre des hommes, 2014: 11).[7] The Quechua word *wawa* is not synonymous with the term child, 'because within the communities the body of an old man encompasses the child and the body of a child likewise the old man' (Carillo Medina and Jaulis, 2012, cited in terre des hommes, 2014: 11). In the case of festivities and rituals, childhood is not equated with a certain age (Carillo Medina and Jaulis, 2012, cited in terre des hommes, 2014: 11):

> Boys and girls of 7 years, 'already know how to spend their lives', that means they already know how to till the

field, they already know how to deal with the animals, and so do 'they already know how to talk with the gods and nature'. In order for the child 'to be able to defend himself in life', the parents and the Ayllu [traditional form of the community] make a vital contribution; they not only enable him, to have 'a good heart for ploughing [chacra]', 'a good heart for the animals', 'a good heart for the production of clothing', 'a good heart for the takeover of responsibility and leadership', but also 'to improve their temperament' and to have a character that will contribute to harmony between people, nature and the Andean gods.[8]

With these critical remarks, I do not want to disesteem the fact that children with the UNCRC for the first time are granted the status of legal subjects under international law, but rather point to its limitations and (contrary to human rights principles) to its conditionality. Nor do I want to deny that the Convention contains a number of wording which includes recognition of other cultures and of the childhoods practised there. Thus it is stated in the preamble that the state agreements enshrined in the Convention and all corresponding measures are to be understood as 'taking due account of the importance of the traditions and cultural values of each people for the protection and harmonious development of the child'. But the UNCRC leaves little scope for imagining other childhoods and child rights concepts that do not correspond to the structural pattern of 'modern' Western childhood.[9] They are indeed practised in some cultures, can even point out the societies and cultures known to us, and are possibly brought forth by children themselves.

Best interests assessments in the pitfalls of universalism and cultural relativism

Regarding the debate between universalism and cultural relativism, I want to highlight some of the problems that arise when applying the principle of the best interests of the child, which is fundamental for the UNCRC.[10] Like international human rights law, the best interest principle takes legitimacy from its claim to universality, but it must be adaptable to different cultures and local circumstances. While the best interests' principle enjoys wide support and was incorporated seemingly without question into the UNCRC (Cantwell, 2016: 19), understanding of what constitutes the best interests of a child and which factors are most important may vary from culture to culture.

For example, living arrangements or child rearing practices commonly seen as neglectful or improper from a Western point of view may for some communities represent normal and important arrangements in community life.

Research in the Australian Aboriginal community, for instance, has shown that household constellations and arrangements which do not conform to European norms, such as extended family households, co-sleeping and the placing of trust and responsibility on older children to care for their younger siblings are often perceived negatively by the non-indigenous community or state authorities. Such practices may be labelled 'overcrowding' or 'parentification' without necessarily understanding whether the situation is really harmful for the children involved (Long and Sephton, 2011: 106). In the Nunga community in Australia it is important that children are taught independence and responsibility for younger siblings, therefore parents give their children trust and freedom in a way which may be viewed as neglectful from a Eurocentric perspective. While a small child, wandering out of the sights of their parent may be seen as an indication of poor parenting by some, from another perspective it indicates the parents' trust in the ability of both the child and their siblings to ensure they are safe.

Such examples demonstrate the difficulty of determining best interests when ideas about what is best for children vary from culture to culture, with the values of the majority culture being likely to dominate the discourse and legal framework. Indigenous children and children who belong to minorities are especially vulnerable to having their way of life interpreted as contrary to their 'best interests' if Eurocentric ideas of childhood are applied without reflection. This vulnerability to the effects of cultural bias is compounded if decision makers are unaware or unwilling to apply the best interests 'test' to ensure the realization of children's rights. Decision makers who allow subjective ideas of what is best for the child to override rights considerations are in greater danger of bringing cultural prejudices into the decision and imposing values on children which may be inconsistent with those of their community, especially if (as is often the case) the decision maker comes from the dominant culture.

The recognition that certain aspects of child rearing may vary between different groups should not lead to the blind acceptance of any practice or view claimed to be 'part of the culture'. Marie-Benedicte Dembour (2001: 56) warns against the dangers of either taking universalism or cultural relativism too far. She characterizes 'universalism as arrogance and relativism as indifference', highlighting that while universalism can exclude the experiences of minorities, relativism taken too far can be used to excuse and justify any action. When applied without reflection or nuance, cultural relativism can be just as harmful to minority groups as Eurocentric universalism because it treats minorities as clearly defined, homogeneous groups and ignores the internal dynamics and diversity of opinion within these communities (Dembour, 2001: 155).

The dominant discourse has been described as comparing culture to biological characteristics, as something a group of people 'has', rather than a diverse and varying set of practices and beliefs, which are developed and used to adapt to different circumstances (Merry, 2001: 42). The danger of this approach is that minority cultures, in particular, are treated as fixed and unmoving, change is seen as inevitably negative, and homogeneity is assumed within the group. While Western or mainstream culture is allowed – and even expected – to develop, activists and academics become consumed with the 'preservation' of indigenous and minority cultures which are then expected to stay stagnant to be seen as successfully preserved (Cowen et al, 2001: 19). This preoccupation with the preservation and perceived authenticity of indigenous and minority cultures ignores the reality of today's interconnected world and limits the possibilities of these communities by painting 'traditional cultures' as in general opposition to international human rights, commerce and communication technologies deemed to be purely 'Western'.

Cultural relativist criticisms of the international human rights framework often focus on human rights mechanisms as instruments of neo-colonialism (Burke, 2010: 133), citing for example the appropriation of women's rights rhetoric to legitimize military interventions in majority world countries (Mies, 2005: 101). While these concerns are justified, such criticisms are apt to ignore how the idea of universal human rights has also been embraced and applied by minorities and colonized peoples (Merry, 2001: 34), often against the opposition of Western powers (Burke, 2010: 114). Ronald Burke points out that the main supporters of cultural relativism in the 1950s were not majority world countries in Africa or Asia, but imperial powers which used cultural relativist arguments to justify denying human rights to people living in their colonies. At this time, 'rights were an anticolonial threat, not a neo-colonial weapon' (Burke, 2010: 114) and colonial powers made substantial efforts to portray human rights as only applicable to 'civilized societies' and as at odds with traditional cultures.

The recognition that cultural relativism has its roots in the racist rhetoric of Western powers is not to deny the value of a relativist perspective or the reality of instrumentalization of human rights by neo-colonialist powers. However, Burke's observations do highlight the importance of treating cultural relativism with caution, especially when it is used to suggest that a certain right is not applicable to a certain group 'because of their culture'. In any best interests assessment, the claim that a particular right is less important to a group of children based on their 'ethnic' background, or that the importance of maintaining a connection with culture justifies the endangerment of other rights, should never been accepted without questioning.

Illustrative of this point is research with Aboriginal activists in Australia who expressed an uncompromising commitment to the principle of acting in the best interests of children, calling into question the claims of some academics who have described the best interests concept as Eurocentric, individualistic and in conflict with the ways of life in collectivist societies (Long and Sephton, 2011: 103). It is really important to recognize the individual thinking that underlies the best interests concept and human rights generally; nevertheless, blanket statements which deem best interests incompatible with 'collectivist cultures' ignore the diversity of opinion and belief within societies. Furthermore, they deny the agency of people including children who use and want to use the best interests concept and the human rights framework in harmony with and support of their practices and beliefs.

Cultural relativism applied without questioning can also endanger the rights of people within minorities. In discussions of practices such as Female Genital Mutilation (FGM), for example, a cultural relativist approach without nuances risks ignoring the fact that FGM does not have the unanimous support within practising communities (Cowen et al, 2001: 5). Affirmations about culture made on behalf of an entire minority group reflect the interests and power structures within that group that should be examined and criticized to the same extent as similar claims in society at large. Indigenous and minority communities, as well as society in general, are made up of privileged members who have the power to represent and even define the group, and members who are silenced or lack power. It is also overlooked that they are made up of individuals who have their own identities that may or may not focus on their ethnicity or other minority status. This process of categorizing individuals and making assumptions about their needs and preferences based on minority status limits them and excludes the possibilities they might have preferred (see Dembour, 2001: 59).

The criticism against Eurocentrism attached to the discourse of human rights must be balanced by also addressing the risks of over-emphasizing cultural relativism. As social subjects whose points of view are usually attributed the least value, children are particularly vulnerable when universalism or cultural relativism are taken dogmatically at all. This is especially true for indigenous children and children belonging to minority groups. They are in danger, on the one hand, of being subjected to the imposition of Eurocentric ideals of childhood through ostensible evaluations of the 'best interests' or, on the other, of being erased as individuals and seen only as members of a certain group.

Case studies on dilemmas of children's rights

Children's rights do not arise or exist in an ahistorical and non-societal space. Their claim for universal validity applies to a world characterized by unequal power and cultural diversity. In order to make visible the contradictions between this claim on one hand and its legitimacy and the possible effects on the other, I will use examples from the Asian and Latin American region to refer to problematic applications of the universality claim.

Dilemmas due to different concepts of children's rights: the case of Vietnam

In a study that deals with the implementation of the UNCRC in Vietnam, Rachel Burr (2006) criticizes the international and local children's relief organizations operating there for propagating conceptions of childhood that by no means correspond with the children's reality and therefore create 'unrealistic and unattainable expectations' (Burr, 2006: 22). Many children need help, but this is only possible if one takes 'the trouble to get to know them and understand their culture' (Burr, 2006: 23). There is a gap between two worlds:

> the world in which the children fought to make a living, often without any understanding that anyone was on their side, and the other world, in which agencies thought they were on the children's side but often had a limited understanding of the children's real problems. (Burr, 2006: 21)

The understanding of human rights and children's rights, which exists in the country itself (see Tai, 1988, 2004–05), is neither taken into account nor taken seriously by the children's aid organizations.

Burr sees one of the reasons for this in the fact that the *Law on Child Protection, Care, and Education*, which was adopted in 1991, was ignored internationally (by UNICEF) and by local relief organizations because it did not correspond to their conceptions of childhood and children's rights (Burr, 2006: 19). It is considered particularly obnoxious that children are expected 'to show love, respect and piety toward grandparents and parents, politeness toward adults, affection towards younger children and solidarity with friends' (Burr, 2006: 19).[11] When rejecting such provisions, it is overlooked that these are not conditions to which the granting of rights is linked but rather moral claims and expectations. It is therefore not appropriate to speak of duties imposed on the children, but rather of the expectation for a kind of shared responsibility. As the quintessence of her study, Rachel Burr still sees Vietnam 'being invaded in a more subtle but nevertheless nefarious manner, this time by cultural hijackers' (Burr, 2006: 25), even after the formal end of the colonial rule.

As further examples, I will go into more detail on two case studies from India and Indonesia. They are concerned with children who are dependent on the streets and other public spaces of large cities as sites of work and living. When they are commonly referred to as street children, the impression is made that they are members of a single group, who are a social problem and particularly needy. It is easily forgotten that 'the street' is used by them in quite different ways and has different meanings for them. Some children use the public space for work, for example, and then return to their family. Other children depend on it because they have no home or family, so that it becomes their central place in life. In turn, others practically live with their families in the public space or change their place of life according to necessity and own interests. The term 'street child' is also problematic because it suggests negative associations and can contribute to additional discrimination against children, which is why the children almost never call themselves or want to be designated as street children. Since the term is used in the case studies discussed here, I cannot avoid using it in the following presentation, but its problematic aspects are always to be considered.

Dilemmas due to unequal positions of children and adults: the case of Calcutta, India

In three examples of street children's projects in the Indian metropolis of Calcutta, Sarada Balagopalan (2013, 2014) shows how unexpectedly and determinedly the children understood the rights which are granted to them, and how they dealt with them. Consequently, it becomes visible what dilemmas may arise in social and educational projects when children claim their rights.

Example 1: A local NGO that worked with street children had invited children to demonstrate in a public skit that they have rights. An educator suggested to a group of 20 street children: 'This sketch should show the audience that all children have rights, you too. You have a right to food, education, to sleep beneath a mosquito net.' Shankar, one of the older boys who liked to perform as an actor said: "We are doing this skit so people really understand the way we live, the way we stay." Liton, a smaller boy who seldom said a word, interfered with the question: "Will they give us money when we tell them that we have rights?" Immediately the other boys took this up and argued loudly how this could be done. The educator answered loudly: "NO all we want is their understanding." Liton, keen not to lose out on the role added: "I know the perfect first line for the play. I can open the dialogue saying to the rest of the boys as if my character is not one of them, 'Why should the babus [middle class man] listen to you? After all they make money from people like you'" (Balagopalan, 2013: 13).

Example 2: Some NGOs wanted to organize a demonstration for children's rights together with children. All children who came had, as far as they could, dressed up. Whereas normally they would walk in simple sandals, some of the children had somehow organized shoes this time. Or they wore pretty shirts that had never been seen before. At the demonstration, which went through the business district of the city and through a residential area of wealthy people, the children held up banners and shouted slogans that the educators had given and taught them. After 15 minutes the interest of the children had ceased, the older boys handed the banners to the younger ones and complained that there was not anything to drink. Observed by the disapproving views of the educators, some began to collect pieces of metal they found on the street and which they obviously thought they could use. The demonstration ended in a high school which had never been attended by any of the participating children. Here, a stage was set up, from where NGO officials held speeches against child labour. Some children started collecting plastic cups and empty coke bottles that were lying around while the speeches were made, to be able to watch a movie at night with the money earned. When asked, some older children who only observed the activities said they would rather not dirty their nice clothes as they were not meant for working.

Example 3: As almost always at markets in countries of the South, also in Calcutta there are many children busy collecting left over vegetables and fruit. Sometimes, they also steal things from stands. Mostly they appear in groups and split the work between each other. Whereas some collect or steal, others carry away the loot in small sacks in order to distribute it among each other later or to re-sell the goods in other corners of the market. One morning, some children brought a small boy to the meeting point of an aid organization and said that the boy had been caught by a tradesman and had been beaten up by the police then and there. The boy was bleeding in many places and looked really bad. When the boy was somewhat fixed up he was told that the policeman had acted in an unjust way and must be sanctioned for his doing. After having listened carefully, the boy said:

> 'Aunty, it would have been much worse if he had arrested me. They would have put me in the lock-up until I got bail and in the lock-up worse things would have happened. He was doing his job and helping me by beating me at the market itself. I know him because during the times that I have fought with someone at the shelter and decide to sleep on the station platform he often asks me to run small errands for him and gives me a blanket to cover myself at night.' (Balagopalan, 2013: 17)

Obviously, the children thought it to be of little use to be made aware of their rights. They could not imagine how reference to these rights could help to improve their situation. However, it would be short-sighted to see a lack of understanding of children's rights in this. The problem is, on one hand, the manner in which the children were imparted their rights and how they were introduced to them; on the other, the socio-political constellation in which the children are and which makes it nearly impossible for them to understand that they are subjects of rights.[12]

In the case of the skit and the demonstration (examples 1 and 2) children were to show their rights to better-off people in order to clearly demonstrate that their situation is unjust and to reach understanding. This approach contradicted their whole life experience. The wealthy people, whom they were to address, are mainly experienced as ruthless and even as the origin of their problems. How were they to expect that the people who exploit and abuse them would *do* anything *for* them? In addition, the children probably felt hurt in their pride and dignity by this approach, as they must have felt like some sort of beggar asking for pity from the better-off. It is not a coincidence that most children hate begging and that they rather steal or be active in some other way in order to deal with their miserable situation.

In the case of the skit, the children interestingly did not reject the idea of having their own rights but rather gave this idea an unexpected interpretation of their own. They took them up not to promote understanding for them but to point out those responsible for their situation and to make fun of them. The children did not trust that the rights speak for them or have any effect but wanted to show that the law is rather often used by the powerful to their advantage at the expense of the children. What seems like a violation of rights in our eyes is, for the children, the normality of the social and rights system in which they live.

In example 2, the children did not participate in the demonstration because they were convinced of its sense, but rather in order not to disappoint the educators. That they dressed up (and likely stole to be able to do so) shows that they interpreted their role differently from the organizers of the demonstration. Whereas the NGO wanted to achieve authenticity in recognizing children's rights by showing the visible misery of ragged children, the children made sure to be seen in their best light and to avoid the impression of being dependent on other people's pity. Instead of trusting in verbal appeals to businessmen and well-to-do pedestrians, some children seemed to find it more effective to use the anonymity of the demonstration to do something for their living and enjoyment.

The small boy's refusal to insist on his rights towards the police officer that had abused him (example 3) shows that generally formulated rights can have very different meanings according to situation and experience. The boy had not only had more complex experiences with the police than his caregiver was able to understand, but he also had more in mind than only the recently experienced abuse. As he was to count with further encounters with the police officer in his daily (and nightly) life, it was very obvious for him to weigh up the advantages and disadvantages of a legal claim. Far from an attitude of submissiveness, he proved to have an extraordinary sense for the existing dependencies and power hierarchies and knew how to use them for his own good.

The behaviour of the children shown in the three examples may be disappointing for some children's rights advocates, yet it demonstrates even more clearly the necessity of not propagating rights without taking into account the actual life context of the children concerned and to be sure of the experiences and views of the local children.[13] Sarada Balagopalan clearly depicts that it is not her intention to regard children's rights principally as useless and senseless for children in street situation in India because of their liberal Western origin. She also does not want to give way to impunity and rights violations and accept the existing power hierarchies and injustices or trust in survival tricks of the less powerful. She does insist however on dealing with children's rights (and human rights in general) in a contextual and situational way.

This means children's rights cannot be only 'implemented' but must be culturally 'translated' and be imparted with local ways of reasoning and according to local customs as well as legal views and practices. This includes understanding children's rights not only in the sense of individual claims, but also as mutual connections and obligations between members of different generations. This further includes, notwithstanding the cultural and regional particularities, taking care that rights do not come into force merely by being 'naturally' ascribed to persons or being written in laws and regulations. To refer to them is only useful if they are not undermined by factual power and ownership differences. In view of their often marginalized status this holds particularly true for children who live in extreme poverty and oppression.

Like the children in India, there are many children around the world whose rights are massively violated and who have little reason to believe in the 'power of rights'. Many of these children are not willing to give in to being seen and treated as victims of adverse circumstances but rather, lacking other possibilities, try to find solutions for their problems themselves. This I will point out by a case study from the Indonesian city of Yokyakarta, located on the island of Java, where street children were fighting against a proposed law of the provincial government which was supposed to protect them (van Daalen et al, 2016; see also Beazley, 2000, 2003).

Dilemmas due to unequal local power relations: the case of Yokyakarta, Indonesia

The planned law foresees protecting 'children who have troubles on the street'[14] by forbidding them 'hanging around' and begging on streets and public places. The police should not only be empowered to stop these activities, but also to take action against people who give money or other goods to the children (this should be explicitly punishable).[15] In contrast to other Indonesian provinces, where similar laws were adopted by local parliaments, the provincial government of Yokyakarta invited 'representatives of the civil society' to comment on their draft law. The local children's aid organizations saw that the law legitimized police raids that had previously taken place, and declined it unanimously. Remarkably, this time, the directly affected children also spoke up.

Along with adults, for whom the streets and public places are a working and living space, hundreds of children who had painted their faces and bodies, accompanied by traditional Javanese music, repeatedly rang through the streets and before the regional parliament and called slogans like the following: 'Reject, reject, reject the draft!' 'Fight, fight, fight!' 'Those who reject this draft must say it out loud, REJECT!' 'Let us pass these streets, hands off our streets!' 'The draft is hell!' 'The draft is bullshit!' 'Piece of shit regulation!' On other posters, the children made known, how they understood their right to live in the city: 'Stop the violence to street people!' 'The street is our house!' 'Let us live here!' 'This is our country; it is our right to be here!'[16]

The protests had the effect that the government agreed to negotiate the proposed law. In the negotiation commission formed on the initiative of the international NGO Save the Children, officials of the government and members of the parliament met with representatives of local children's aid organizations and some adults of the so-called *Gerakan Kaum Jalanan Merdeka* (independent street movement).[17] Children were not invited; they showed little interest in participating in the two-year debates on details of the law anyhow.[18] It seemed to them most important that the draft law had been withdrawn. During the negotiations, however, they repeatedly drew attention to their own actions in which they stressed their right to work and live on the street and thus support their families. They did not always articulate with words, but by demonstratively using the street space for various acrobatic showings, chants and other music performances. This could be interpreted as a creative response to their actual exclusion from the political negotiations, but could also have underlined the fact that the children preferred other forms of political participation to those practised by the adults.

In the Law on the Protection of Children Living on the Street, which was finally agreed in the negotiations between adults and adopted in 2011, the expectations and demands of the children are in no way considered. In the law, which expressly refers to the UNCRC, a concept of protection prevailed which is fundamentally different from the children's understanding of rights as articulated by them during the protests. Although the law with great éclat of all children's charitable organizations does not include repressive measures against the children, the streets were again defined as places that are damaging for the children's development. The only way to protect the children and their right to a child-friendly life is to remove the children from the street and keep them away.[19] Instead, they should be returned to their families and, as far as possible, be looked after in social projects. In doing so, it is generally assumed that children who use the street for life-related activities and/or for their pleasure have no family contacts, are in particular need of assistance and must be 'saved'. The law does not elaborate how it could be possible to remove them from the street without the use of compulsory measures, and ultimately is left to the imagination and the pleasure of the lawmakers.

In their analysis of the case, van Daalen et al (2016) conclude that the adults who participated in the negotiations, who understood themselves as defenders of children's rights and spoke in the name of street children, were not at all clear about the discrepancy between children's perceptions of their rights and their own interpretation of children's rights. While the adults were only concerned about how the activities carried out on the street and assessed as genuinely harmful could be prevented, the children were concerned with how they can now exercise them under safe and humane conditions. This not only conceals various concepts of protection, or of what is good for children, but also the question of whether and, if so, how the legal conceptions of the children can be transformed into positive law. In the opinion of the authors of the case study, a new conceptual framework must be found that transcends the hitherto dominant practice of rights and law. They describe this concept as 'living rights' (van Daalen et al, 2016: 818):

> Living rights should be understood as, first, entitlements of agentic persons or collectives who can act upon the inevitable contradictions and tensions they often contain. This implies, second, that rights cannot be static and settled once and for all and that what were once only norms or even taboos may be transformed into legal rights and vice versa. Living rights are therefore continuously reinvented in the face of changed circumstances. Finally, even before they are codified and find their way into law, living rights are already there, in the daily lives and struggles of people confronting the challenges of everyday life and trying to make the most of their situation. Our point is that this is *also* true of the rights of those, such as street children, whom the state and even the outsiders who claim to speak in their name 'from below', exclude.

In the case of children's rights, the concept of living rights includes the necessity for the children to be directly and continuously involved in law-making and legal practice as social subjects of rights. It has to be acknowledged and politically enforced that norms and practices claimed and created by children become valid only in formal law, in a state-codified form, but also get recognized in social life and have real impacts.[20] To achieve this, the authors insist that the children's perceptions and expectations are taken up by adult persons and 'translated' in a solidarity manner, that is, publicly communicated and supported. They are conscious – and this is shown in the case study – of this translation work being confronted with numerous difficulties and inconsistencies (van Daalen et al, 2016: 821):

> The study of Yogyakarta's street children's rights illustrates that the implementation of rights is not limited to the translation between the international, national and local levels. Translations also occur between different organisations, between headquarter and field levels within the same organisations, and between organisations and the people they claim to represent. As our case study suggests, translations of children's rights take place in many of these 'transitional spaces' (Flax, 1993) between an indeterminate number of actors functioning at different governance levels and adhering to different worldviews. In each of these spaces and between all these actors, different forms of translation occur. We see living rights and translations primarily as conceptual tools that can help to understand how divergent viewpoints over children's and human rights are played out in particular contexts. However, the notions do not explain the outcome of such translations, which is, as we have highlighted in this article, a question that belongs to the empirical rather than the conceptual domain.

In contrast to the previously discussed study on street children in Calcutta, which reflects the importance of rights for children in the context of power structures, the study of street children in Yogyakarta is more likely to be based on an abstract, rights-theorist level. The question arises as to how the concept of living rights can be concretized so far that it can also be used to criticize and overcome illicit power structures and instrumentalist forms of participation and representation. I will return to this question at the end of this chapter.

Dilemmas due to unequal international power structure: the case of Bolivia

When searching for answers to the postcolonial marginalization, exclusion and exploitation of children, it can be asked to what extent states and state legislation can make a positive contribution. Similar to the appeal to children's rights, in any attempt to improve the situation of children by means of legal regulations without subjecting them to a new foreign rule, ambivalences must be anticipated. As we have seen in the Indonesian case, the postcolonial dilemmas of children's rights are particularly expressed in national laws that seek solutions to children's problems without taking their social and cultural contexts into account. They are usually based on a Western Eurocentric childhood pattern and make this the absolute yardstick for the regulation of different childhoods. Characteristic is the fact that children are excluded from the legislative process and have no chance of bringing their own views to bear. In this way, they contribute to the ongoing colonization of childhoods. One of the few laws that took a different path in its creation is the Bolivian Children's and Adolescents' Code (*Código Niña, Niño y Adolescente*), which came into force on August 2014.

This Code established new guidelines for the appreciation and application of children's rights and the policy on childhood. It is the first law, worldwide, which was carried out with significant participation by children and adolescents, particularly those who work. It interprets children's rights within the framework of the traditions of indigenous communities and respects the social and cultural reality of the country. This applies mainly to provisions concerning the rights of children and adolescents at work. The law established provisions for working children that do not prohibit them from working in general. Instead, they were granted rights and measures to protect them from exploitation and abuse of power, and at the same time they were given a chance to develop and live with dignity.[21]

The law has triggered controversial international debates. In particular, the ILO has rejected the law as incompatible with the ILO conventions on child labour in the sections relating to children's work and has called for their amendment. After three years of opposing this demand, the Bolivian government and parliament finally gave in to pressure from the ILO at the end of 2018, intensified by threats from the US government to restrict commercial trade with Bolivia, and fundamentally changed the controversial paragraphs of the law to the detriment of working children.

Without public debate and without consulting working children and the local organizations and government agencies involved in the implementation of the Code, the Bolivian parliament has substantially amended the Code in accordance with ILO guidelines. All legal protection mechanisms for children under 14 years of age at work have been abolished without substitution, which amounts to a general prohibition. The provisions of the Code and labour guarantees are now fully limited to adolescents between 14 and 18 years of age. At the end of the Code, all that remains for children under the age of 14 is to announce that they will be required to attend school and prohibited from working through supervisory bodies, and that they will depend on the authorities to be more sensitive to their protection. The 'sensitization' now consists of the dissemination of slogans against child labour.

The previous Code was not without its shortcomings and the central government made only scarce efforts to implement it. The necessary funds for the implementation of the protection mechanisms were never available. In order to enable children to work in a manner that respects their rights and ensures their protection and human dignity, the Code established bureaucratic procedures that were difficult to implement in practice. Despite all this, in recent years, many organizations and individuals in the provinces have worked to overcome bureaucratic obstacles and, together with the affected children and adolescents, have committed themselves to implementing the Code. They were and are convinced that the Code was better than anything that existed before in terms of legal regulations. It is strange that the numerous experiences made in the four years since the adoption of the Code have not been evaluated or considered in the new resolution. And it contradicts the spirit of the UNCRC, the Bolivian Constitution and the Code itself that working children were not even heard.

The amendment to the Code is an example for the fact that the understanding and implementation of children's rights is strongly influenced by unequal international power structure. This is particularly true when it comes to children whose way of life and self-understanding contradict the Western pattern of childhood, and legal regulations are sought to solve their problems that are oriented towards non-Western cultures.[22] The example presented here shows that even the promises of a country's constitution can easily vanish into thin air if they contradict the international power relations and the interpretation of international legal norms shaped by them. Nevertheless, the Bolivian code retains its significance – also for other countries – because it has shown that even in law children are not necessarily regarded as 'social cases' or objects of protection measures, but can be recognized as social subjects capable of contributing actively to the necessary changes in society. These, of course, could only have succeeded to the extent that the country is freed from international economic dependence and creates forms of economy and work that correspond to the constitutional principles of *Vivir Bien* (Good Living). In this way, the Code could also have counteracted the colonization of childhoods and contributed to a culture-sensitive children's rights practice.

Conclusion: Ways out of postcolonial dilemmas

I have referred to case studies in this chapter, because ultimately it can only be determined how the Eurocentric and paternalistic bias of children's rights can be undermined and children's rights can be used 'from below' or as 'living rights' by analysing concrete situations and cases. In my opinion, the following conclusions can be drawn from the cases presented here.

Before any appeal to children's rights, it has to be questioned whether, in the given situation, they can be an effective and viable instrument to secure the dignity of children and strengthen their position in society. When we consider children as actors, that is, as acting subjects in their own right, a minimum of prerequisites must be given. This includes the fact that the children not only trust themselves, but also have the necessary space to be able to act at all. This also includes that, at the legal level, they find contact persons who take the rights discourse seriously, and that state structures exist in which human rights are not completely ignored (see Freeman, 2009: 380). Finally, this also includes that the children find allies among the adults in society who are ready to take up and support their legal claims. The origin of these assumptions, just like the emergence of human rights, is not to be understood as a kind of naturalistic fact but as the result of social struggles, and can therefore be induced and changed (see Stammers, 2009, 2013).

In the case studies, it becomes evident that it is not enough for the children to be informed about their own rights. Children have no plausible reason to 'believe' in these rights and to appeal to them when those who have more power than they themselves have control over the rights of the children or instrumentalize them in a self-governing manner and in their own favour (in order to improve their image). Children must have the opportunity to bring their own conceptions of rights and the claims derived from them into play. It is also important to understand children's rights not only as individual but also as collective rights: to accept and, if necessary, support that children – in whatever forms – can join together on the basis of shared interests and act in an organized way (see Kimiagar and Hart, 2017). If children's rights are understood only as individual rights, they at least remain 'helpless' when the implementation of the rights also requires structural changes and calls into question the existing power relations. In this sense, Didier Reynaert and Rudi Rose (2017) distinguish a 'minimalist' and 'maximalist' understanding of children's rights and demonstrate this in dealing with social inequality and child poverty. According to a minimalist understanding, inequality and poverty are the results of inadequate individual use of rights and can be remedied through education to individual responsibility. According to a maximalist understanding, however, the structural causes must be taken into consideration and a redistribution of social wealth must be undertaken.

Van Daalen et al (2016) rightly point out in their case study that different interests intersect and often contradict each other in children's field of action. Children who stand up for their rights can therefore not assume that they are always understood by their children's rights advocates in their sense and that the rights are 'implemented' in their interest. This is a general problem of each kind of advocacy or advocatory ethics (see Oliver and Dalrymple, 2008; Liebel, 2012b). For children in the Global South, it is particularly relevant that children's rights are interpreted neither in an adultist or paternalistic way, nor in a Eurocentric way. In order to counteract this and to give weight to children's own interpretations, there is no way around the question of how to circumvent the universalistic claim to children's rights.

In the face of their claim to universality, children's rights must be understood in an open, dynamic, culture-sensitive and contextualized manner. This includes dealing with the rights codified in the UNCRC in a critical and reflexive way and recognizing that they are not the endpoint of a development but can be changed and developed further (see Reynaert et al, 2015). Particular attention has to be given to the visions and demands of children, especially if they express these themselves in the form of rights or legal claims (for examples, see Liebel, 2012a: 125–42).

The 'guiding principles' highlighted by reference to certain articles of the UNCRC by the UN Committee on the Rights of the Child seem to me to be appropriate points of reference for such a dynamic and culture-sensitive understanding of children's rights. These are the following four legal complexes:

- non-discrimination/equality (Article 2);
- the best interests of the child as a primary consideration (Article 3);
- survival and the best possible development of the child (Article 6); and
- participation/inclusion of the children: express their views in all matters affecting them and give them due weight (Article 12).

As with all human rights, it should be remembered that these principles and the concepts on which they are based are not unambiguous and can be interpreted in various ways. For example, the question arises as to what is meant by the best possible development of the child and by what standards it is to be assessed. Or which criteria are relevant to assess whether discrimination can or must be stated. Or how to define the best interests of the child, which have long justified paternalistic practices towards children, and often still do (see Cantwell, 2016). However, when the above principles are considered in context, they at least tend to underline that every child, regardless of age and other personal characteristics, has to be recognized as an independent subject of rights whose dignity as a person with the same moral status has to be guaranteed under all circumstances. In my view, this implies that there is a worldwide obligation to establish the best possible living conditions for children and to ensure that no child is prevented, disadvantaged, discriminated, exploited or otherwise injured against their dignity. It also means that in every decision to be taken, the best interests of the children are to be considered primarily and with regard to the views of the children concerned.

A distinction must be drawn between general principles on the one hand, which all children of the world have an unrestricted legal claim to comply with, and ideologically or culturally specific determinations on the other hand, which are not fully applicable, but must be interpreted in the respective cultural and social contexts, and, if necessary, be problematized. To the latter, I count, for instance, provisions that require a (chronological) minimum age for certain activities selected or desired by children, or which limit the right to education to the obligation to attend school. It is also to be critically reflected that certain rights can be in a contradictory relationship with one another and possibly mutually exclude or hinder one another. This is, for example, the case where protective rights are interpreted as being equivalent to the incitement of children and their status as subjects to which the right to participation and self-determination is due. Or, if development and provision rights are understood only as an obligation of state authorities, but not as subjective rights of the children, which they themselves can concretize, co-construct and practically demand.

In general, the guiding principles, which apply without restriction, are violated in the world of today at least in two ways:

- The postcolonial world order has the effect that the vast majority of children, especially in the Global South, are exposed to preventable distress, violence, diseases and constraints that violate their human dignity and impede their best development.
- Everywhere in the world, there are various ideologically or religiously justified practices that disregard the moral and legal rights of the children to recognize their subjectivity, to safeguard

their human dignity, and to participate in actions and decisions concerning them.

This shall be explained by a number of areas that seem particularly important to me. If the European-Western childhood pattern dominates in dealing with children's rights, it is obvious to practice the protection of children in a paternalistic way at the expense of their (relative) autonomy and participation. However, a childhood understanding, which is more common in the Global South and which emphasizes the child's shared responsibility, also carries the danger of disregarding the same moral status and the right of children to make independent decisions about their lives and take part in decisions of social and governmental institutions that are important to them.

Postcolonial material inequality, intensified by capitalist globalization, increases the risk of children who live in poverty and precarious social conditions to having their human dignity violated and being exposed to greater risks. Since they have fewer options for their own decisions, they are particularly exposed to the risk of economic exploitation as well as the threat to their health and even their life (also by destroying the natural habitats and the living environment). Likewise, they are prevented from exercising their right to an education, which is useful to them and connected with their lives. This can also be the result of education systems that make access dependent on material resources and that disregard the specific life situation and the knowledge resulting from the children's everyday experiences. The postcolonial world order is not least linked to forms of social inequality, which are based on the unequal assessment of people of different origins and skin colour. They can condense into racist practices that lead to multiple ('intersectional') forms of discrimination and disability in conjunction with other visible personality traits.

It is more difficult to deal with the 'traditional practices' (UNCRC).[23] They can harm children, for example, by causing pain and prolonged physical impairment. This applies to, for instance, often religiously justified traditions, such as FGM or circumcision of boys in the first months or years of life. Even the custom of marrying girls or boys at an early age against their will disregards the subjectivity of the children. It can jeopardize their integrity in both physical and psychological terms, be associated with adverse effects on their health, and limit their life prospects. But instead of condemning and forbidding them as an expression of a 'barbaric culture', it would be a cultural-sensitive understanding of children's rights to seek a respectful dialogue with the people and communities who are involved, and look for solutions that provide more advantages than disadvantages and enable the children ultimately to make their own decisions about their lives (see CRIN, 2018). Since the children are further integrated into their sociocultural communities, solutions in the interest of the children cannot be brought from outside, but must be found within these communities (for examples of misguided and successful practice, see Richter, 2016; Hopgood, 2017; Wessels and Kostelny, 2017).

The lack of recognition of the moral equality of the sexes ('sexism') or of 'deviant' sexual orientations ('homophobia') can lead to social disadvantage and discrimination as well as the lack of recognition of moral equality solely because of the low age of the children ('adultism'). However, these are not the special characteristics of 'postcolonial' world regions, but rather the expression of societies, which are heavily hierarchically structured and overlook equality principles. Nevertheless, they may also be closely linked to colonial or quasi-colonial ways of thinking and practices in that they depreciate and exclude those people and lifestyles that do not correspond to the ideas and interests dominating in the world or within particular societies. They can even be a result of colonization or religious proselytization.[24] Therefore, when dealing with traditional customs, care must be taken that they are not condemned simply with the know-all gesture of the supposed enlightened man. Like human rights and children's rights in general, they must also be understood in their respective historical contexts and valued in a sensitive manner. It should always be borne in mind that traditional knowledge can even embody a knowledge that has been marginalized by the process of colonization and whose resurgence benefits people (for example, natural healing methods).

The recognition and interpretation of leading principles of children's rights, as exemplified here, is not yet a guarantor for them being practised in the sense of the children affected by an infringement. For this purpose, it is indispensable to observe and include children's views, and to understand children's rights in such a way that they can be used individually and collectively by the children themselves. In this sense, children's rights must be understood not only as individual but also as collective rights. Furthermore, it must be borne in mind that the rights themselves are only of practical importance if they are accompanied by structural changes in the respective societies which lead to more egalitarianism and social justice and, in particular, strengthen the social position of the children. This does not exclude the representation of the children by adults and state institutions, but it requires that each representation by 'others' is also associated with risks which can only be countered by a comprehensive participation and self-organization of the children.[25]

Notes

[1]   This also means taking a look at the fact that the European history of human and children's rights has been shaped by influences from other regions of the world and by historical periods (see, for example, Frankopan, 2015). The Declaration of the Persian leader Cyrus II in Babylon from the year 539 BC is considered the first charter of human rights and is also recognized as such by the United Nations. It should be noted that even in Europe, traditions of human and children's rights can be identified which have hitherto been largely hidden behind their dominant Eurocentric understanding and use.

[2]   The French sinologist François Jullien (2017) proposes putting the universal against universalism, imposing its hegemony on others, and believing that it can claim universality. The universal thing to fight for is a rebellious universal that is never complete; or say a negative universal that counteracts the comfort of any arrested positivity. It is not totalizing (satisfying), on the contrary: it puts the totality once again into being by referring to the missing. Jullien locates it in the 'in between' and in the 'dialogue' of the cultures, which in turn are constantly changing and therefore cannot claim a fixed 'cultural identity' but are open and challenged to think about their own assumptions and transformations. The 'universal' he presents always remains open to the 'common' with other cultures. If the term 'inter-cultural' is to have meaning, according to him, it can only consist in bringing to fruition this intermediate, this dialogue as a new dimension of the world and of culture.

[3]   With respect to the vocation to human dignity, however, it is worth considering Frantz Fanon's demand ([1961]2005: 9) that it is not allowed to remain on the plane of 'the abstract, universal values', but to rather take into account the concrete situation of those who are revolting against colonization. Fanon's reminder refers to the fact that the colonial powers had often turned to human dignity for legitimating their practice as a humanitarian and civilizing mission, for example, when they claimed the 'liberation of women' for themselves.

[4]   This committee consists of 18 independent experts nominated by the States Parties and elected by the UN General Assembly to review the implementation of the UNCRC in the States Parties, to make recommendations and to interpret and concretize the UNCRC in General Comments.

[5]   This was underlined in later years by other authors, such as Pupavac (1998); 2001); Scheper-Hughes and Sargent (1998); Ennew (2002); Cussiánovich (2010) or Holzscheiter (2010).

[6]   By interpreting the right to be heard as a collective right of children, the UN Committee on the Rights of the Child (in the General Comment N° 12, 2009) tries to strengthen children as a social group and counteract adultist power relations.

[7]   Cordero Arce (2018) points out that the question of the subject of children's rights requires not only an abstract understanding of the child as a 'legal subject', but also a 'dialectical' view of the child in its concrete contexts. According to him, the life reality of the child is characterized by 'autonomous interdependence'. The co-responsibility of children practiced in non-Western cultures must therefore not be understood as a restriction but can be understood as an extension of the rights of the child. In this way, the child is both a beneficiary ('rights-holder') and an actor of his/her rights ('duty-bearer'), or, in other words, a 'subject-as-citizen'.

As examples of corresponding legal regulations, he refers to the African Charter of the Rights and Welfare of the Child of 1990 and the Bolivian Children and Adolescents Code of 2014.

[8] It should also be pointed out that the presence of the ancestors presented in the Andean as well as other indigenous cultures of America and Africa suggests a different relationship between generations than in cultures in which the world of the living is strictly separated from the 'beyond' of the dead. This is expressed in a novel by the Nigerian author Ben Okri (1993), in which a child returns from the spirit world of the dead to the world of the living and observes the actions of the adults in bewilderment.

[9] In order to understand such concepts, a look at cultural anthropological and social geography-oriented childhood studies can be revealing (see André, 2015; Aitken, 2015; Montgomery, 2017).

[10] In this section, I follow some considerations by Elizabeth Dieckermann, a student in the Master of Childhood Studies and Children's Rights at the University of Applied Sciences Potsdam (Dieckermann, 2018).

[11] Similar formulations can be found in the African Charter of the Rights and Welfare of the Child (African Union, 1990) and the new Children and Adolescents Code of Bolivia in 2014 (see Liebel, 2015).

[12] In this context, the problem is that a conception of individual rights, as laid down in the UNCRC, remains helpless against the structural conditions of social inequality, poverty, violence and oppression (see Boyden, [1990]1997: 220).

[13] Another impressive example of the need for a contextual approach is the study by Heather Montgomery (2001) on child prostitution in Thailand.

[14] This formulation obscures the fact that the children were actually understood as people who 'make trouble'.

[15] Similar laws exist in many countries of the Global South. They also resemble the attempts made in the Global North to prohibit the use of public spaces for young people, a practice which is usually described as 'status offenses' (see CRIN, 2016). While the laws and decrees on this subject were formerly legitimized by the 'irregular' behaviour of young people, they are now widely declared as measures to protect minors (see Liebel, 2014).

[16] Translations of the chants and signs: Edward van Daalen and Hanna Marinda.

[17] This movement had initially made the following demands with the participation of the children: '(1) Reject the draft. (2) The government must meet its obligation to ensure decent jobs and livelihoods for communities. (3) Stop the razzias against the street community. (4) Refrain from all other forms of violence on the streets. (5) Revoke regulations which violate the rights of the urban poor. (6) Revoke similar local regulations in all other provinces throughout Indonesia. (7) Provide the street community with identity cards' (translated by Edward van Daalen and Hanna Marinda; cited in van Daalen et al, 2016: 810).

[18] Some children were only present in a conversation with two deputies, but soon turned away, plucked on the guitars, smoked and made jokes.

[19] Article 3 of the Law provides: 'The protection of children living on the street aims to: a. Remove children from street life; b. Ensure the fulfilment of children's rights to live, grow, develop and participate optimally in accordance with human dignity and values, and; c. Provide protection against discrimination, exploitation and violence, for the realization of qualified, noble, and prosperous children.'

[20] Van Daalen et al (2016) discuss these questions in retrospect and in the context of theories on legal pluralism. In these, it is assumed that the law consists not only

of state-sanctioned laws, but of various sources such as habitual rights, traditional local legal systems as well as legal conceptions and claims of social groups and movements. It is assumed that law can be created and renewed through the agency of social actors (see Kleinhans and Macdonald, 1997; Webber, 2006; Tamanaha, 2011; Inksater, 2010; Ndulo, 2011; Messner, 2012). In these legal theories, however, hardly any reference is made to children. On the importance of custom law for the understanding of children's rights in Africa, see Himonga (2008).

[21] The process and details of the law are discussed in Liebel (2015).

[22] The international conflicts in the implementation of the law are analysed by Fontana and Grugel (2016) and Van Daalen and Mabillard (2019). In addition to the Bolivian case, Liebel (2017) and Liebel and Invernizzi (2018) discuss the difficulties of bringing the views of working children to bear internationally.

[23] Article 24.3 UNCRC provides: 'States Parties shall take all affective and appropriate measures with a view to abolishing traditional practices prejudicial to the health of children.' This formulation raises the question of whether 'modern' practices that are associated with the capitalization of societies and 'technological progress' (for example, those based on beauty ideals propagated by commercial advertising and induced by way of plastic surgery) can have harmful effects as well. The ideas and practices associated with the new reproductive medicine and genetic technologies which are aimed at the 'perfect (desirable) child' can also have extremely negative consequences for children (see, for example, the debate about the so-called liberal eugenics as a part of the 'genetic supermarket': Robertson, 1996; Habermas, 2003; Sandel, 2007; Sorgner, 2015). They have also led to the emergence of a flourishing branch of business in the Global South for the recruitment of surrogate mothers (for this and other examples, see Cregan and Cuthbert, 2014: 147–64).

[24] For example, Karl Hanson and Roberta Ruggiero (2013) in the pursuit of so-called 'witch kids'.

[25] At the very least, it should be noted that this must also have consequences for childhood and children's rights studies in the sense that research does not degrade the children to objects in the research process, but tries to illuminate and understand their lives and always handles children's rights from the perspective of the children themselves (see Bessell et al, 2017).

8

Beyond paternalism: Plea for the de-paternalization of children's protection and participation

For some, paternalism can be an attitude of arrogance and highmindedness, best detected by recipients whose dignity has been injured. For others paternalism exists when outsiders presume that they know what is best for others. And others want to reserve paternalism for when some form of coercion is used to impose one's views on another on the grounds that it is in her best interests. Paternalism, just like care and power, comes in many different forms. (Michael N. Barnett, *Paternalism beyond Borders*, 2017: 5)

Introduction

When we want to characterize the quasi-colonial relationship between adults and children,[1] the concept of paternalism is sometimes used. The term is used in different ways and I intend not only to present it, but also to determine to what extent it is really apt to analyse, qualify and design the relationships between adults and children in different social and cultural contexts. To this end, I will place particular emphasis on issues of child protection and child participation.

At first, I will explain the concept of paternalism and I will question the arguments with which the so-called pedagogical paternalism or soft paternalism is usually justified. In a second step, I will analyse to what extent the rights of children and certain variants of paternalism can be compatible with each other or can contradict themselves. Then I will explain in two steps and with regard to several examples of child protection and participation how they are marked by paternalist thought patterns and how these patterns can be overcome. Finally, I will present some suggestions on how to deal with children to overcome paternalism.

How to understand paternalism

The concept of paternalism is discussed primarily in moral and legal philosophy, but has also entered into various disciplines dealing with practical questions about relationships between people and their social positioning in society. With regard to children, the question of paternalism now plays an important role, for instance, in pedagogy, childcare and welfare, as well as in social science and ethical and legal contributions to the understanding of children's rights. The debate often distinguishes between different forms of paternalism, for example, between strong and weak, hard and soft, direct and indirect, active and passive, symmetrical and asymmetrical paternalism, as well as between paternalism and anti-paternalism.

Likewise, the general definitions of paternalism differ, as a look into popular dictionaries may demonstrate. The *Merriam Webster* dictionary defines it as 'the attitude or actions of a person, organization, etc., that protects people and gives them what they need but does not give them any responsibility or freedom of choice'. According to the *Oxford Dictionary*, paternalism is 'the policy or practice on the part of people in positions of authority of restricting the freedom and responsibilities of these subordinate to them in the subordinates' best interest'. Other definitions highlight not the attempt by one person to improve the circumstances of another, but instead the intent to 'prevent him from harming himself, either when he would harm himself voluntarily or when he would do so involuntarily' (Claassen, 2014: 61). According to Ronald Dworkin, one of the protagonists of the debate that has been predominantly conducted in the US since the 1970s, the analysis of paternalism involves at least the following elements (Dworkin, 2017[2]):

> It involves some kind of limitation on the freedom or autonomy of some agent and it does so for a particular class of reasons. As with many other concepts used in normative debate determining the exact boundaries of the concept is a contested issue.[3]

I cannot go into the various controversially discussed concepts of paternalism here in detail.[4] By all means, it is always a matter of whether paternalistic action lies in the 'objective' or 'best interest(s)' of the persons concerned and is thus morally commanded and justified, or whether the (adults') autonomy is implicitly impaired by paternalist action, and they are shamed as persons and injured in their human dignity. In contrast to mere compulsion, every concept of paternalism is linked to the aspiration to strive for the welfare of the persons to whom paternalistic action relates. In my opinion, the question whether paternalistic actions are based on certain moral norms that are to be enforced by individuals and in society as a whole ('moral paternalism') is of particular importance.

A recent concept, influential at a political level and highly controversial, is the so-called libertarian paternalism. It is based on the concepts of behavioural economists Cass Sunstein and Richard Thaler (2008) which claim that through so-called nudges and in a discrete way, consumerism as well as health and social behaviour of people shall be channelled in a certain direction which is considered to be positive. Paternalism here is that the persons concerned are not given explanations and they are not aware, why they (should) make certain decisions.[5]

Liberal philosopher John Stuart Mill is considered one of the first critics and at the same time theorists of paternalism. Without resorting to the term paternalism (which did not emerge until the end of the 19th century), Mill in his work *On Liberty* (Mill, [1859]2001), published in the mid-19th century, criticized the guardianship of people by authoritarian and arbitrary interference in their personal lives by powerful people and higher authorities. At the same time, he established a moderate variant of paternalism considered by him to be reasonable. A classic example of Mill is that: A man prepares to cross a bridge that is about to collapse. Mill maintains that in this case not only is it allowed but it is necessary to retain the man and inform him about the state of the bridge so that he can decide if, having this information, he still wants to cross the bridge. In this, it is presupposed that what the man wants is not to fall to the precipice but to reach the other side of the bridge safe and sound. Therefore, it is about helping the man to know what his will is, implementing it successfully and accepting without hesitation the decision made by him. However, it needs mentioning that Mill excludes two groups from this intellectual experiment which for him have common characteristics: children and 'the mentally ill'. Therefore, the philosopher of ethics Jean-Claude Wolf (2006: 60) has been motivated to make the following observation:

> It seems that [Mill] considers paternalism [hard or strong] in front of children is not a problem at all, and that he himself has suffered under the rigorous educational experiments of his father and lived first-hand the sufferings that implied the

ruthless forced education, complaining in his autobiography that he has not had a childhood like other children.

Here, the term paternalism suggests that it is based on a constellation father-son/daughter or parents-son/daughter. Some authors prefer the term *parentalism* in order to avoid the negative connotation of the expression paternalism and to take account of gender neutrality (see Kultgen, 1995: 60). According to this model, 'parents, superior in their understanding and experience ..., take care of the welfare and development of their minor children, if necessary also without consideration of their own desires' (Grunert, 2006: 9). In fact, this is probably one of the reasons why

> an important part of the authors, on the one hand, looks for convincing definitions for the phenomenon of "paternalism" and, on the other hand, tries to find justifications that attenuate or dissolve the problematic of paternalism seen primarily as a moral issue (Grunert, 2006: 9).

Unlike what is called adultism or adult-centrism, paternalism against children is generally considered inevitable or at least certain variants are justified arguing that they are for the benefit of the children's welfare or correspond to their interests. In this sense, some authors come out in defence of a 'protective paternalism', a 'pedagogical paternalism' or a 'soft paternalism'. For my part, I will show that paternalism towards children is always morally problematic, that it goes against the vision of children's human rights and that it is avoidable – at least with a view to the future.

The concept of paternalism does not necessarily refer only to the relationship between adults and children. In fact, it can refer both to the relationship between people – regardless of their ages – as well as to the relationship between the state and citizens or between social institutions and the people subjected to them or cared for by them. In the first case, it is a constellation of superiority and inferiority, in which the superiors make decisions that affect the inferiors without consulting them or are even against their will. The second case is the so-called legal paternalism. Here, the state or its institutions intervene in the freedom of action of its citizens through certain laws or administrative measures, for example, when a law or a provision obliges citizens to assume a certain behaviour or prohibits another. Generally speaking, it is the legal power of state authorities to make decisions about other people without prior consent (Alemany, 2005). Its application entails a reduction of the freedom and autonomy of the person or group subject to paternalistic treatment. The invasion of individual autonomy by legal norms is justified with the inability or ineptitude of citizens to make certain decisions that the state considers correct.

State or legal paternalism is criticized from fundamentally different perspectives. On the one hand, liberal and neoliberal positions require distinction and on the other radical democratic positions. Liberal and neoliberal positions understand state paternalism as impermissible restriction of individual freedom of choice. They equate the democratically legitimized welfare state with the pre-democratic authoritarian state and plead for a 'slim state'. This is to be distinguished from the radical democratic critique of paternalism. It does not deny the state taking precautions, but criticizes its insufficient democratic legitimacy ('crisis of representation'). It does not content itself with a 'slimming' or 'de-bureaucratization' of the state, but calls for the state to be tied back to the society of the citizens. Freedom for them means not boundless individualism, but the creation of a maximum of democracy on the basis of social equality and justice (see Chapter 9 on concepts of citizenship).

Legal paternalism is not a moral issue. The question is whether it is right to grant the state or international authorities an elevated right that enables them to proceed without considering the will of the people affected. In the case of social institutions the question is: Can the professionals working in these institutions make decisions about the people they are in charge of and for whom they are responsible? And if yes, to what extent? Primarily, paternalism is conceived as a measure of protection in favour of people who are attributed the lack of basic skills or who are defined as 'basically incompetent' (Garzón Valdés, 1988: 167). Paternalism is justified with the presumption that these people cannot articulate their will, make their own judgements or make timely decisions due to lack of capacity or 'reason'. On one hand, it is considered that the inferior or dependent persons are incapable or incompetent to act according to their own interests, which apparently needs assistance, protection, education or representation by a person or higher institution. On the other hand, people or higher institutions have the pretence that their action directly or indirectly benefits the people whom they are in charge of or who depend on them.

Although the limits between paternalism justified with moral or legal reasons and paternalism exercised by individuals and institutions are not clear, it seems appropriate to speak of paternalism only when personal, state or institutional action justifies or consolidates dominant relationships, or when certain social groups are disadvantaged compared to others and are trapped in an inferior social position. However, when we speak of the action of state or that of international institutions, for practical reasons, it may be inevitable that norms and behaviour rules for people are established without consulting each and every one of them if they agree or disagree. The classic example are the legal norms in the so-called welfare states whose purpose is to socially insure people in need (for example, through compulsory health insurance) or people who are likely to need help or material support in the course of their life (for example, retirement provisions, or compulsory work disability payments). What is not to be forgotten are the norms and rules that force certain groups of people to take care of others when they are jointly responsible for their situation of need (for example, compensation of family expenses, payment of alimony in divorce situations). At the international or global level, these conditions are expressed in binding norms for exercising economic power or for protecting the environment.

Concerning legal norms that are established by state or international institutions, there is a need to clearly distinguish between provisions that solidify certain privileges and provisions, and those that counteract social inequalities or actions of powerful entities (such as multinational companies or banks), which are detrimental to the majority of the population in one country or of the world as entity. Examples for the latter are (international) tax laws, norms that regulate financial markets or provisions regarding the protection of the environment. All these norms are subject to a democratic legitimization, and should be qualified as paternalistic only when they mean putting the weakest or the majority of the population in a disadvantaged position.

Paternalism against children

In the relationship between adults and children, the term paternalism, in my opinion, should be used when adults, for the supposed good or interest of the children, interfere in their life against their expressed or likely will, despite the fact that the children are capable of making a decision that corresponds to their interests. Therefore, it is not paternalism when someone feeds a baby who, for physical reasons, cannot eat or choose only their food, or when someone carries a baby because they still cannot walk. On the other hand, it is a paternalistic behaviour when someone feeds a baby when in reality they do not like food or when someone lifts up a baby even though they want to crawl. In fact, childcare becomes paternalism when the children's freedom of action is restricted against their visible or presumed will. The argument for the protection or welfare of the child is not a sufficient justification. Speaking of legal paternalism, I will refer to the subject only as regards the direct relationship between adults and children.

Paternalism against children is similar to what is generally called *adultism* or *adult-centrism* (see Liebel, 2014; LeFrançois, 2014) when the tutelage of children is justified by adults arguing that it is (only) a *child*. That is when the main justification for intervening in children's life is their being a child. In this case, the judgement of the adult on which the paternalistic behaviour is based is 'suggested' to be appropriate, justifying it with physical characteristics that have nothing to do with the actual relevant capacities demanded by the situation. A very common argument, for example, is that the child is smaller and physically weaker than the adult. In this case, the characteristic of the paternalistic or adultist attitude is to make the children 'smaller' or 'weaker' than they really are, instead of supporting and helping them to compensate for the disadvantages of being small or weak. The same can be said for the argument that children lack experience. The child may have less experience than the adult, but there are also *other* experiences, from which other experiences, other perspectives and other points of view are born, and they must be considered and respected.

The Polish-Jewish pedagogue Janusz Korczak (see Lifton, 1994; Eichsteller, 2009; Liebel, 2018a) presents numerous examples for this kind of anti-paternalist thinking. In fact, in his pedagogical practice, Korczak perceived characteristics in children that are not only different from those of adults, but can be even superior to those of adults. In this regard, in his ground-breaking book *How to Love a Child* (Korczak [1919–20]1999b: 77) published shortly after the First World War, he points out that the children's 'feelings are more powerful than ours because they are not yet restricted by any kind of shame'. Regarding their intellectual capacity, despite all the differences, Korczak considers that the children equal the adults (Korczak [1919–20]1999b: 101): 'The child cannot "think like an adult", but in a childlike way he/she can reflect on serious problems of adults; the lack of knowledge and experience imposes another way of thinking.'

When evaluating the supposedly inferior capacities and abilities of the child, as in the question of experiences, it is necessary to ask whether we measure them in a 'rationality' that only adults consider 'normal' and indispensable. In fact, in current societies, it is generally an instrumental rationality that serves as a means to a certain external end. However, behind it another rationality is hidden in which affections and feelings are not a disturbing factor but an integral part. It is probable that this type of rationality is more frequent in children than in already more conditioned adults. Therefore, if we want to counteract paternalism against children, it is important to question such rationality that measures human beings only and exclusively in their functional utility in the capitalist social and economic system in which we currently live. We must understand that, instead, it is about seeing the subjectivity of people in their complex diversity, and then we will realize that the 'suitability' of the criteria for a supposedly rational decision depends not only on facts that can supposedly be measured objectively, but also from the perspective and perception of each of the subjects involved. I am going to illustrate what I have just explained with the help of a scene in a German kindergarten in which educators guide their work by the principle of understanding children in their diverse subjectivity and encouraging their participation (Richter and Lehmann, 2016: 57):

> The educator is cold. She knows that because she often freezes, as she says, 'especially when I'm outside.' She sees a girl who has gone into the garden only in a T-shirt. She then goes to the girl three times and asks if she is okay and if she can feel her temperature. The girl accepts the need for action of the educator and allows her to do so. But when the teacher comes a fourth time and asks again if she is feeling well or if she is cold and if she should feel, the girl turns around and says, 'Are you cold? Then put on your jacket! I'm fine'. The educator takes this hint and thinks for herself: 'Wow! I'm gonna go, then'.

The action of the educator is anti-paternalistic insofar as she is not guided by the twofold competence of the child, but by the consciousness of the difference between her own perception and that of the girl. The educator admits that her feelings cannot be transferred seamlessly to the feelings of the child, so that an adult cannot easily know what is best for the child. Richter and Lehmann (2016: 57) note:

> In this interaction example, not the possible consequences of the child's decision, but ultimately the arguments of the child are used to justify pedagogical action. The child is given the opportunity to 'keep the last word' and to assume responsibility independently.

Such an attitude of the educator could have been inspired by Korczak's pedagogy. For Korczak, it was central that the adult educator cannot know what is best for the child. He must acquire this knowledge together with the child and constantly question it in his interaction with the child. For him, this also means questioning the power constitutive for pedagogical action and being ready to meet the children on an equal footing and being ready to learn from them. Here is an example in which Korczak describes his learning experience in a summer colony:

> I had understood that children are a power that can be encouraged to participate and raised against oneself by disrespecting them, but which you definitely have to reckon with. … The next day, during a chat at the walk in the woods, for the first time I did not talk to the children, but with the children; I did not talk about what I want them to be, but what they wanted and could be. Maybe that's the first time I've convinced myself that one can learn a lot from children, that they, too, make demands and conditions and object, and that they have a right to do so. (Korczak, [1919–20]1999b: 222)

Every adult faces the challenge of respecting children as equals and, wherever possible, understanding their point of view and acknowledging their will. Korczak is not concerned with 'empowering' or 'involving' children, but with creating conditions that will enable children of all ages to express their views and will. From Korczak's point of view, children do not have to 'mature' to express themselves freely and participate in decision making, but it is the educator who must look for the conditions that the child can do it *now*. Korczak carries out this search together with the children. In his book *Happy Education*, he gives to consider (Korczak, [1919]1999a: 459): 'Note: Either the life of adults – on the verge of children's lives. Or the lives of children – on the verge of adult life. – When will that moment of frankness arise, since the lives of adults and children will stand side by side?'

The social structure of a childhood that is strictly separated from the adult world and clearly differentiated from it is what encourages paternalistic behaviour towards children, their underestimation and their disadvantaged situation, retaining them in their inferiority status. This dichotomy or division of society manifests itself in the institutionalization of childhood, that is, in the location of children in social spaces specially constituted for them. Some authors refer to this situation as 'insularization' (Zeiher and Zeiher, 1994).

The alleged inability of children to make their own decisions not only responds to laws of nature but may also be the consequence of the inability of adults to recognize and consider what the needs of children are. Moreover, the behaviour of adults can contribute to curbing or even destroying the development of children (see Young, 1980: 185; Lansdown, 2005). This phenomenon can be observed mainly in certain concepts and measures of the so-called child protection, but also in some concepts and forms of participation designed especially for children. However, before referring to some issues of child protection and participation, let me explain the constellation between paternalism and the rights of children.

Paternalism and children's rights

The fact that children have their own rights can question and limit paternalism. But this depends on how these rights are conceived. It can be argued that, not because of their mere existence, children's rights are capable of dismantling social constellations in which children are subject to adults or dependent of them in such a way that the latter can exercise power over them. By looking at the history of children's rights, we can identify two main streams. The first focuses above all on the protection of children from dangers and risks. It speaks of children's rights, but it does not understand them as the subjective rights of children, but rather as the responsibility and obligation of adults or states to ensure their wellbeing. It is an obviously paternalistic trend, and its first expression was the Geneva Declaration on the Rights of the Child promulgated by the League of Nations in 1924. The other trend, less well known, argues that the rights of children must be understood, as an expression and means to achieve the emancipation and equal rights of children within the framework of human rights as a whole. As this tendency has come from the hand of different social movements that aimed to transform political and social situations, I call it 'rights from below' (Liebel, 2012a). It was manifested, for example, in the works and educational practice of Janusz Korczak (2007, 2009; see Liebel, 2018a) or in the Moscow Declaration on the Rights of the Child in 1918 (see Liebel, 2016). Without freeing states and the international community from their responsibility in the application of the rights of children, this argument is directed against all kinds of paternalism in dealing with children.

In 1989, the General Assembly adopted the UNCRC. It is the most important document of international law in the field of children's rights and brings together the two currents mentioned above in a sometimes contradictory way. In fact, the UNCRC still has a foot in the traditional line of paternalism but, at the same time, includes elements that go beyond. However, this does not depend on the rights themselves but how they are interpreted and on the constellations of power that rule in each society and in the world.

A tendency that reinforces the paternalistic bias of the UNCRC is to deny that children's rights are human rights in the literal sense of the word and to declare them special rights for children instead. This happens explicitly, for example, in a recent contribution by Gunter Graf (2017), understood as 'child ethics', when he emphasizes that 'to accord children the same human rights in the same way as adults would lead them to classify their will as authoritative' (Graf, 2017: 127). In this case, the author seems to fear a development that will put children 'in power' and oppress the adults. It is therefore not surprising that he cares about the 'strong paternalistic element' (Graf, 2017: 128), which he sees anchored in the UNCRC. This tendency ties in seamlessly with positions in the legal and moral philosophy that deny children any rights of their own because they are unable to recognize their interests and act 'autonomously' with their own will.[6]

Although since the 1970s, law and philosophy have been discussing questions of paternalism and anti-paternalism and subtle concepts have been worked out, only few authors have dealt with these issues with respect to children's rights. While paternalistic positions were explicitly questioned in the 1970s and 1980s, the recent philosophical and legal literature on children's rights tends to reject paternalism in its 'strong' or 'hard' forms, but to justify it in its 'weak' or 'soft' variants as inevitable. This I want to demonstrate with two theoretical studies examining the relationship between children's rights and paternalism under legal, philosophical and ethical aspects.

In her work *Human Rights of Children: A Proposal for Grounds*, Mexican jurist Mónica González Contró (2008, see also González Contró, 2006) initially criticizes that in the legal debate on the rights of children 'certain characteristics are tacitly attributed to this group, especially related to rationality and as a consequence the exercise of autonomy' (González Contró, 2008: 3). As an example, she refers to the frequent use of terms such as 'disability', 'lack of maturity' or 'lack of rationality'. According to the author, such terms start

> from an adult perspective that has as the consequence that the characteristics are defined in terms of shortcomings, ignoring the studies that show that each stage of childhood has its own mental structures, that is, that its logic or reasoning is peculiar and differs from the adult's (González Contró, 2008: 3).

Consequently, the author rejects hard paternalism – 'moral-legal perfectionism' in her words – but makes an allegation for a 'soft' legal paternalism that is based on what she calls 'the basic needs' of children with the intention of considering the different stages of life as well as social and cultural contexts.

From this point of view, for González Contró paternalism is therefore inevitable due to the natural characteristics of childhood that are manifested in the children's dependence on adults and their vulnerability, which include the need to balance the interests of the child, as a child and as a future adult. In fact, when referring to basic needs, the author not only considers paternalism justified but also limited because these needs are supported by protection and provision rights, which particularly guarantee the right to life, development and human dignity. Because it is a stage of life in the evolutionary process in which the child's abilities are developing, the author is convinced and has the confidence that paternalism will be gradually reduced until full autonomy is achieved.

The other work I want to refer to was done by the German philosopher Christoph Schickhardt (2012). His attempt to formulate the foundations for a rights-based 'child ethics' can be summed up as follows: when children have been granted their own rights as legally binding under the UNCRC, every action by adults based on the interests of the child which intervenes in children's lives must be morally justified. According to him, it is no longer acceptable for adults to treat children as they see fit at their own discretion. However, due to the fact that children have limited (but during the course of their life changing) rational competencies for making their own choices, it is inevitable that adults act on children's behalf and intervene in their lives in certain situations. Schickhardt describes such behaviour as paternalistic. Since the children now have their own rights, however, a 'hard paternalism' in the sense of an arbitrary action – no matter how well-intentioned – is no longer acceptable. The rights-based paternalism, which is always dependent on justification, is described by the author as 'soft paternalism'. Like Mónica González Contró, he considers it inevitable.

Schickhardt continues that the child's interests cannot be determined solely by focusing on positive law but requires a deeper understanding of the rights of the child that must necessarily include moral rights. Thus, for Schickhardt, the foundation for children to claim moral rights is what he calls the 'moral status' of children, understanding that this status implies that children must be recognized as full persons and treated as equals to adults. It ascribes children the right to a moral status and that, therefore, it is essential to reflect in detail on their interests. In his attempt to define the content of these interests, Schickhardt deals in a detailed way with the question of what is 'good living' of children, relying on the legal concept of 'child welfare' (in German *Kindeswohl*) – the idea of which is unclear but anyway very common in German social law – equating it nominally with children's good living. Schickhardt states that the concept of child welfare determines 'what is good for the child as long as the child cannot do it on its own' (Schickhardt, 2012: 187). He admits that the concept of child welfare 'is less apt than legal language to give the necessary weight and attention to the interests of children in the social normative system' (Schickhardt, 2012: 188). Referring to the German legal system, he even considers justified the suspicion that 'with the concept of child welfare, children are given an instrument for the formulation and vindication of their interests that does not go beyond being of the second category' (Schickhardt, 2012: 188). Despite all this, Schickhardt believes that the term is inevitable because children still do not have the necessary skills and the 'qualified will' (2012: 193) that allows them to assess their own wellbeing in every conceivable way and act accordingly.

Therefore, and following Schickhardt, in each stage and situation of their lives, children depend on the different ways in which an adult person makes decisions on their behalf. According to the author, these decisions respond to a 'soft paternalism' and are acceptable only under certain circumstances and as an 'emergency solution', that is to say, their justification must be permanently questioned. He clarifies that they are morally problematic when they occur 'in front of the child for the sake of the child' (Schickhardt, 2012: 192), that is, against his or her expressed or presumed will. 'The main moral problem of paternalism against children is knowing under what circumstances it is permissible or even necessary to assume a paternalistic behaviour *against* their will or above their head to preserve or promote their well-being' (Schickhardt, 2012: 191; italics in original).

In summary, according to the considerations of 'child ethics' (Schickhardt, 2012) or 'ethical constructivism' (González Contró, 2006, 2008), the hard variant of paternalism means that the child does not have a moral status or personality, they remain seen as a pure object, and other people can make decisions without any prior or subsequent consent of the child. Unlike this one, the soft variant of paternalism grants the child a moral status as a human being, mainly equal to the adult, and each decision must be justified later by the affected person, usually when they come of age. For the conceptualization and management of children's rights, it seems reasonable then to ask: to what extent and in what areas is paternalism considered inevitable or acceptable? An example is found in the establishment of minimum legal ages for certain activities or responsibilities of children (for example, marriage, suffrage, criminal responsibility or consent in sexual relationships). Usually, minimum ages are justified with the need to protect children (not always their rights), but may also have the effect of limiting their autonomy and participation.

It is undeniable that in today's societies, there are different situations in the life of children in which they depend on adults making decisions for them without being consulted or having negotiated this decision. I will offer an obvious example that is often alleged, also in Schickhardt's book. A boy is about to run to a busy street to pick up a ball that has escaped him. The mother holds him back, intervening in his freedom against his will. The soft paternalism would justify the action of the mother arguing that the child could not have implemented his will to pick up the ball because, very likely, he would have been hit by a car before he could fulfil his intention. Therefore, the mother did not prevent the child from achieving his goal but saved him from serious consequences that were not the child's will. We could point to hundreds of examples and similar cases.

However, there are many situations in which adults intervene in the lives of children that are not as obvious and easy to justify as the example we have just seen. Schickhardt points out several cases, especially in the medical area, in which adult interventions in children's lives seem inevitable but continue to be questionable, as there is still doubt as to whether there were no other solutions that were more in the interest of the child than the decision made by adults. In any case, according to him, it is necessary to make 'preventive efforts for the long term to reduce the situations in which paternalistic interventions are an option' (Schickhardt, 2012: 211). The question is whether these preventive measures are desirable only in the area of medicine or in other fields of action that affect children. Going back to the example of the child who runs behind his ball, we could ask ourselves if it were possible to eliminate the risk of being run over by a car by adapting the street or all of citizen life to the needs of children. Obviously, this would not be possible overnight, but the idea shows that the need for paternalistic interventions could be reduced as far as possible to equalize priorities and power constellations in a society.

Analysing the matter under this aspect, it seems to me that one of the problems of Schickhardt's argument is that, with all the caution and doubts he exposes, it always leads to the justification of paternalistic action instead of analysing in more detail how we might face this type of situation, and avoid or reduce them. It is worth saying the same for the concept of Mónica González Contró, because, although she tries to consider social and cultural contexts, she deduces the basic needs of children to nature, understanding the development of the child as an endogenous process, naturally predetermined, as suggested by the patterns of classical evolutionary psychology. In effect, neither González Contró nor Schickhardt consider that the relationship between adults and children is a constellation of inequitable power that is not determined by mere and simple anthropological or biological conditions but, to a considerable extent, is due to the adultist structures of contemporary societies. These adultist structures are revealed, for example, in the fact that it is adults who determine what is valued and recognized as 'rational capacities' (see Palmeri, 1980: 160). Although Schickhardt (2012: 204) emphasizes that paternalism is always paternalism 'in a concrete situation', he tends to consider it as generally inevitable. Therefore, instead of defending paternalism in its soft or moderate variant, we should study in more detail how to overcome conflict situations for children's interests in the sense of a shared responsibility between adults and children.

Undoubtedly, this proposal implies rethinking and reconceptualizing the rights of children, since current discourse and practice still move within a protectionist and legalistic framework, and children's rights are still more often conceived as a legal obligation of adults or state bodies to act for the benefit of children, instead of trying to expand the possibilities and options of the children themselves to make use of their rights (see Liebel, 2012a; Cordero Arce, 2012, 2018). In my opinion, the two alternatives are not mutually exclusive. It is about changing the emphasis towards a more equitable constellation of power. In the next section, I will illustrate this idea in more detail by applying it to child protection and children's participation.

Child protection between paternalism and participation

Until today, in most cases, child protection is understood and managed in a tutelary sense. According to this logic, the way in which children should receive 'protection' is one in which adults or adult society covers them with protective wings taking care of their welfare and avoiding dangers and threats. However, this type of protection often 'is not much more than a mask to conceal paternalistic practices that undermine the autonomy of children and go against the implementation of their rights' (Franklin, 1994: 61). In all this, it is assumed that, given their young age and their consequent 'weakness' and due to their 'lack of life experience', children do not have the necessary competence to assume an active and responsible role in their protection against hazards and caring for their wellbeing.

Indeed, the assumption that adults are strong and children are weak is correct for most contemporary societies and in many situations of daily life. Nevertheless, it should be noted that it is not a simply 'natural' relationship but rather the result of a constellation of power that attributes a fundamentally different status to the children and the elderly. Therefore, from the point of view of paternalistic protection, it is not advisable to question the power constellations between children and adults and to give children the possibility of acting on the same level as adults. But doing so would not mean that adults or society as a whole should not assume their responsibility. It would mean that the children and young people themselves could influence the protection provided to them to be really in line with their interests and that protection does not imply incapacitating them for everything almost automatically as is happening up to now.

This vision of protection is based on a concept that, contrary to what is happening currently, does not concentrate on avoiding or totally isolating children from all dangerous situations ('protection against …') but points at overcoming the situation through the active engagement of those directly affected ('protection through …'). Obviously, this look is not exempt from certain risks. Thus, it is worth asking whether children are always able to correctly assess the danger a given situation may entail, if they are always able to recognize 'their best interests' or to distinguish between short- and long-term interests. But it would also be a very short-term view to think that the concept of avoiding hazards is risk-free. In fact, it not only tends to cement childhood dependence further at the expense of their freedom and participation and to continue preventing them from developing the skills necessary to act appropriately in different situations. It is also totally blind and inflexible in the face of the concrete living conditions of children in their respective social positions and the diverse cultural contexts they live in.

Thus, we must consider that, on numerous occasions, those children who grow up in difficult living conditions learn from a very young age to assume responsibilities, to take care of themselves and others and, with it, develop skills and abilities to overcome risks and situations that afford it. In many societies, childhood is not a phase of preparation for life that is based on the support provided by adults – as it is in Western Europe and Northern America today – but children and adolescents take on an active role in life both socially and economically (see

Liebel, 2004; Newman, 2005). For this reason, it is still very common to hear that *childhood is the future*, placing children in the usual social moratorium in which they have been located.

For the non-paternalistic concepts of child protection that understand protection as a right and that take it seriously as such, it is fundamental to see how children can be supported and strengthened. In fact, these concepts do not consider children only under the aspect of dangers and threats – real or potential – but consider them as subjects with their diverse characteristics and in their vital context. Therefore, concepts of this type will not aim, in the first place, at keeping children away from any danger but will try – wherever possible – to accompany them and generate the capacities so that they themselves can face potential risks and threats in an active manner and learn to resist them. This implies that children must not only participate in decisions regarding the type and form of the most timely protection they will receive, but also take into account what dangers they want to be protected from and which they may not. In all of this, of course it is not about leaving children 'to do whatever they want'. It is about establishing and working a relationship with them in which their points of view and their competences are respected.

In no way does this vision of child protection mean that children always know better what their interests are or that they realize possible dangers for them better than adults. But neither does it suggest the opposite: that adults always have a wider (quasi-perfect) vision and that they always act in the best interests of the children. What it does do is explicitly take into account the existence of differences between children and adults, in points of view, in social position and, therefore, in the corresponding interests. That is why it is essential to reach an agreement on what is the best way to correspond to the best interests of children, and also on the subject of their own protection. And the foundation of this agreement must be to understand that children and adults need each other and that we must (be able to) accept this 'generational interdependence'.

Regarding the possibilities of realizing non-paternalistic concepts of child protection, we can analyse them from a macro and a micro perspective. At the micro level, we come across the issue of how children handle possible imminent dangers in specific cases and how they can protect themselves. On the other hand, at the macro level, it is about seeing how to strengthen the position of children as a social group within society and how to enlarge their power of influence in political decisions that affect them – which means, by the way, almost all of those decisions.

In order to develop in children the capacity for criticism, decision-making capacity and self-responsibility, the *micro* perspective points to a concept of educational child protection. However, until now, educational protection has nearly always been based on a unilateral understanding of children and adults. It is the adults who identify the dangers and who must train children to protect themselves from them. However, children can only gain confidence in their skills and a critical vision of their life circumstances if in their daily life they have the possibility to really face these circumstances. To do this, it is necessary to provide them with possibilities and encourage them to ensure their individual and collective interests and rights, and allow them to organize (they have the right to do so), whether in children's or youth groups, local or social networks, or in larger children's movements. It is in this type of group where children can be better aware of their strengths and give a practical dimension to their competencies. In fact, as shown by Martínez Muñoz and Cabrerizo Sanz (2015: 15) in a self-evaluation guide on the strengthening of children's organizations, the experiences of organizations of children and adolescents

> … have entered the political arena. Introducing new ways of doing and organizing (in their styles, in their grammar, in their speeches) with a fresh air in their communicative forms through which they have managed to offer solutions and make visible conflicts gain greater legitimacy in recent years. … This has implied that a traditionally inactive population has gained more visibility and social empowerment in public affairs. This role has a double aspect: a convivial role (within their own organizations) and a political protagonism in which they interact in order to achieve changes that improve their daily lives.

It is evident that this is not applicable to all children in the same way and to the same extent, but it is not restricted to older children either. Even in the case of young children it is possible to make them see and experience that they can support and strengthen each other and to teach them how to do it (for instance, in schools or kindergartens). Experiencing this type of interaction in their group or in their network is the best way to overcome the feeling of helplessness and to learn how to defend oneself if a dangerous situation arises, especially for girls and children who live in particular situations of disadvantage and who, therefore, may be more vulnerable.

The *macro* perspective is located in the structural protection, because it tries to transform the general living conditions in order to improve the welfare of children and reduce dangers. The problem is that – similarly to what happens with the educational concept – structural protection is also implemented without consulting children, since it sees them as 'beneficiaries' of decisions and political measures. In order to free structural child protection from its paternalistic boundaries, children should have the possibility to participate in the decisions and political measures taken for their benefit. A good way to do this would be to accept children as citizens who have the same political rights as adults and who have the right to exercise their rights actively and effectively. This not only implies recognizing that children have civil and political rights but expanding them, for example, with the right to vote. Society and its institutions must create a culture of participation that takes children as competent citizens seriously, with specific characteristics and interests, giving them a real opportunity to assert their ideas of what would be a better life, beyond punctual and demonstrative experiences of participation, with more publicity than real impact in their lives (see Collins, 2017, for the field of international child protection).

It is true that neither the self-organization nor the citizenship of children are a guarantee that they are really protected from risks and dangers. But they would place the protection of their rights on a new basis, because they would change the vision adults have of the children, their need for protection and their skills, and children would have better opportunities for themselves to actively enforce their views and interests. In fact, the foundation of child protection would no longer be exclusion and prohibition, but the recognition and promotion of skills and competences, motivation and mutual solidarity. Children would have a better chance of taking their protection into their own hands, of taking part in the decisions and measures taken to protect them. Above all, it would no longer be a question of safeguarding children and adolescents from different dangers and threats, but they would have the possibility of participating in the improvement of society, asserting their interests and, consequently, changing their own life circumstances. In fact, the critical awareness of being a subject of rights increases as each child has their associative experience within their organization.

In order to better protect children from risks, a number of projects in recent years have focused on capacity and competence building, often referred to as resilience. It is important that these projects do not confine themselves to promoting individual skills and consider them as a private matter, where everyone is responsible for themselves, but also ensure that the conditions that give rise to risks are changed.

Children must be considered as a public issue and their wellbeing must be guaranteed through public policies with their consideration.

Children's participation between paternalism and protagonism

Participation cannot only be manifested in various forms but it can also have many meanings, for the individual as well as for their neighbours or society as a whole. While the term 'participation' is an empty signifier that can be filled in different ways, discourses and concepts of participation always contain normative components. They include certain expectations as to what is desirable and appropriate, how far it can go participation as it relates, what purpose it has, who should benefit from it, and so on. However, these normative components rarely appear openly, and that is why I consider that one of the most important tasks that we must face is to make these hidden aspects visible: the implicit objectives and the admitted consequences of participation. When we talk about participation, it does not necessarily mean that it is free of paternalistic concepts and intentions – especially when it comes to child participation that adults intend.

When we talk about participation today, we usually think about projects and models that are established for or with children. In all this, many times, we forget the fact that, first of all, participation is a matter of daily life, beyond any kind of pedagogical or legal considerations. As social beings, people of all ages participate in social life. They are actors, express their needs, organize their lives, and try to participate in the organization of their environment, seek their position in their interrelations with other people, measure the scope of their influence, assume tasks and functions, fulfil their responsibilities or oppose them. Children do the same, in their particular way and according to their age and their life situation in such a way that the important thing is to understand and take seriously the different forms of expression as forms of participation or as a vindication thereof.

Generally, it is implicitly assumed that for the stage of life that we commonly call childhood, specific conditions apply that differ from those applicable to adults, for instance specific interests according to age or generation, greater vulnerability, need for protection or certain requirements of development. As participation 'adapted to children', it is located in pedagogical institutions or as a kind of previous or symbolic form of political participation in special places outside the world of adults. It is based on the supposed separation between the sphere of adulthood and the sphere of childhood, and it is very rare that this assumption is questioned (Liebel, 2018b; Brando Cadena, 2018). Childhood is not defined as an integral part of the community, but rather as a preliminary state and a stage of development on the way to an adult being (supposedly capable of thinking and acting rationally). Therefore, child participation is usually conceived and designed primarily by adults and for learning purposes. It is true that some influence is at times expected in adult decisions but, nearly always, this power of influence is restricted to consultations in which adults are free to ignore the opinions and expectations expressed by the children. Thus, that children have decision-making power in matters that go beyond their personal life normally continues to be a taboo.

One of the fundamental problems of many participatory projects and initiatives is that they are designed by adults and are conceived in a *functional* or *instrumental* sense (top-down approach), its *usefulness* being important, so that there is participation only as far as it suits adults. Thus, participation serves, in the first place, to generate identification in children and to mitigate resistance. We can observe this concept of participation, for instance, in schools, where it serves to motivate bored students or to avoid conflicts and problems with rebellious children. Or in planning projects at the community level, where child (and youth) participation is expected to generate greater efficiency or means a comparative innovative advantage in the competition to win investors and jobs.

Now, to understand participation in an existential sense and as a right that belongs to a person, that serves someone or does not serve anyone, is a fundamentally different understanding of participation. According to this perspective, participation is inherent to the acting subject, and it expands its action space and saves it from being degraded to an object for heteronomous purposes. The UNCRC grants this right also to children, but to a limited extent linked to the degree of 'maturity' and 'capacity'. The vision of participation as a right is based on a concept of humanity according to which, in principle, every human being has an interest and is capable of making use of that right.

However, to determine whether this concept of child participation really benefits the emancipation and equality of rights, here too, it is necessary to see what the basic interests of the children are and what the concrete conditions for implementation are. Only then can we determine whether children can really exercise participation and if it makes sense to them. In effect, the concepts of participation based on the rights of children are often disconnected from the concrete realities of life and the interests of children, particularly those in socially disadvantaged living situations. They are limited to evoke the sense of rights and democracy for children in (potential) citizens or tend to take child participation as a pedagogical resource or means for educational policy with the purpose to educate them, so that someday they will be 'real' and 'competent' citizens. Therefore, as well as participation-oriented approaches to utility, child rights-based approaches are also not free of instrumentalizing children in a paternalistic sense and for heteronomous purposes.

In order to overcome this hitherto dominant understanding of participation and to do justice to the everyday, hardly noticed forms of children's participation, especially in non-Western cultures, Savyasaachi and Mandel Butler (2014) consider it necessary to 'decolonize' the notion of participation with regard to children and young people:

> Firstly, we can seek to decolonize children and young people's participation by analyzing and becoming mindful of the historical origins and cultural specific baggage of 'participation' as commonly used in theories and practices within this field. This means becoming aware of the values and assumptions that inform such theories and practices. Secondly, by critiquing the dominant concept and practices of participation, we can analyze how it may be used and for whose benefit, highlighting the power relations perpetuated by theories and practices. Thirdly, by appreciating the pluralistic possibilities of participation through listening to stories, histories, values, practices and concepts at a local level, we can open up different spaces and forms of participation and give them greater visibility within the worlds of adults. Lastly, combining these three approaches can prepare the ground for listening to children and young people and for rejuvenating theories and practices of participation. (Savyasaachi and Mandel Butler, 2014: 47)

According to these considerations and if we understand participation as an individual right, we must ask ourselves what the concept of the relationship between the individual and society is. Thus, there is, for example, the liberal concept that emerged in the era of European rationalism and bourgeois society, which suggests that the individual must be understood in an 'individualistic' sense: it exists in front of society, but in a separated way from it. In this understanding, the individual is a non- or pre-social being that unites with other subjects only later, in an 'artificial' way and according to 'legal norms'.

However, there are several relationship concepts between individuals and society that contradict this liberal-individualist approach. They do not conceive the individual as a 'last unit' or a kind of atom that can no longer be subdivided, but they consider it a social being that is always part of society and that is affected by it.

> If the human being exists fundamentally through similar ones, if only for these others is what he/she is, then what defines him/her is not in the first place his/her indivisibility and his/her singularity, but the fact of necessarily being part of the other and his/her ability to communicate. Before being an individual, the human being is similar, is a neighbour; before linking him/herself with herself explicitly, he/she links with others; he/she is an instant in the whole of relationships, before – perhaps – some time to be able to define him/herself (Institut für Sozialforschung, 1956: 42).

Therefore, society as 'the whole' is always included in the individual, just as, conversely, the whole could not exist or make sense without other living human (and non-human) beings.

The 'everything' in the sense of society, community, and so on, must always be understood from a historical perspective and as something with an internal structure. We are always a part, but the position we occupy in this 'everything' can vary; we can have or not have power, we can be recognized or belittled. The more equitable and open for 'all' is conceived, the less oppression, coercion or submission entails. Taken to the extreme, this conception can lead to the negation of sociability, as is the case, for example, in neoliberal messages. However, the other extreme is also possible: the individual is 'devoured' by society – that is, they are totally ignored in their personal characteristics, in their needs and interests. It happens, for example, in the German fascist motto that the '*Volksgemeinschaft*' is everything, but the individual is nothing.

My proposal is to understand participation as a way of freedom as well as of belonging and to pay special attention to the relationship that can exist between both. In this sense, we can understand participation as a possibility or opportunity for the individual to gain more room for action, more power and influence in an 'inequitable' and 'not free' society (liberation, empowerment), but also as an individual possibility or opportunity to escape from a marginal position and to achieve more social recognition and greater 'belonging' (inclusion, having part). In fact, instead of thinking about categories of 'or this or that', we should look at the interdependencies. Being autonomous alone can also mean being alone, feeling abandoned and useless. The human being needs to relate to other people, that is, they need 'participation'. Thus, working children in countries of the South, for example, feel proud of being able to help their family, that is to say to get a feeling of belonging, recognition or mutual solidarity, but at the same time, they nearly always insist on disposing of the gained money themselves, that is to say to get autonomy or individual freedom (see Liebel, 2004; Bourdillon et al, 2010; Jijon, 2019).

When engaging in a comparative analysis regarding different cultures, it is important to avoid qualifying the different concepts or participation practices as historically advanced or retrograded. In this sense, modernizing or developmentalist theories that consider 'modern' societies as 'developed' or 'advanced', trying to make them be seen as an example, model and norm for 'traditional' societies, do not work. The aim is to understand the different practices and concepts of participation with their immanent meaning and their importance for the people who live in the respective society– in our case for the stage of life or the age group we call 'childhood'.

Unlike the issue of participation in general, a comparative analysis of children's participation in different cultures requires additional assumptions about the specific position, the status of children in relation to the 'adults' in society, in the generational constellations, in the way in which society practices or conceives the (extended) reproduction of society. In fact, these specific conceptions of what childhood is, are fundamental to the way in which participation and social spaces that are considered legitimate for children's participation are conceived (see Thomas, 2007: 206–07 and 215).

All human societies divide the process of development and aging of people into different phases that, in general, have some denomination. But while in today's Western societies, childhood is seen as a special phase of life that is fundamentally different from the stage of adulthood, there are numerous non-Western societies in which children are considered an integral part of the whole and they take part in the activities of the 'adults'. For these societies, there is no distinct 'childhood' as in Western cultures, but they do know age structures that, in some cases, are more differentiated than the simple distinction between children and adults. Generally, the ages of life are not classified in years, and people are not categorized according to their age, but according to their physical condition and ability to perform certain tasks. Thus, in many indigenous cultures, children are not seen as a particular species that differs fundamentally from adults, but are considered 'small people' (about such cultures, see Liebel, 2004: 77–111).

However, despite these specific generational rules in different cultures, it is to be assumed that children and adults have different interests and points of view insofar as children are relegated to a position of impotence or inferiority (see Alanen and Mayall, 2001). If this is the case, it is necessary for adults to adopt a new vision of children or, in other words, for 'big' people to look at 'little ones' in a different way. Speaking of the different forms of participation, this leads us to the need to ask each one of them to what extent the interests and points of view of children are taken into account. If we consider it necessary to expand child participation, it is not about interfering in the structures of a certain culture, but about giving the same importance to the interests of adults and children, of giving them the same value. Thus, children are also part of society and that is why they should have the possibility to influence the organization of it according to their interests.

In this sense, I understand participation as a right that children have, regardless of whether or not the state laws foresee or establish them. This concept does not oppose the fact that, in some cultures, children are expected to participate in social affairs and assume a certain responsibility. Whether participation is considered a 'right' or an 'obligation' depends on the rules that the culture or society has in this respect and on whether they are explicitly differentiated. In the case of children, it depends on – among things – the existing comprehension of the different age groups or phases and of the position, of the functions, responsibilities, liberties, and so on, that are considered adequate for them, that is, of the generational constellations. Thus, it is possible, for example, that children assume a great deal of responsibility and participate widely in social events without having the explicit right to do so. Conversely, children may have broad rights, but their participation in social life may be minimal.

With the recognition and general acceptance of the concept of human rights and the conventions and corresponding international treaties, normative principles have been established throughout the world that set mutual rights and obligations. However, this model is often limited to the level of the (national) state and to the relations between the state and 'citizens'. In the case of children's rights, the rules may bring more protection, recognition, freedom or participation for children, but they may also generate specific restrictions on their freedom of action and participation that may lead to their total exclusion or marginalization. This situation is reflected, for example, in the minimum age rules for the active practice of certain rights, tasks and responsibilities (for example the right to vote or some child protection standards).

In many societies and cultures considered 'underdeveloped' or 'retrograde', child participation takes different forms and may even be 'broader' than in so-called developed or advanced societies. There, children are perceived as integral members of the community with specific characteristics but whose life does not take place apart from the existence of the 'adult' members of the community. Moreover, according to their abilities (which, incidentally, are not necessarily defined by chronological age), children are expected to assume certain important tasks for the community. They can be social, economic or political tasks, for instance in domestic or work on the farm, and even public positions in the community. Also, there are often rules that give children certain specific goods (farms, domestic animals), as a living legacy of the parents or as a contribution from the community. It should be noted that this is not private property that can be disposed of in any way but social property (see Liebel, 2004: 93–6). We can understand these expectations and rules as a condition for participation but also as a form of participation – without it being denominated in this way or dealing with an individual right. When it comes to the position and power of influence of children in society, these rules can go beyond what is usually understood by participation, since children are considered responsible members of their community.

Such consideration is also relevant to what we can understand by political participation. Many times, this type of participation only gets official recognition and approval when it takes place in contexts predefined by adults. When the activity of children goes beyond these previously delimited forms, the debate about participation simply does not take it into account. In a study on the forms of participation in an indigenous community in Mexico, for example, the author states (Smith, 2007: 50):

> The children of Loxicha are not part of a children's group set up to empower them or to promote their participation, they do not attend strategy meetings, do not have 'agendas', do not plan protest actions, have not been given titles or roles by the adults around them (e.g., 'group leader' or 'young MP'), and they have not been politicized in a specified or agency-led format. They have grown up within a politically charged environment, where protests, marches,

sit-ins, press photo calls, and hunger strikes are all part of their childhoods.

The variously shaped life of children and the political dimension of their agency therefore can only be understood if it is studied with an open concept of childhood that takes its starting point in local realities. The normative notions of childhood that are usually contained in aid activities and media coverage conflict with such an appraisal and make it impossible to link the child rights discourse with children's real lives.

That they work and contribute to the family income, are responsible for feeding and looking after younger siblings, or go on political marches is not at any point identified by the Loxicha children as exceptional elements of their lives. Nor do they define such roles as a movement between the established worlds of childhood and adulthood. This may be simply due to the fact that children do not question the ins and outs of their childhood to the extent that adults do. Another explanation is that these are only 'exceptional' activities if they are viewed from a normative and fixed standpoint. Therein also lies a crucial issue at the core of the debates: it is adults who lead discussions about 'who' children are, 'what' childhood is, and 'how' they should participate in society. According to Anne-Marie Smith (2007: 52),

> The Loxicha children do not fit a neat research category such as 'street child' or 'working child'. They move between worlds – they are indigenous children from a rural home who now move in an urban environment, they are displaced as the result of a situation of political violence, they are involved in a day-to-day struggle for the recognition of the rights of their community, they go to school, they feed and care for younger siblings, and they sometimes work. They do not fit into most local NGOs' criteria for inclusion in their programs. While some adults may argue that the Loxicha children's participation in marches and sit-ins does not constitute 'political activism', the fact that these activities are difficult to categorize does not mean they do not 'count'.

The way in which Loxicha children participate in the political struggle of their community is belittled and devalued because it does not fit the experts' criteria of what a 'nice' participation is, especially in those that are generally run by NGOs. The author concludes (Smith, 2007: 52):

The lives of the Loxicha children in Oaxaca clearly present a 'type' of children's participation not envisaged by the CRC and its ideals. An acknowledgment of the roles children can play in political activity has not been forthcoming in the advocacy for children's rights, in particular within debates around their participation rights. Their voices are being listened to and their views incorporated into many areas of decision-making, facts that would have been inconceivable at the beginning of the twentieth century. It is perhaps time, however, for notions of children's participation to move beyond the present vision which, while having opened hitherto unexplored territory for many young people, remains nonetheless carefully contained by clear (and adult-imposed) conceptual and linguistic parameters.[7]

In Latin America, this form of anti-paternalist participation is often called *child protagonism* or *protagonist participation* (see Liebel, 2004, 2007a; Cussiánovich, 2001; Cussiánovich and Márquez, 2002). These terms emphasize that children do not act only within the framework of predetermined participation patterns but that they generate self-organized forms of participation linked to their life circumstances. They are not limited to a restricted area of children but intervene in social and political fields that have been seen as reserved for adults. With this, they contribute in an organized and autonomous way to the transformation of society and politics. In a figurative sense, as well as anti-paternalist approaches to child protection, anti-paternalist participation can also be understood as decolonization of the relationship between children and adults and the inferior social status of childhood in society.

Conclusion: Beyond paternalism

To adopt a perspective that overcomes paternalism, it is important not to equate paternalism with child protection, or see participation as overcoming paternalism. The difference is that protection guarantees a certain level of security, while paternalism means that adults or state institutions always have the power to make decisions about children and make decisions *on behalf of and in their place*, including against their will. Children always depend on a certain degree of protection by adults, but this protection must not be exercised in a paternalistic way. In addition, it must be taken into account that with the participation of children in the measures that concern them ('best interests'), protection becomes less necessary because the risks in society as a whole are reduced.

This occurs when social inequality and power (based on generational logics) are replaced by more equality and social security, and a culture of mutual recognition and respect, even among different age groups. In the same way, participation itself will have to be identified in the middle of daily life, taking into account the forms that emerge from it in different social situations and cultures.

To imagine other perspectives beyond paternalism with respect to children, we will have to continue to deepen a participatory concept of protection and a protagonist concept of participation such as those explained in the previous paragraphs. It is true that participation can in itself be a form of protection because it contributes to reducing the vulnerability of children. But it is not enough just to look at the children's performance and their capacity for agency; at the same time we must address and question the inequalities of power, whether due to social conditions (poverty, exploitation, social exclusion), or because of discrimination based on prejudices about race, gender and/or age.

Paternalism against children corresponds to a restrictive interpretation of the concept of evolving capacities of the child codified in the UNCRC. This interpretation attributes the presumed dependency and vulnerability of children to a lack of skills instead of considering that skills are largely the result of social experiences. Children who are strictly separated from the world of adults have fewer opportunities to expand and deepen their capacities than children who are involved in the exercise of responsibilities, in social relationships based on mutual respect. Likewise, the supposed basic needs of the child, which – according to González Contró (2008) – serve both as a justification and as a limitation of legal paternalism, are not simply a natural expression but are socially constructed and depend largely on the opportunities society makes possible and facilitates.

Instead of simply waiting for paternalism to be gradually reduced in the course of life, we should promote and pursue fundamental changes in the power structure of society and adult–child relationships that allow us to overcome paternalism as such. In a society of social equality and mutual respect, there is no need or justification for paternalism. It is true that paternalism cannot be overcome 'by decree', but the implementation of participatory protection and protagonist participation of children could gradually advance their improvement. Such a process is not a question of development or progress towards 'modern' societies but the synthesis of social practices that exist in different cultures of history. Likewise, liberating and emancipatory currents in the history of children's rights can serve as a source of inspiration.

In essence, as adults, we are obliged to act in a way that children's position in society becomes stronger and their political participation and citizenship is expanded, to which, in particular, social movements and organizations led by children and adolescents can contribute. Such organizations can contribute to the dynamization of multiple processes, reaching the public instances of decision making, and taking the voice of children as a collective. Such actions also contribute to reverting power relations in the spaces in which children carry out their activities, in order to have a greater public presence in places traditionally run by adults.

Notes

[1] See the explanations of the 'colonization of childhood' in Chapter 2, which is based in turn on what is called 'colonial paternalism'.

[2] The quote is taken from an article first written in 2002 and revised in February 2017.

[3] In an earlier, often quoted definition, Dworkin (1972: 70) had described paternalism as 'the interference with a person's liberty of action justified by reasons referring exclusively to the welfare, good, happiness, needs, interests or values of the person being coerced'.

[4] For the genesis and meanings of the term, see Zude (2010); on different definitions and their location in the history of philosophy and law see Shiffrin (2000), Coons and Weber (2013) and Dworkin (2017).

[5] For the critique of 'libertarian paternalism', see White (2013) and Dworkin (2017).

[6] On the question of children's interests and their relation to rights, see Liebel (2018).

[7] For more details, see Liebel (2012a: 176–9).

9

Children's movements as citizenship from below

Adults miss the point. When is a child considered skilful enough to contribute and participate actively? If you do not give them the opportunity to participate, they will not acquire the skills. Give us the chance early and see how we fly. (Khairul Azri, 17, Malaysian delegate to the UN 'Special Session on Children' in 2002; UNICEF, 2002: 1)

Citizens before the revolution were apathetic and careless. We didn't care about what is happening because we felt the country was not ours. But now the revolution has succeeded, everyone feels this country is theirs and that's why we will try to rebuild it and make it a better place. (Jihad, 14, Cairo, Egypt, April 2011; cited in BBC News, 2011)

Introduction

In today's political discourse on the role of children in society, it would be a breach of etiquette not to emphasize children's citizenship. Most of the time, the discussants limit themselves to insist on children being citizens, though without specifying or supporting their assertion. Where children's citizenship is further described, it is usually defined as a becoming status, which children can acquire in a step-by-step process ('citizens in the making'). The acquisition of citizenship is depicted as a learning process through which children have to go by themselves or be guided by an educator. In this context, children are invited to fight for their interests by participating in activities and programmes organized for them. To engage in such a program is seen as a practical test to prove that children are on the verge of turning into citizens or just became citizens.

This understanding of children's citizenship seems to me to be inadequate and wrong. In my opinion, children's citizenship is not merely a preparation for a future status, nor is it exhausted in a point by point or symbolic participation. It is also not covered by the so-called participation rights, which have been approved in the UNCRC for the first time under binding international law. The right of children to be heard and to take their views according to their age and maturity into account, as laid down in Article 12 of the UNCRC, reserves the final decision making for adults and the bodies they dominate. It is certainly not to be underestimated that children are assured that they can inform themselves and freely express their thoughts, freely join others and gather peacefully (Articles 13 and 15). However, these articles also contain restrictions imposed by adults, and they do not guarantee the children the necessary conditions to exercise such rights (such as the right to hold meetings or establish their own associations in any country legally depends on age limits or the consent of adults). Political rights, such as universal suffrage, have not yet been granted to children. It cannot therefore be said that the UNCRC and the laws of the nation states have so far given children a citizenship in the full sense of the term.

Nevertheless, the citizenship of children is not a ghost. Just as human rights arose from social movements and struggles, change and expansion (see Stammers, 2009), the citizenship of children can arise and expand through their own movements and struggles, too. It must, however, be borne in mind that citizenship cannot be restricted to formal procedures within the framework of established political orders, but must prove itself as a 'lived citizenship' (Lister, 2003) in everyday life. I understand this kind of citizenship as 'citizenship from below', as it is brought out and pushed forward by social movements for more social and political justice, in which children can also play a decisive role. This all is true for other marginalized social groups as well.

In my opinion, citizenship of children implies that they can assume political co-responsibility in society on an ongoing basis, as well as influence societal processes and political decisions, not only in the future, but in the present. To understand children as citizens means that they can do so in a particular, but equal and equivalent, way. This must be accompanied by the development of a culture of children's rights in society, which takes children seriously as legal subjects and grants them, in particular, participation rights, which enable them to make their own decisions in all areas of life and in society including questions, which touch the interests of adults. This requires not only the recognition of children's competencies, but also the creation of conditions that enable children to develop their agency competences and use them in practice. In doing so, I have a conception of citizenship in mind, which is appropriate for the life situation and the life experiences of children.

First, I outline what can be understood by citizenship in general and what problems are associated with the term. Then I discuss concepts of citizenship that relate directly to children and their relatively impotent social status. In the main section, I explain what I understand with regard to children under the term 'citizenship from below' and how this can emerge from social movements of children, which I primarily locate in the Global South.[1]

What does citizenship mean?

When speaking of citizenship there are close links to ideas about democracy and participation. It is a product of urbanized societies emergence and the aspiration of the urban inhabitants not to leave public affairs to a sovereign authority, but to take them into their own hands. This urban origin is visible not only in the English term *citizen*ship but also in corresponding terms of other languages like in French (*citoyenneté*) or Spanish (*ciudadanía*).[2] With the emergence of bourgeois societies and the associated claim of the rising bourgeois class to dispose of a territorially demarcated state, which serves their interests, the citizenship of 18th century Europe gradually became a national affair. With the enforcement of universal suffrage, citizenship was extended, at least formally, to all (electorate) nationals of the nation state, and increasingly also to interstate and supranational political systems. However, transnational citizenships or even a world or global citizenship[3] are still abstract notions without clear contours and assertiveness (see Bobbio, 1996; Dower and Williams, 2002). The reference to a 'global citizenship' sometimes also veils the continuing and even growing social inequality between people in different regions of the world (see Mignolo, 2006; Boatcă, 2015).

Ambivalences and contradictions of citizenship

Citizenship is a specific form of political participation that is not free of ambivalences. It is bound by the fact that a person belongs to a territorially defined community, nowadays usually a nation state, which is expressed by the possession of appropriate documents of their national identity (birth certificate, identity card, passport, or residence status). This becomes evident with the fact that the relevant declaration of the French Revolution stated a difference between 'men's rights' (that is to say human rights) and 'civil rights'. To this day, there is dispute whether and which international human rights are valid for all people regardless of their nationality, or whether they must first be converted into national law, and consequently can only be claimed by those who are recognized as citizens of this state.

The fact that, since the First World War in the 20th century, a large number of people strayed around the world who did not have such recognition or were even 'expatriated' by states ('stateless persons') motivated German-Jewish philosopher Hannah Arendt ([1951]1973), to claim 'the right to have rights' as fundamental for every human being. This leads to a cosmopolitan or universal understanding of citizenship, which goes beyond the 'state-centric' model of citizenship (Benhabib, 2004), which is still dominant today. As far as I know, Ecuador is the only country that, in its 2008 Constitution, has defined the principle of 'universal citizenship' (*ciudadanía universal*), with the result that no person living in the country is treated as 'illegal' or 'stateless'.

As an essential achievement of the modern construction of national citizenship, it does not measure people by their inherited affiliation (for example, as nobleman), social qualities (for example, to have a certain amount of property) or 'natural' characteristics (for example, to be a male), but confer the same rights on all nationals of a country. However, it must be borne in mind that in the reality of nation states not all people were granted the same civil rights. For example, women were not granted the right to vote as an integral part of citizenship until 1918 in Germany and 1944 in France, and the inhabitants of the European overseas colonies were completely excluded. Children are still denied the right to vote. In addition, should be borne in mind that just as this type of citizenship claims to be 'internally inclusive', it is 'externally exclusive', that is to say, it maintains access to the same rights to those who 'belong' (Brubaker, 1994). This also applies to people who live within the borders of a country but who are not recognized as 'nationals' (for example, migrants, refugees). Therefore, it can be said that citizenship is also internally exclusive, especially when it is about societies with strong immigration (Mackert, 1999).[4]

No matter how the affiliation is defined and acquired, be it by so-called blood relations (*ius sanguinis*), place of birth (*ius soli*) or the application of other criteria, it always excludes others who do not meet these criteria. A so far little noticed aspect of this contradiction – Boatcǎ (2015: 190) speaks of a 'blind spot' of Citizen Studies – consists in the fact that this form of citizenship also contains elements of heredity, similar to the membership criteria of pre-bourgeois ('feudalist') societies. It is transmitted from generation to generation through the grace or misfortune of birth, and can by no means be freely chosen. This intergenerational transmission of citizenship privileges those who are growing up in the wealthy countries of the world, as their citizenship offers more options than that of poorer countries. It thus contributes to the deepening of social inequality in the world, contrary to the promise of inclusion by citizenship (Shachar and Hirschl, 2007; Shachar, 2009).

Especially in the postcolonial debate, there are claims that citizenship has different qualities depending on nationality and geopolitical location (Boatcă, 2015: 117). For example, an EU national or a US citizen can travel to and stay in many more countries for a longer period of time than people who, for example, (only) have the nationality of an African, Latin American or Asian country (there are, in particular, differences between Asian countries). As wealth is concentrated in the first group of countries and poverty is concentrated in the second group, citizenship tends to cement the advantages of one against the disadvantages of others. This is particularly evident today in the migratory movements from the South to the North. The migrants from the South are faced with great difficulties in crossing the borders with the countries of the North, and often they must pay their flight with their lives. Even if they have succeeded, they remain second-class citizens in the country of arrival, provided they obtain a legal residence permit at all. In contrast to local citizens, their status as a resident is subject to restrictions and discrimination, which can make life a source of agony and significantly curtail the prospects of life.

Walter Mignolo (2006), who represents a Latin American variant of postcolonial theory, warns against the construction of (national) citizenship as a way of overcoming social inequality, or of reaching a 'global citizenship' which benefits all people equally (he calls it 'a myth'). Instead, he sees in it the late stage of enforcing Western dominance and the production of 'otherness'. According to him, the negative quality of being different was equated in the antique Greek and Roman Empire with the 'barbarians', in the colonial epoch with the 'primitives', and in postcolonial times with the 'underdeveloped'.

This hierarchization of citizenship is also reflected in the fact that it is portrayed as an autonomous achievement of Western modernity to be exported from the 'developed' Global North to the still 'developing' Global South, as it describes a form of development aid for 'good governance'.[5] Without doubt, the idea of citizenship emerged with the European Enlightenment and the emergence of nation states, and was a product of the bourgeoisie emancipated from the fetters of feudalist societies, but other subaltern classes (the 'Third Estate') contributed to their success. Nevertheless, these processes were closely linked to the 'discovery' and plundering of the 'new world' called America, and later to the colonialization of other Southern regions of the world.

It is true that the world is now organized in formally independent nation states, but these represent only a rough scaffolding, which often opposes rather than favours the emancipation of its citizens. When citizenship in the formerly colonialized regions of the world arises, this does not necessarily follow the pattern practised in Europe. Instead, it is necessary to ensure who is the protagonist of the emancipation and liberation processes in these regions of the world, and which forms of statehood and citizenship they bring forth. This is expressed, for example, in Latin America, when citizenship in the context of a new concept of 'political subjectivities' is understood as a comprehensive self-organization of society, rooted in the everyday life of the people but not bound to a centralized nation state (Díaz Gómez, 2005; Alvarado et al, 2008, González Rey, 2012).

Liberal and republican citizenship

Two fundamentally different concepts of citizenship can be distinguished: on the one hand the liberal concept and on the other hand the republican one (see Fernández Steinko, 2004). The latter is sometimes also referred to as 'social citizenship'. These different concepts are based primarily on observations of social and political processes in modern Europe, but are not limited to them. If they are used in a heuristic way, they can provide a conceptual framework for understanding, criticizing and shaping citizenship in other parts of the world.

The *liberal* concept stresses the individual liberty of the citizen, and assigns to the state the function of guaranteeing private property as well as the scope for action of each individual citizen based on corresponding constitutions and laws. The function assigned to the state here is not a forming but a regulating one. The role of the citizens in public affairs is confined to periodic elections of representative bodies whereas basic decisions (such as those related to economic and financial policy) are shifted to 'post-democratic' expert committees. The emphasis is on 'participation' in the private sphere, whether in economic or family matters. In neoliberal variants of citizenship, this can reach the point where the public sphere, when relating to matters of 'public welfare', is completely commodified – absorbed into the private or commercial sphere. In this case, public tasks are subordinated under the functional principles of private enterprises, and 'citizens' are transformed into 'customers' (Crouch, 2005, 2015).

The most recent variant of neoliberal citizenship is to make citizens themselves the commodity that can be acquired with money ('citizenship-by-investment'). There is a logic behind the fact that only the citizenship of certain countries is desirable, as it brings particular economic and political advantages, such as citizenship of the countries of the European Union (examples are Hungary, Malta and Cyprus; see Dzankic, 2014). Other countries (or islands) attractive for such a kind of 'citizenship' are the so-called tax-havens, where properties can be hidden and multiplied (such as the Cayman Islands, which also offer the advantage of belonging to the British Commonwealth; see Shachar, 2014). For their part, the power elites of these countries are, of course, only interested in those new citizens who have the necessary capital to 'revive' the national economy. Special agencies have made this commitment itself a business model (see, for example, Henley & Partners, 2014). The new kind of citizenship, which is now caricatured by critics as *ius pecuniae* or right based on payment (Stern, 2011; Dzankic, 2012), not only contributes to bringing the states themselves into further dependence on commercial enterprises, but also amplifies the social division in the respective country as well as between the Global North and the Global South.

The *republican* (or *social*) conception of citizenship, in contrast, stresses the dominance of the public sphere and of the community, based on solidarity of all citizens identified with it, regardless of their private possessions or their individual social position. The individual's scope for action is seen as dependent on economically conditioned positions of power, and the state is expected to intervene in the interests of social levelling. The liberty of the citizens is then expressed, conversely, by the fact that they are able to exert a continual and as far as possible extensive influence on public affairs. The corresponding state form is mostly termed 'participatory' or 'direct', newly also as 'communitarian', in contrast to 'representative' democracy.

In contrast to socialist (or social democratic) views, libertarian (or anarchistic) variants of the republican conception of citizenship ascribe greater significance to citizens' self-organization beyond the state than to the state itself. However, in contrast to the (neo-) liberal conception, society is not regarded as a conglomeration of private individuals; instead, the social interrelations and mutual obligations of the members of society are stressed.

Today, the fundamental differences between (neo-) liberal and republican concepts of citizenship have sometimes been extended by the notion of 'active citizenship'. This term implies that citizens – as in traditional socialist or social democratic conceptions – not only function as (passive) recipients of governmental provision services but as individuals that actively participate in society. What 'own activity' implies can, however, vary largely. Here again, the neoliberal understanding of replacing state responsibility by complete individual self-responsibility (which leaves those perceived as too 'passive' to their own fate) is opposed by a social or republican understanding, which aims at extending the citizens' realm of action and their responsibilities, yet in a sense of extended influence on political decisions as well as state action.[6]

In the European sphere, the republican concept of citizenship has had a transitory opportunity of realization only in situations of social upheaval, for instance during the Paris Commune of 1871, in the revolutionary years following the First World War,[7] in republican Spain in the 1930s, or immediately after the victory over fascism. During these times, it became visible what a huge fund of energy and ability can be triggered, not least in those who are socially disadvantaged and have been pushed to the fringe of society. In countries of the Global South, the concept meets the interests of the excluded and the despised, and can become a moving element that challenges the national authorities and bureaucracies formed according to the colonial model. The republican idea of citizenship is, contrary to the assertions of the ideological mainstream of today, anything but a relic of the past. Precisely at the present time, when struggles for shares in the distribution of wealth are on the rise, and the relation between state and society is being re-examined, it can provide suggestions for possible alternatives of social and political participation. At the same time, it can serve as a frame of reference in the critical debate on neoliberal 'reform' politics and for fundamental social changes in the interests of the underprivileged and excluded.

The ideas and strivings for a citizenship of children presented below will be discussed in the light of the republican conception of citizenship. However, I do not refer to the European origins of citizenship here in the sense of offering them to other continents and cultures as an ideal model. In the design of citizenship, consideration of specific ways in which people have dealt with dominating conditions will always be necessary and how concepts of liberation, autonomy and participation in social affairs have been produced. In this context, it is important to keep in mind the anticolonial movements and the discussion on the colonial legacy in postcolonial societies.[8] The concept of citizenship discussed below refers explicitly to such processes in the countries of the Global South.

Children and citizenship

In the social sciences that deal with children, scholars agree that there is no 'citizenship as a whole of rights' (Jans, 2004: 38), not even in states with democratic constitutions. This takes into account that, together with civil rights, political, social, economic and cultural rights[9] are fundamental to citizenship. Jens Qvortrup (2005: 11) expresses this succinctly in the statement that 'children do not enjoy economic and political rights as autonomous citizens'. However, there are differing ideas of children's citizenship and possible ways for its implementation.

Child-specific or equal citizenship?

On one hand, there is support for the idea that children have the possibility to influence society not only in 'children's affairs', but also in all matters affecting the present and future of societies. This position is at times described as '*equality* between children and adults' yet does not – as the history of the children's rights movements demonstrates (see Liebel, 2012a: 29–42) – automatically imply an *equation* of children and adults. On the other hand, there is support for 'child-friendly' or 'child-size' forms of citizenship that are understood as preparation for future (full) citizenship and are therefore seen more than anything as a learning process (see Jans, 2004; Roche, 1999). An equal citizenship is seen as being problematic since it would burden the children with full responsibility, and would ignore or endanger specific peculiarities and needs of children that are based on human development. This understanding of child-friendly or child-size citizenship is therefore also critically termed 'partial citizenship' by Invernizzi and Milne (2005: 3), and connected to the question whether the citizenship of children requires special 'children's structures', or whether we are to understand them 'as inclusion and collaboration with adults'.[10]

Based on the above described republican concept of citizenship, I will next argue to what extent an equal citizenship of children can not only consider differences between children and adults but is virtually dependent on considering the inferior social status of children. To this end it seems useful to imagine citizenship not only in a legal sense as a 'bundle of rights', but in a sociological sense as a social relationship, in which norms, institutional practices, meanings, cultural assumptions, and the sense of belonging are combined (see Isin and Turner, 2002). This understanding of 'lived citizenship' (Lister, 2007) is based on a dynamic, process-oriented understanding of rights. Following Ruth Lister (2007), this is particularly important for 'societies where rights are under-developed or are under threat or for groups who are denied full citizenship rights'.

Tom Cockburn notes, with reference to the citizenship concept of Thomas H. Marshall (1950), that the full citizenship of children is prevented by their marginal social status. 'Children cannot own property and are excluded from legal decisions about family matters' (Cockburn, 1998: 101). Their parents are directly responsible for them or – in exceptional cases – the state is. Meanwhile children have certain rights, such as the right not to be killed or be physically abused, nevertheless they remain dependent on the goodwill of adults. In conceptions of political citizenship, children are by definition non-political subjects with the right neither to vote nor to strike, and have only limited and, as a rule, strictly controlled access to the media (see also Cockburn, 2005). In this context, Cockburn calls to mind that over the past 150 years, children have successively been excluded from almost all spheres of public life (see in detail Cockburn, 2013).

According to the notions of childhood that predominate in the world today, children are primarily regarded as potential for the future or as future citizens. Like women in earlier times, and as 'ethnic' minorities still are today, they are considered as 'outsiders', who (still) fail to possess all the qualities that are required of a 'proper citizen'. 'Children are almost everything that the non-citizen is: they are irrational, incapable, undeveloped or dependent and are defined in terms of what they are not, that is adult, responsible, rational and autonomous' (Cockburn, 1998: 107). Their lack of qualification for citizenship is, as a rule, 'justified on grounds of children's need for protection and their dependence on adults' (Lister, 2006: 24).

Certainly, one particular feature of children's citizenship consists of the fact that children require a special degree of protection, and their dependence on adults can mean vital security and support, too. Arguments in support of children's citizenship do not need to claim (or insist) that they have to be like adults, or possess the same qualities that are ascribed to them, or which adults claim for themselves. Indeed, children may possess other qualities that can be particularly fundamental to citizenship, such as the 'intuitive' feeling for what is phoney, or for discrepancies between words and deeds. Their supposed lack of competence is also not an argument against their citizenship, as this cannot simply be deduced from their lifetime, but is connected with specific circumstances of their lives and with their experience. According to Cockburn (1998: 109), 'incompetence is not something natural or innate but is socially produced'.

According to Marshall (1950), social and economic rights and safeguards are the necessary precondition for the actual ability to exercise civil and political rights. This connection, which is formulated in particular with a view to socially disadvantaged and excluded sections of the population, does not, however, include children. Although

Marshall sees the right of children to education as a sign of their 'social citizenship', he also claims that: 'Fundamentally it should be regarded not as a right of the child to go to school but of the adult citizen to have been educated' (Marshall, 1950: 25). Moreover, with the expansion of compulsory schooling and the length of school attendance, children are denied the opportunity to engage in generally recognized and paid 'productive work', even if it takes place under conditions which bring positive and vital experiences for children.

Taking Marshall's position further, a view that 'social citizenship' has been extended to children could also be supported, in the sense that they are able to claim a degree of protection, that society is responsible for them. Nevertheless, so far, this has not been combined with the right for children to exercise political power themselves. Children have merely a 'welfare role' that grants them a certain amount of care and protection, but which conversely plays down their social and economic contributions (Cordero Arce, 2012). Moreover, during the past 30 years, the social citizenship of children, even in the relatively affluent societies of the North, has been undermined by a dramatic growth of poverty. The attitude towards rights and laws that has spread under neoliberal influence since the 1980s devalues social citizenship, while stressing a form of citizenship that is to a high degree individualistic and market-related. Euphemistically, these forms are also referred to as 'active citizenship' in order to underline the self-responsibility of each person for their welfare.

Here, the question is not least whether the concept of citizenship is related to the community or rather to the market, whether a citizen is seen mainly as consumer or as (potential) member of the labour force.[11] According to the latter concept – which may be termed neoliberal – the public and private spheres are no longer distinguished; the relation to the community is replaced by individual behaviour of choice in the sense of personal advantage (such as the ability to choose from a large number of TV channels). This concept is currently being furthered in European Union countries, for example, by an increase in the 'economic orientation' of the (still state-run) school system and its opening up for 'marketing' of large enterprises.[12] Likewise, the previous strategies of protection, welfare and the extension of education to children were not always beneficial for them and had little to do with the expansion of rights and citizenship (see Cannella and Viruru, 2004, Close, 2014). Children have found the attention of the authorities largely as delinquents that threaten security and property, as future workers who must be trained, or as future soldiers who must remain healthy and fit.

Some authors refer – with the UK in mind – to the children who, because their parents live in poverty or are otherwise handicapped, have to take on responsibilities within the family, especially in the frame of taking part in looking after other family members (younger siblings, sick or handicapped parents, or other relatives).[13] Roche (1999: 478) calls it 'ironic that those children who act in that highly responsible way … in relation to their family are "made to disappear" by adult practice. … What the young carers are doing does not really have to be taken seriously, they are just "helping out".' Aldridge and Becker (2002: 218) point out that in the media children are represented either as 'little angels' or 'little victims' of exploitative practices.[14]

In the case of the children in countries of the Global South, who live in great poverty, this paradoxical situation is even more pressing. The 'privilege' of being largely unburdened by duties and responsibilities promised by the status of childhood in the relatively affluent countries of the North is totally denied to them. Although the UNCRC asserts their rights to care and protection as well as participation, in practice they are hardly able to avail themselves of these, and have little but duties. Indeed, even when, for instance, out of a feeling of solidarity with their families, they fulfil these duties, they receive no recognition for this in society or from political quarters. Their situation becomes completely paradoxical when, as working children who are forbidden to work, and whose work is aimed at being abolished, they are placed in a situation of lacking rights, which can extend even to their criminalization.

Citizenship despite powerlessness?

One constant topic in research and writings on children's rights is the fact that children and young people have a profound feeling of impotence and exclusion (see Lansdown, 2002; Hill et al, 2004; Wyness et al, 2004). Hence, this begs the question what this means for the view of children as subjects or actors, which is a central element of childhood studies of today (see Esser et al, 2016). Answers are needed whether children are degraded to the status of objects by exclusion, marginalization and the withholding of political rights, or if the feeling of impotence and exclusion is precisely an indication of the fact that children do regard themselves as subjects, which prevents them from resigning from their reduction to the status of objects. In other words, the question is whether it is possible to imagine that children could effectively influence political life, or at least attempt to do so, despite their feeling of impotence and the inadequate political rights they (do not) have.

I see the key to the answer in the fact that children are becoming aware of being involved in many ways in social and economic life today. This way of participation frequently takes on forms, which, as shown above, bring disadvantages rather than advantages for the children, and as a rule is not valued with appropriate recognition. Nevertheless, it can form a basis for children to be assured of their importance to society, and to claim a not merely recognized but also influential role in society.

Citizenship in this sense is the result of a learning process among children (and among adults in relation to the children). I do not, however, see this learning process in the yet common concepts of education for citizenship – namely that the children need to be made capable of citizenship by means of an induced growth of competence – but instead that it relates to concrete experiences of 'being needed' and of children's own contributions to societal life, and become aware of their own 'importance'. The framework of such learning processes can be either educational projects directed towards the empowerment of children and the fostering of their self-confidence, or social movements organized and managed by the children themselves (frequently with support from solidary acting adults).

In all societies – whether in the North or the South – 'children are social participants – participating in homeworking, child labour, political protest, caring, keeping the family "on the road", etc.' (Roche, 1999: 484). This participation takes very diverse forms; ranging from participation in the 'functional' sense of acting out different predefined roles or social integration into the existing society and its improved functioning[15] to the 'transformational' sense of a critical exertion of influence aiming at an improvement of living conditions and social recognition. For this kind of citizenship, the local (municipal) environment and the nation state are just as relevant as a global perspective, which takes into account the evolving process of globalization and the increasing global interdependence.

While in the 'classical' participation research political participation has been understood as democratic participation in elections, parties and parliaments, since the 1980s, intercultural-oriented democracy and participation research amplified the concept of participation from the formal-democratic boundaries to 'informal' aspects of political participation, for instance, social protest movements or self-help networks. According to Herriger (1997: 186),

... building solidary communities and the demand for participation and co-responsibility on the level of (local) public politics are essential. Political empowerment is thus realized in processes of changing selves (seen as an expansion of the reserves of personal competencies for forming the environment) as well as in processes of social change. This is realized when people, together with others, become critical actors on the level of local citizens' public and enter into 'spheres of justice' through collegial resistance and critical action.

From this, a concept of citizenship can emerge that does not only focus on the dependence of children on adults, but also brings out the mutual interdependence of children and adults (as a rule concealed) in the sense of 'giving and taking' (Alderson, 2008a: 62). Or, in the words of Tom Cockburn (1998: 109–10):

Children are clearly dependent upon others .... However, all members of society are dependent upon children for their society's continuation and future existence. ... A starting point for any reformulation of citizenship must begin with a re-evaluation of citizenship not as property centred but rather based on solidaristic, non-contractual interdependence.

This also applies to quite young children who, although they are more dependent on adults than older children, can be also important to the adults. Parents can learn from them how to treat their 'following' children (for instance younger siblings), or educators in public institutions can be relieved of the daily burden by children participating actively. Furthermore, as Priscilla Alderson (2008b: 117) points out, taking on tasks and self-responsibility of children from an early age can contribute to making the services 'more cost-effective', meaning this can have immediate economic impact: '[A] review of children's under-recognized citizenship and economic contributions to their families and communities suggests that concepts of "delivering" health care and education services misunderstand the crucial contributions that children can make within more cost-effective public services.'

When speaking of citizenship, children should not be seen and treated as if they were adults, but can be met with recognition on the basis of 'social difference'. According to Ruth Lister (2006: 25), 'children should be regarded as equal citizens with the right to belong as "differently equal" members of society'.[16] We must also remember that not all children are equal, but differ according to age, situation in life, and social competences. Where these differences are not taken into account and expressly picked out as a central theme, there is a risk that children from privileged social backgrounds will dominate over socially disadvantaged children, and thus add to discrimination against them.

At times, there is a warning that the issue of autonomy will be the crucial question of children's citizenship. Although it could help to strengthen the social position of the children, Cockburn (1998: 116) considers it ultimately a 'liberal illusion' in view of the factual interdependencies and 'polymorphic' power relations. Anyone who comes to such a problematic conclusion in my opinion has a liberal understanding of autonomy, which understands individuals not as interdependent social subjects, but as isolated monads (Liebel and Saadi, 2012; Mühlbacher and Sutterlüty, 2019). In my opinion, the claim to autonomy is indispensable if the idea of difference, based on equality, is to be taken seriously. In the case of children's citizenship, this means that children must have the right and the opportunity to articulate their own group-specific interests and to make them manifest in society, even if they differ from the expectations of the dominating adults (Liebel, 2018b). To reach this, they need social spaces in which they are 'at home' and can feel free to be themselves.

Citizenship from below

From what has been said so far it is clear that citizenship cannot be understood in a purely legal sense or even less only in the way 'to be in the position of being governed' (Roche, 1999: 484). Instead, it is to be understood as a form of everyday action, which can be called on by way of rights, but can also be entirely independent of them, for instance, in protest movements targeting encroachments, whose actors do not wait until they are granted rights.[17]

In any case, it would be truncating to understand citizenship only in the sense of being based on state recognition and affiliation or within a framework of formal institutions. This would be particularly problematic for children, since formally only few political rights have been granted to them. In addition, as shown above, the participation rights anchored in the UNCRC are limited to a pre-political space and do not directly permit children's influence on political decision-making processes. Especially in the case of children it would be appropriate to consider a form of citizenship 'which looks at relations within civil society and how children are positioned, because then new relations are revealed and new questions of power, requiring justification, emerge' (Roche, 1999: 476).

In what I call citizenship from below, I see a specific form of citizenship which is tailored more to children (and adolescents) than to adults. I understand it as a form of everyday action that may appeal to rights but can also take place totally independently from them, for example, in protest movements with deliberate infringements of rules, whose actors do not wait for their rights to be granted. Precisely due to the fact that these children organized in movements are often accused of being 'bad citizens' (Milne, 2007; Smith et al, 2005: 437), it is important to take note of the manner in which protest is performed, and to recognize the way 'in which children do resist and challenge adult practices, though not necessarily in obvious or constructive ways' (Roche, 1999: 478). Faced with a world of adults, in which children are hardly listened to and whom political rights are largely denied, they do not have many opportunities to take part in publicly recognized political action. 'Children have to start from where they are socially positioned. This means that they have to make their own space in spaces not of their making' (Roche, 1999: 479).

In this context, German sociologist Oskar Negt (1997) speaks of *Kinderöffentlichkeit* (children's public) as a 'semi-autonomous protest form'. It emerges when childhood turns into a 'life cycle' which has been separated from the adult society and has become 'an object of public interest' as a 'privatized' living space (Negt, 1997: 95). According to Negt, thus it is to be understood as

> ... expression of domination and protest in one. It gives the children the interpretative frame for their needs, their behaviour and the thought they need, in order not to remain mere objects. As individuals, they cannot break the supremacy of the adult; they are dependent on the public as a collective form of protest because they thus can only free themselves from the feeling of absolute impotence (Negt, 1997: 95).

However, always according to Negt, the children's public should not be confused with a 'reserve' that adults offer and establish for children, it rather means the 'use of their own means of expression' (Negt, 1997: 96). It can only form beyond the private space in which the self-directed activity of children becomes possible. Thus, an essential element of childhood is the 'producing process of experiences', provided that this is 'based on the self-organization of the children' (Negt, 1997: 97–8).

Citizenship from below is in this sense not an individual matter, subject to the whim of individual children. The only way it can be realized is through an awareness of common interests among the acting children. This is not possible for all children in the same way or to the same extent, for common interests are not only a question of a common age group (a 3-year old and a 13-year old may not have much in common, but they certainly share the desire for distinction). Huge differences might also separate a child living in poverty from one that does not lack any material goods. As with adults, a fusion of interests must first take place, in which similar experiences are put together in an impetus for common action. Here, social movements of children are instructive examples for demonstrating how such a union of interests might occur and what can result from it.

Children's movements in the Global South as citizenship from below

Children's social movements as indicated here are to be found today mainly in the Global South (see Liebel, 2004, 19–37; 2007a).[18] They arise partly from projects that are initiated by adults and then become independent. Others emerge as a protest against adults' refusals to give children an independent role in social and political life. In addition, the movements are also inspired by the rights that children are entitled to under the UNCRC, and which they invoke.

Usually it is not a matter of 'pure' children's movements; mostly children interact with young people and adults. However, children are not only active in these movements as some kind of assistants for adults and their agendas or for reasons of learning, they also play a decisive role in decision making. They see themselves as equal political and social subjects. In some movements, children themselves are the driving force and insist on their autonomy. Nevertheless, they never understand themselves only as children, but always as members of *certain social groups or communities*, whose problems, worries and interests they share. Sometimes there is tension between children and adults, especially when the children have the impression that adults want to patronize them or disrespect them and their own views. This can become a serious problem because children are nearly always dependent on adults for their protection and support.

In the Global South, children are often already involved in social and political conflicts and are called on as actors from a young age.

In their life environment and for themselves, it is self-evident to take responsibility and interfere. Anyone who may conceive childhood as an exclusively sheltered space far from the 'seriousness of life' will not even notice children in such interrelationships, or will see in them only regrettable victims of grievous circumstances or irresponsible adults. The US-American social scientist Diane Rodgers (2005: 241), on the other hand, has pointed out that children have long been playing an important role in social movements that are committed to social change:

> To discuss children's actual participation in social movements not only uncovers questions about childhood, innocence and their socio-political location, it alters the discussion of inequalities and oppression that effect children and includes the possibility of children having a voice in their own lives and even taking action.[19]

Most of these movements are organized by children who, at first sight, start from the worst conditions for claiming attention self-confidently. In their lives, they face multiple challenges. As children, they are not taken seriously. As children living in poverty, they have comparatively few educational opportunities, are frequently discriminated against and have little opportunities of making positive experiences which would increase their self-esteem. Children from ethnic minorities in addition face racist prejudice and exclusion. Girls are often prevented from taking part in social activities outside the home that involve young people of their same age group. In a sense, these children can be understood as a group or class of persons whom the Italian philosopher and political activist Antonio Gramsci (1971) has termed 'subalterns'. He wanted to emphasize that due to the culturally connoted political hegemony of ruling groups and classes, they have no opportunity to exert themselves in society and to be acknowledged and achieve their collective interests (see Smith, 2010; Reed, 2013). In the case of children, this hegemony is established by the institutionalization of the bourgeois childhood pattern, which makes the children who do not conform to this pattern 'outsiders of society'.

If, nevertheless, these children appeal to their rights and insist on rights, this is no doubt to do with the fact that with their activities in the movements they have fought for and acquired social domains of their own, in which they can experience mutual respect and can apply their own rules. The rights that they formulate are, as a fact, influenced by the discourse on children's rights that, since the UNCRC has been passed, has been welcomed by the children too, but the rights articulated by them are primarily founded on their own experience, and are immediately related to the reality of their lives. They are not formulas of compromise or general principles that leave broad, almost unlimited scope for interpretation, but concrete programs of action in experienced or conceivable situations in life.

In the children's movements of the Global South, what is doubtless the main motor of common action is the shared experience of fulfilling vital tasks in everyday life despite widespread disadvantage and discrimination. The necessity to do something in order to survive leads many children to take part in the spontaneous formation of groups whose self-help is frequently denigrated and criminalized as an early or concealed form of delinquency. While these spontaneous groups often see themselves in the paradoxical situation of offending laws in order to realize their rights, in the more organized forms of children's movements a marked sense of justice arises. They act intrepidly, expressly demanding the realization of rights, and in some cases even formulating and claiming such themselves.

This is remarkable inasmuch as thinking in terms of codified rights is alien to children in everyday life. In general, they have a sceptical attitude towards everything to do with the law, or show little interest in it. The sphere of laws is a domain of adults. Children can (until this day) neither pass laws nor administer justice. As a rule, laws are accompanied by unpleasant experiences for children, by primarily restricting their freedom of action, either by certain actions being prohibited for them as 'minors', or by laws that only apply to adults (from a particular age) when they involve advantages. For instance, African children are confronted by laws dating from the colonial era, which forbid them to engage in 'hawking' or 'loitering' in the street in order to sell things or beg (Coly and Terenzio, 2007). Children who work in the street in Latin America are at present experiencing how laws and conventions which are supposed to be for their protection lead to harassment by the police or 'social cleansing' operations.[20] Such laws place children, particularly those who live in poverty and try to assist their families, in a state of illegality which means even greater problems for them than that of merely having no rights (Liebel, 2004). In many – even European – countries, the everyday behaviour of children and young people, especially when it deviates from common ideas and norms about what children belong to or what they are entitled to, is also called 'unsocial' or 'asocial' behaviour and combatted with repressive measures (such as in the UK by so-called Antisocial Behaviour Orders).[21]

However, when children and young people are called on to exercise rights and insist on their rights as citizens, this is probably due to the fact that, with their movements and actions, they have eked out their own social spaces, where they experience mutual respect and the use of their own rules. The rights that they formulate are influenced by the discourse on children's rights, which, since the adoption of the UNCRC, also raises the children's interest, but they are based primarily on their own experiences and are directly related to their reality. They are not compromising formulas and general principles that leave wide, almost arbitrary space for interpretations, but rather concrete instructions in lived or imaginable life situations.

In order to provide an idea of the areas in which social movements of children originate in the Global South, likewise of the manner in which a citizenship from below is embodied, I give some examples[22]:

- Children and adolescents of individual villages or districts, which are often affected by epidemics due to precarious living conditions, are working together to promote better environmental and health conditions; they are involved in appropriate initiatives and campaigns (for example, vaccination campaigns against malaria).[23]
- Children and adolescents of indigenous communities are committed to the revival of indigenous cultures and their recognition and anchoring in social relations and state structures; they are taking part in protests against measures and 'development projects' which violate the rights of these communities and endanger their habitat (for examples in Mexico, see Smith, 2007; Corona Caraveo et al, 2010).
- Children and adolescents who are active in non-commercial communication media (such as communal radio stations), and in some cases have their own programmes, are organized on a regional basis as 'communicators' and are committed to a stronger presence of children in the media (examples can be found in India, Latin America and South Africa, among others; see, for example, Acharya, 2010).
- Children and adolescents are committed to more participation and the representation of the interests of children and adolescents in their communities (for example village parliaments in indigenous areas of India, the so-called Makkala Panchayats; see Bhima Sangha and Makkala Panchayat, 2001; Pal, 2008).[24]
- Children and adolescents who are affected by armed conflicts in their habitats are engaged in groups against violence and for peaceful coexistence (see Özerdem and Podder, 2015: 184–220; Huynh et al, 2015: 185–211; on Latin America, see Peterson and Almere Read, 2002; Feinstein et al, 2010; Vinyamata i Camp and Benavides Vanegas, 2011; Rojas Suárez, 2012).

- In August 2018, on the occasion of the killing of a girl and a boy in traffic, several thousand children and young people in Dhaka, the capital of Bangladesh, refused to go to school. They blocked and even regulated traffic in order to demonstrate against corruption and for more safety on the streets. The government had the protest removed by the police and temporarily blocked the mobile internet.[25]
- Children who work and often experience exploitation and violence organize themselves in a kind of labour union to oppose their exploitation and discrimination, and to improve their living and working conditions. They describe themselves as movements of working children and adolescents.

I will go into the latter example in more detail, since in these movements it is particularly clear which dimensions citizenship from below can assume. Having first arisen in the late 1970s, these movements have already existed over several generations, and have succeeded in ensuring this continuity on their own. The two main reasons are probably that the children explicitly understand themselves as *working* children and they have retained to a great extent their independence from adults. For the children who are active in these movements, besides the fact that they are children, the work they do has a high significance for defining their identities and it strengthens their mutual bond. It also helps making them more independent from adults and to gain greater recognition in their family and their neighbourhood. In parts, this raises their subordinate status as children and can give them a stronger self-confidence. In addition, the children in their self-organized movements can make experiences that they are denied in their everyday environment and especially in school. They are experienced among each other as competent subjects who can make their own decisions in matters which are important to them, and who are able to cope with them independently, self-responsibly and on mutual support. This in turn gives them the strength to resist violence, exploitation, discrimination and other disadvantages they are exposed to as working children in social life and in work. Often, this also leads to the demand for fundamental changes in society, which are in the interest of all working children, and sometimes they succeed in implementing them.

However, the movements of working children and adolescents are not only trying to influence state action by making demands and making suggestions, but are also acting to improve their living conditions directly. One example is the small enterprises or cooperatives founded by working children and adolescents, in which they produce their own products needed for living in their city district. Sometimes the products are also exported to other countries. These cooperatives are seen as part of a solidarity economy that enables children to work under dignified conditions and contribute to their own and the livelihood of their families. In some cases, the workshops are linked to a kind of production school in which adults teach, but the children practice a kind of self-government.[26]

Conclusion

Citizenship from below, which is manifested in social movements of children (and young people) as well as in concrete action, goes beyond a state-centred and nationally limited understanding of citizenship. It includes demands on the state, for example, for better laws which amplify and guarantee the rights of the children, or seeking agreements with governmental authorities to improve access to government services. But it also articulates itself in direct actions and the creation of solidarity networks, which strengthen the social position of children in daily life and make the living conditions, especially of socially disadvantaged and marginalized children and adolescents, safer and more humane. The children's rights on which the demands and initiatives of children's movements are based could 'benefit from the conceptual advances within indigenous peoples' rights law' (Desmet, 2017: 141). They could strengthen the collective rights of children as a group and, in particular, advance their right to free, prior and informed consent. This could also counteract the 'adverse consequences of idealised constructions' (Desmet, 2017: 141).

The citizenship, which becomes visible in children's movements, is ultimately aimed at a community that does not end at territorial borders, nor does it require formal membership or a certain legal status. It is a citizenship in which the recognition of differentness is accompanied by the claim to be regarded as equitable and of the same value in the here and now.

Notes

[1]   In the chapter, I continue to reflect ideas, which I had formulated in part in earlier publications (Liebel, 2008; 2012a).

[2]   German political scientists Jürgen Mackert and Hans-Peter Mueller (2007: 10) emphasize that 'citizenship refers much more to citizens' rights and thus to the active, participatory role of citizens in public affairs than the German concept of *Staatsbürgerschaft*, that accentuate the membership of a state'.

3 German philosopher Immanuel Kant had this in mind already at the time of the French Revolution as the basis of a world peace order, which today is concerned with the system of the United Nations or with transnational civil society networks.

4 In the debate about the inclusive and exclusive functions of citizenship, the almost complete exclusion of children is almost never referred to. Mackert (1999) points out that children are often given cultural rights, such as the right to education, regardless of their nationality, but does not question their exclusion from other rights.

5 This perspective is expressed in the concept of citizenship formulated by the German sociologist Max Weber ([1921/22]2013) at the beginning of the 20th century as a rational and legal form of rule based on the hypothesis of the particular progress and superiority of the 'modern' nation state, based on 'urban life' and its allegedly neutral 'bureaucratic' institutions. It is reproduced not only in early modernization theories that divide the world into progressive 'modern' and backward 'traditional' societies and social spheres (for example, Parsons, 1965, 1971), but also, for example, in the more recent theory of a so-called 'multiple modernity', formulated by the Israeli sociologist Shmuel N. Eisenstadt (2002; 2004; see Boatcă, 2015: 177–99).

6 Cutting across this distinction, in reactions to the citizenship concept of Thomas H. Marshall (1950), which is concerned with the integration and participation of the working class in the democratic nation state, other approaches are also represented. In recognition of the social and cultural characteristics and self-definitions of various groups of the population, some plea for a 'differentiated' view of citizenship(s) (for example, Young, 1989; Kymlicka and Norman, 1995; Lister, 2003), or others, in view of the dwindling significance of the nation state, consider a 'multiple', 'global' or 'trans-national' concept of citizenship more appropriate (for example Held, 1995, 2004; Soysal, 1994, 1996; Dower and Williams, 2002; Benhabib, 2004; Cabrera, 2010). From a postcolonial perspective, such concepts, in reference to transnational social movements, are understood as a step to a 'subaltern cosmopolitan legality', which does not emerge 'top-down' but 'bottom-up' by the collective self-empowerment of the subaltern subjects (see de Sousa Santos and Rodríguez-Garavito, 2005; Rajagopal, 2003).

7 A child-centered example is the Moscow Declaration on the Rights of the Child, which emerged at the beginning of the Russian Revolution of 1917/18 and went far beyond the provisions of the UNCRC with regard to the citizenship of children (Liebel, 2016).

8 In particular, I refer to contributions from the so-called Postcolonial Studies (for example, Mbembe, 2001; Mignolo, 2000; Young, 2003; Parry, 2004; Moraña et al, 2008), and the Latin American debate on the concept of *Buen Vivir* (Good Living) in which pre-colonial cosmovisions are taken up (Walsh, 2010). Parallels will also be drawn between the European colonialization of supposedly uncivilized territories and the conceptualization of childhood as an 'infantile' precursor to adulthood the Austrian education scientist Peter Gstettner (1981) and the US-American education scholars Gaile Cannella and Radhiku Viruru (2004) elaborated.

9 Other authors add other rights, for instance ecological or reproductive rights (for example Held, 1989) – however, these are limited to adults.

10 Elizabeth Cohen (2005: 237) talks of 'semi-citizenship'. To this end, Aoife Nolan (2010) has written an illuminating essay in which, with a view to different countries, she reveals the 'participation gaps' for children within legal regulations.

[11] In French, this corresponds to the distinction between *citoyen* and *bourgeois*.

[12] On the UK, see Scott (2002); on Germany, see Liebel (2007b).

[13] However, children's care work cannot be itself, as Anne Wihstutz (2016) claims, regarded as a form of citizenship because it is denied recognition (by the state).

[14] Another term contrary to 'little angels' that is particularly popular in the media is 'little devils' (Prout, 2003).

[15] In development politics, functional participation is seen as a prerequisite to the efficiency and effectiveness of projects.

[16] This is worked out with regard to children in the feminist-inspired concept of 'difference-centred citizenship' by Mehmoona Moosa-Mitha (2005; for discussion see Liebel, 2012a: 183–95).

[17] This is also emphasized in concepts of cosmopolitan legality and citizenship 'from below' (see de Sousa Santos and Rodríguez-Garavito, 2005).

[18] However, not exclusively, as evidenced by the riots against police repression and racist discrimination in the poor districts of French or British cities. They were started mainly by young people (adolescents), but also children were decisively involved.

[19] Rodgers (2005: 249) describes the initial situation of children's movements with the following words: 'Children have been subject to oppressive conditions that are even difficult for adults to withstand. Despite our image of childhood as a protected safe space, for many children this space is full of dangers and hardships. Children have never been excluded from any of the conditions that might lead to resistance or participation in a social movement. They are involved in such situations as war, slavery, abuse, homelessness, poverty, racism and sexism. Even if a child does not experience severe oppression first hand, she/he may otherwise develop a social consciousness. What distinguishes a child as an active participant? Beyond the exposure to certain oppressive conditions themselves and resulting awareness of social injustice or social movement goals, the child must then decide to voluntarily participate in a social movement.'

[20] As has happened in Bolivia, Paraguay, Peru, Ecuador, Colombia and other countries in Latin America, with reference to the ILO Convention No. 182 on the 'worst forms of child labour', occasionally in connection with laws or regulations against begging.

[21] I discuss such and other measures in Liebel (2014) in terms of age-specific discrimination. For an analysis of the antisocial behavior orders in the UK, see also Squires (2008).

[22] Similar initiatives and movements of children can also be found in the Global North. One example is the school strike movement 'Fridays for Future', which is standing up against the destruction of planet earth and for a sustainable climate policy. This movement has taken on global dimensions but has less resonance with children in the Global South who have to live in precarious conditions, as for these children problems of current survival are of greater urgency. Another example is the school student movement 'March for our lives', which was triggered by a massacre at a school in the USA and advocates effective restrictions on the possession of weapons.

[23] These movements are often associated with approaches of so-called child-to-child education or peer education (see Pridmore and Stephens, 2000) and are not always immune to being instrumentalized by commercial social enterprises such as the Child-to-Child Trust (www.child-to-child.org/), which are active in this area.

[24] See also the film *Power to the children*: www.powertothechildren-film.com/de/

[25] See: https://en.wikipedia.org/wiki/2018_Bangladesh_road-safety_protests or www.theguardian.com/world/2018/aug/10/none-will-be-spared-students-fear-reprisals-over-bangladesh-unrest

[26] On the movements of working children, see Liebel et al (2001); Liebel (2004, 2007a, 2012b); Nieuwenhuys (2009); Reddy (2017); and Taft (2019).

Epilogue

Childhoods and children's rights beyond postcolonial paternalism

The children living in the world today are still in the clutches of postcolonial paternalism. It materializes in what I have called postcolonial childhoods, and manifests itself in various interrelated forms:

- in the inequality of power and material living conditions between the Global North and the Global South, which has persisted since the colonial era, and the associated global inequality and even the growing discrepancy in children's prospects for life;
- in the dominance of forms of knowledge, ways of thinking and seeing that make the childhoods of the Global South invisible or only distort their expression and lead to disregard, discrimination and negation of the vast majority of the world's children;
- in the persistence of racist violence against children who do not meet the standards of what is supposedly the only 'real' childhood in Europe or who insist on a life that contradicts these standards;
- in the oppression and degradation of children as immature and incompetent contemporaries, their social and political exclusion and their instrumentalization as potential human capital in the interest of a globalized capitalist economy; and
- in the distortion and malapropism of human and children's rights within the framework of a Eurocentric development and aid policy of gracious goodwill towards the 'poor children' of the Global South.

In the book, I have tried to present postcolonial childhoods in various aspects and to make the presumptions for the children associated with them visible and understandable. This could obviously only be done in excerpts and calls for further, more comprehensive and in-depth research. Although I have tried to consider the children not only as objects of given circumstances, but also as (possible) actors, further research should place even greater emphasis on the agency of children (without essentializing it). There are a few questions that I would at least like to adumbrate.

They include the question of the importance of independent child and youth movements, how they come to terms with the unreasonable impertinence of postcolonial paternalism, what visions of a 'better childhood' they produce and how they can be supported and strengthened. This could be linked to the question of whether a worldwide citizenship of children can be imagined that contributes to overcoming postcolonial paternalism, which approaches can be identified, but also which pitfalls can be associated with it. In this context, the question also arises what demands should be made on political action that strengthens the social position of children both globally and locally and expands their possibilities for action. This includes asking in what way legal regulations at international and national level can contribute to this (whereby here too attention would have to be paid to the possible pitfalls of a policy dependent on state power).

If such a policy wants to contribute to overcoming postcolonial paternalism, it must ensure social conditions and quality of life worldwide and locally, and meet the minimum requirements of social and ecological justice (see Stainton Rogers, 2004; Alderson, 2016). It is obvious that this cannot be a policy that is pursued over the children's heads, but in which the children themselves should be able to play a decisive role, especially since those whose childhoods have so far been ignored or made invisible. Regardless of their origin, skin colour and place of life, they should have the real opportunity to defend themselves against any injustice they feel. As orientation points for this I consider the following:

- the right of children to a world in which no child is no longer subject to the power of persons and institutions who can dispose of them without regard to their interests and rights;
- the right of children to a life in which they no longer suffer and have to submit to others who have power over them;
- the right of children to a childhood that is recognized as an equal part of society and in which children have a significant say in all issues affecting their present and future; and
- the right of children to be visible and to be recognized and respected with their history, their identities, their peculiarities and their views.

To show how these rights can become part of practical politics, at the end of the book I would like to present some experiences I had in February 2017 in Senegal, West Africa.

Saint-Louis, in the north of Senegal near the border to Mauritania, is a morbidly charming city that, in colonial times, was the capital of French West Africa. In the streets, hundreds of very young boys, usually in groups, persistently approach pedestrians with white painted cans and boxes in their hands.

They are *talibés*, students of Islamic schools who collect money on behalf of their religious teachers, called *marabouts*. In these schools, called *daaras*, they are taught to read and recite the Quran. It seems that, except for some occasional tourists, no one is annoyed by the begging kids. In the Islamic society of Senegal, it is a common practice to offer something to someone in need a gift, especially if it is believed to be for charity.

One afternoon I have a meeting with the local section of the African Movement of Working Children and Youth (AMWCY). To my surprise, a group of young women, approximately 12 to 18 years old, await me and some friends in a courtyard in the city centre. They present themselves as the elected delegates of the 18 grassroots groups belonging to the movement in the Saint-Louis area. They have come specially to meet us from the suburbs where the movement, according to our hosts, includes no less than 1,800 members – that is, on average, 100 in each group.

The delegates inform us that both men and women are organized in the movement. They are children and young people who earn money for themselves and their families through various jobs in third-party homes, markets, stores or workshops. Others take care of their younger siblings or take on household chores (what they call 'real work' that deserves recognition). They do not like to beg. They do, however, maintain contact with various Islamic schools, and in some cases where *talibés* expanded their activities, they were allowed to associate with the groups of the movement. They do not understand their movement as in rivalry with the Islamic schools, but would prefer that system to better enable *talibés* to lead autonomous lives as well.

One of the main activities of the grassroots groups is learning to read and write in French. French is the official language in Senegal, which is mainly used in administration and formal education. Senegal contains many other languages – of which Wolof is the most widespread – but in general, they are not used in schools. There are efforts to change this, but not much progress has yet been made. At the Saint-Louis meeting, the girls speak in Wolof and our guide translates. The girls emphasize that their own language is important to them but, to get ahead in life, it seems essential to them to be literate in French.

Almost none of our interlocutors have been in school or, if they have, only for short periods of time. They feel that one of their tasks is to provide access to school for all working children, a goal they pursue by helping children to find spots in school as well as offering extracurricular classes guided by tutors. They also believe their work experience should earn them respect within the school system, as they have already proven their ability to manage their life on their own. School, like work, is thus a place where they can learn things that are useful for life (explicitly including sex education, as well as encouraging girls in particular to trust in their capacities and put limits on others who want to take possession of them). When a group member finds work difficult, others come together to give her extra support.

Another important task of the grassroots groups is to train themselves for activities that allow them to achieve a better life and a better future. This does not just include technical and professional skills, but skills that allow them to 'work with dignity' and establish self-sustaining joint projects (called 'income-generating activities'). They hold training workshops, for example, on sewing, embroidery, and computer use, as well as on creating small gardens to generate their own food.

As child domestic workers, they are frequently abused and exploited. Our interlocutors tell us that they often have to work seven days a week and earn the equivalent of only €22 to €38 a month. Even in Senegal such an amount is not enough to maintain a livelihood. With the creation of small cooperatives, where they produce for their own basic necessities and make all the decisions on their own, they hope to find better life prospects for themselves. Such systems are already in place elsewhere in Senegal, for example the women collectives that together ensure their livelihoods by producing soap, food, and various clothing items.

The tasks set by the movement go beyond learning and preparation for a dignified work life. The grassroots groups are understood as a kind of 'older siblings' ('ainées'), which encourage children to defend themselves against all types of violence, including the forced marriage of children (still common in Senegal).

The movement also supports children who have lost their families or have migrated alone to Senegal and must now survive in the streets (many talibés are part of this group). These children are integrated into the grassroots groups and given 'mentors', who explain their rights as children in Senegal and encourage them to actively remind neighbours and government authorities of their responsibility to children (called 'sensitization' by the movement).

In our discussions, we got the impression that the movement is not keen to advocate openly for public policies, but rather focuses on assisting each other to achieve a better life. They do not attribute much importance to state laws in practical matters, but they invite the local authorities to attend their meetings and see utility in concluding agreements with them where possible. The most important thing for the members of the movement is to strengthen their self-confidence and capacities through solidarity and to improve their positions as socially disadvantaged children in society.

In Saint-Louis, our interlocutors stressed that it is by no means exceptional in Senegal for girls to be elected as delegates. In fact in Thiès, the second largest city in Senegal, I met, shortly afterwards, another group of delegates with a single boy. All the others were girls. Indeed, girls were instrumental in the movement's very foundation. In the 1990s, there were young domestic workers, known in French as '*petites bonnes*', who carried banners through the streets of Dakar on 1 May to claim their dignity and their rights. This was the seed of a movement that has now grown to include over 1 million members across 27 African countries. One that has been officially recognized as representing the interests of working children and youth and is accredited as an observer organization by the African Union.

References

ABA (2011) *Tierra y territorio, espacio de crianza y compartir. Nuestras responsabilidades para el buen vivir*, Ayacucho (mimeo).

Abebe, T. (2013) 'Interdependent rights and agency: the role of children in collective livelihood strategies in rural Ethiopia', in K. Hanson and O. Nieuwenhuys (eds), *Reconceptualizing Children's Rights in International Development: Living Rights, Social Justice, Translations*, New York and Cambridge: Cambridge University Press, pp 71–92.

Abusch, A. (1950) 'Die Geistige Coca-Kolonisierung – und der Friede', *Sonntag – Wochenzeitung für Kultur, Politik und Unterhaltung* (Berlin, DDR), 22 January.

Acharya, L. (2010) 'Child reporters as agents of change', in B. Percy-Smith and N. Thomas (eds), *A Handbook of Children and Young People's Participation: Perspectives from Theory and Practice*, London and New York: Routledge, pp 204–14.

Acosta, A. (2013) *El Buen Vivir. Sumak Kawsay, una Oportunidad para Imaginar Otros Mundos*, Barcelona: Icaria.

Adichie, C.N. (2004) *Purple Hibiscus*, London: Harper Perennial.

Adichie, C.N. (2007) *Half of a Yellow Sun*, London: Harper Perennial.

Adick, C. (2013) 'Bildung in Subsahara-Afrika', in C. Adick (ed), *Bildungsentwicklungen und Schulsysteme in Afrika, Asien, Lateinamerika und der Karibik*, Münster: Waxmann, pp 125–46.

African Union (1990) *African Charter on the Rights and Welfare of the Child*, Addis Ababa: African Union.

Aitken, S.C. (2015) 'Children's rights: A critical geographic perspective', in W. Vandenhole, E. Desmet, D. Reynaert and S. Lembrechts (eds), *Routledge International Handbook of Children's Rights Studies*, London and New York: Routledge, pp 131–46.

Alanen, L. (1992) *Modern Childhood? Exploring the 'Child Question' in Sociology*, Jyväskylä: University of Jyväskylä.

Alanen, L. and Mayall, B. (eds) (2001) *Conceptualising Child-Adult Relations*, New York: Routledge.

Alderson, P. (2008a) *Young Children's Rights: Exploring Beliefs, Principles and Practice*, London and Philadelphia: Jessica Kingsley.

Alderson, P. (2008b) 'When does citizenship begin? Economics and early childhood', in A. Invernizzi and J. Williams (eds), *Children and Citizenship*, London: Sage, pp 108–19.

Alderson, P. (2013) *Childhoods Real and Imagined*, London and New York: Routledge.

Alderson, P. (2016) *The Politics of Childhoods Real and Imagined: Practical Application of Critical Realism and Childhood Studies*, London and New York: Routledge.

Alderson, P. and Yoshida, T. (2016) 'Meanings of children's agency. When and where does agency begin and end', in F. Esser, M.-S. Baader, T. Betz and B. Hungerland (eds), *Reconceptualising Agency and Childhood: New Perspectives in Childhood Studies*, London and New York: Routledge, pp 75–88.

Aldridge, J. and Becker, S. (2002) 'Children who care: rights and wrongs in debate and policy on young carers', in B. Franklin (ed), *The New Handbook of Children's Rights*. London and New York: Routledge, pp 208–22.

Alemany, M. (2005) 'El concepto y la justificación del paternalismo', *DOXA – Cuadernos de Filosofía del Derecho*, 28: 265–303.

Alston, P. (1994) 'The best interest principle: Towards a reconciliation of culture and human rights', *International Journal of Law, Policy, and the Family*, 8(1): 1–25.

Alvarado, S.V., Ospina, H.F., Botero, P. and Muñoz, G. (2008) 'Las tramas de la subjetividad política y los desafíos a la formación ciudadana en jóvenes', *Revista Argentina de Sociología*, 6(11): 19–43.

Ampofo, A.A. (2013) 'Gender and Society in Africa – An Introduction', in T. Manuh and E. Sutherland-Addy (eds), *Africa in Contemporary Perspective: A Textbook for Undergraduate Students*, Legon-Accra (Ghana): Sub Saharan Publishers, pp 94–115.

Anderson, B.R. (2006) *Imagined Communities: Reflections on the Origin and Spread of Nationalism*, London: Verso.

André, G. (2015) 'Anthropologists, ethnographers and children's rights', in W. Vandenhole, E. Desmet, D. Reynaert and S. Lembrechts (eds), *Routledge International Handbook of Children's Rights Studies*. London and New York: Routledge, pp 112–30.

Andreotti, V. (2011) *Actionable Postcolonial Theory in Education*, Basingstoke: Palgrave Macmillan.

Anta Diop, C. (1959) *L'Unité culturelle de l'Afrique Noire*, Paris: Présence Africaine (published in translation as *The Cultural Unity of Black Africa*, Chicago: Third World Press, 1974).

Anta Diop, C. (1960) *L'Afrique Noire Précolonial*, Paris: Présence Africaine (published in translation as *Precolonial Black Africa*, Westport: Lawrence Hill and Co, 1987).

Appadurai, A. (2006) *Fear of Small Numbers: An Essay of the Geography of Anger*, Durham, NC: Duke University Press.

Archambault, C. (2010) 'Fixing families of mobile children: Recreating kinship and belonging among Maasai adoptees in Kenya', *Childhood*, 17(2): 229–42.

Arendt, H. ([1955]1994) *The Origins of Totalitarianism*, New York: Harcourt Books.

Arewa, A. (2014) 'The humanist basis of African communitarianism as viable third alternative theory of developmentalism', in O. Onazi (ed), *African Legal Theory and Contemporary Problems: Critical Essays*, Dordrecht: Springer, pp 241–64.

Ariès, P. (1960) *L'enfant et la Vie Familiale sous l'Ancien Régime*, Paris: Plon.

Ariès, P. (1962) *Centuries of Childhood: A Social History of Family Life*, New York: Vintage Books.

Ashcroft, B. (2001) *On Post-Colonial Futures: Transformations of Colonial Culture*, London and New York: Continuum.

Ashcroft, B., Griffiths, G. and Tiffin, H. (2013) *Post-Colonial Studies: The Key Concepts* (3rd edn), London and New York: Routledge.

Atkinson-Sheppard, S. (2017) 'Street children and "protective agency": Exploring young people's involvement in organised crime in Dhaka, Bangladesh', *Childhood*, 24(3): 416–29.

Aufseeser, D. (2014a) 'Control, protection and rights: A critical review of Peru's Begging Bill', *International Journal of Children's Rights*, 22(2): 241–67.

Aufseeser, D. (2014b) 'Limited spaces of informal learning among street children in Peru', in S. Mills and P. Kraftl (eds), *Informal Education, Childhood and Youth: Geographies, Histories, Practices*, Basingstoke: Palgrave Macmillan, pp 112–23.

Bâ, M. (1979) *Une si Longue Lettre*, Dakar: Les Nouvelles Editions Africaine.

Bâ, M. (1981) *Un Chant Écarlate*, Dakar: Les Nouvelles Editions Africaine.

Báez, C. and Mason, P. (2006) *Zoológicos Humanos: Fotografías de fueginos y mapuche en el*, Jardin d'Acclimatation de Paris, siglo XIX, Santiago de Chile: Pehuén Editores.

Balagopalan, S. (2013) 'The politics of failure: Street children and the circulation of rights discourses in Kolkata (Calcutta), India', in K. Hanson and O. Nieuwenhuys (eds), *Reconceptualizing Children's Rights in International Development: Living Rights, Social Justice, Translations*, New York and Cambridge: Cambridge University Press, pp 133–51.

Balagopalan, S. (2014) *Inhabiting 'Childhood': Children, Labour and Schooling in Postcolonial India*, Basingstoke: Palgrave Macmillan.

Balagopalan, S. (2018) 'Childhood, Culture, History: Redeploying "Multiple Childhoods"', in S. Spyrou, R. Rosen and D.T. Cook (eds), *Reimagining Childhood Studies*, London and New York: Bloomsbury Academic, pp 23–40.

Barber, C.L. (1964) *The Story of Language*, London: Pan Books.

Barnett, M.N. (ed) (2017) *Paternalism beyond Borders*, Cambridge: Cambridge University Press.

BBC News (2011) 'Egyptian children tell revolution tales', 9 May, www.bbc.co.uk/news/education-13312429

Bean, P. and Melville, J. (1990) *Lost Children of the Empire: The Untold Story of British Child Migrants*, London: Unwin Hyman.

Beazley, H. (2000) 'Street boys in Yogyakarta: Social and spatial exclusion in the public spaces of the city', in G. Bridge and S. Watson (eds), *A Companion to the City*, London: Willey Blackwell, pp 472–88.

Beazley, H. (2003) 'The construction and protection of individual and collective identities by street children and youth in Indonesia', *Children, Youth and Environments*, 13(1): 105–33.

Bell, A. (2017) 'Working from where we are: a response from Aotearoa New Zealand', *Higher Education Research and Development*, 36(1): 16–20.

Bengoa, J. (2014) *Mapuche, Colonos y Estado Nacional*, Santiago de Chile: Catalonia.

Benhabib, S. (2004) *The Rights of Others: Aliens, Residents, and Citizens*, Cambridge: Cambridge University Press.

Bentley, K.A. (2005) 'Can there be any universal children's rights?' *International Journal of Human Rights*, 9(1): 107–23.

Bessell, S., Beazley, H. and Waterson, R. (2017) 'The Methodology and Ethics of Rights-Based Research with Children', in A. Invernizzi, M. Liebel, B. Milne and R. Budde (eds), *'Children out of Place' and Human Rights. In Memory of Judith Ennew*, Cham: Springer International Switzerland, pp 211–31.

Bhabha, H.K. (1994) *The Location of Culture*, London and New York: Routledge.

Bhambra, G.K. (2007) *Rethinking Modernity: Postcolonialism and the Sociological Imagination*, Basingstoke: Palgrave Macmillan.

Bhengu, M.J. (2006) *Ubuntu: The Global Philosophy for Humankind*, Cape Town: Lotsha Publications.

Bhima Sangha and Makkala Panchayat (2001) *Our Survey Story*, Bangalore: Concerned for Working Children.

Blackstock, C. (2007) 'Residential schools: Did they really close or just morph into child welfare?', *Indigenous Law Journal*, 6(1): 71–8.

Blazek, M. (2016) *Rematerialising Children's Agency: Everyday practices in a post-socialist estate*, Bristol: Policy Press.

Boatcă, M. (2015) *Global Inequalities beyond Occidentalism*, Farnham and Burlington: Ashgate.

Bobbio, N. (1996) *The Age of Rights*, Cambridge and New York: Polity.

Bolados García, P. (2017) *Orígenes versus Originarios. La disputa por el control de la salud indígena atacameña*, Valparaíso: Editorial UV de la Universidad de Valparaíso.

Bordonaro, L. (2012) 'Agency does not mean freedom: Cape Verdean street children and the politics of children's agency', *Children's Geographies*, 10(4): 413–36.

Bordonaro, L. and Payne, R. (2012) 'Ambiguous agency: Critical perspectives on social interventions with children and youth in Africa', *Children's Geographies*, 10(4): 365–72.

Borg, L. (2015) 'Are human rights exclusive to humans?' Sapere Aude, August 18; www.daretoknowpublications.com/single-post/2015/08/17/Are-Human-Rights-Exclusive-to-Humans

Bourdieu, P. (1986) 'The forms of capital', in J.F. Richardson (ed), *Handbook of Theory of Research for the Sociology of Education*, Santa Barbara, CA: Greenwood Press, pp 241–58.

Bourdillon, M., Levison, D., Myers, W. and White, B. (2010) *Rights and Wrongs of Children's Work*, New Brunswick, NJ and London: Rutgers University Press.

Boyden, J. ([1990]1997) 'Childhood and the policy makers: a comparative perspective on the globalization of childhood', in A. James and A. Prout (eds), *Constructing and Reconstructing Childhood*, London and Bristol: Falmer Press, pp 190–229.

Boyden, J. (2003) 'Children under fire: challenging assumptions about children's resilience', *Children, Youth and Environments*, 13(1): 1–29.

Boyden, J. and Howard, N. (2013) 'Why does child trafficking policy need to be reformed? The moral economy of children's movement in Benin and Ethiopia', *Children's Geographies*, 11(3): 354–68.

Brando Cadena, N. (2018) 'Not just for kids: childhood, equality and the limits of freedom in liberal theory', PhD dissertation, Doctoral School Humanities and Social Sciences, KU Leuven.

Brems, E. (2007) 'Children's Rights and Universality', in C.M. Williams (ed), *Developmental and Autonomy Rights of Children: Empowering Children, Caregivers and Communities*, Antwerp, Oxford and New York: Intersentia, pp 11–37.

Brett, R. and Specht, I. (2004) *Young Soldiers: Why They Choose to Fight*, Boulder, CO and London: Lynne Rienner.

Bristol, L.S.M. (2012) *Plantation Pedagogy: A Postcolonial and Global Perspective*, New York: Peter Lang.

Brock-Utne, B. (2000) *Whose Education For All? The Recolonization of the African Mind*, New York and London: Falmer Press.

Brock-Utne, B. and Holmarsdottir, H.B. (2004) 'Language policies and practices in Tanzania and South Africa: problems and challenges', *International Journal of Educational Development*, 24: 67–83.

Brown, G. (2010) 'Apology to Child Migrants', 24 February, House of Commons, www.parliament.uk/business/news/2010/02/prime-ministers-statement-child-migration/

Brubaker, R. (1994) *Citizenship and Nationhood in France and Germany*, Cambridge, MA: Harvard University Press.

Buckingham, D. (2003) *After the Death of Childhood: Growing up in the Age of Electronic Media*, Cambridge: Polity.

Bühler-Niederberger, D. (2011) *Lebensphase Kindheit: Theoretische Ansätze, Akteure und Handlungsräume*, Weinheim and Munich: Juventa.

Bühler-Niederberger, D. and van Krieken, A. (2008) 'Persisting inequalities: Childhood between global influences and local traditions', *Childhood*, 15(2): 147–55.

Burke, R. (2010) *Decolonization and the Evolution of International Human Rights*, Philadelphia: University of Pennsylvania Press.

Burman, E. (1994) 'Innocents abroad: Western fantasies of childhood and the iconography of emergencies', *Disasters*, 18(3): 238–53.

Burman, E. (1996) 'Local, global or globalised? Child development and international child rights legislation', *Childhood*, 3(1): 45–66.

Burman, E. (2016) 'Fanon's other children: psychopolitical and pedagogical implications', *Race Ethnicity and Education*, March, www.tandfonline.com/doi/full/10.1080/13613324.2016.1150832.

Burr, R. (2004) 'Children's Rights: international policy and lived practice', in M.J. Kehily (ed), *An Introduction to Childhood Studies*, Maidenhead: Open University Press, pp 145–59.

Burr, R. (2006) *Vietnam's Children in a Changing World*, Brunswick, NJ and London: Rutgers University Press.

Cabrera, L. (2010) *The Practice of Global Citizenship*, Cambridge: Cambridge University Press.

Cannella, G.S. and Viruru, R. (2004) *Childhood and Postcolonization: Power, Education, and Contemporary Practice*, New York and London: Routledge-Falmer.

Cantwell, N. (2016) 'The best interests of the Child: What does it add to children's human rights?', in M. Sormunen (ed), *The Best Interests of the Child: A Dialogue between Theory and Practice*, Strasbourg: Council of Europe Publishing, pp 18–26.

Carillo Medina, P. and Jaulis, P. (2012) *Una exploración sobre derechos de los niños y niñas en comunidades andinas: Roles vitales y sagrados de los niños y niñas en comunidades alto-andinas de Ayacucho*, Ayacucho (mimeo).

Carneiro, S. (2005) 'Ennegrecer el feminismo. La situación de la mujer negra en América Latina desde una perspectiva de género', *Nouvelles Quéstions Féministes. Revue Internationale Francophone*; edición especial en castellano: Feminismos disidentes en América Latina y el caribe, 24(2): 21–26, http://catedraunescodh.unam.mx/catedra/SeminarioCETis/Documentos/Doc_basicos/5_biblioteca_virtual/5_participacion_politica/10.pdf.

Carpena-Méndez, F. (2007) 'Our lives are like a sock inside-out': Children's work and youth identity in neoliberal rural Mexico', in R. Panelli, S. Punch and E. Robson (eds), *Global Perspectives on Rural Childhood and Youth*, New York and London: Routledge, pp 41–55.

Casas, F. (1998) *Infancia: Perspectivas Psicosociales*, Barcelona: Paidós.

Cassidy, J. (2006) 'The best interests of the child? The stolen generations in Canada and Australia', *Griffith Law Review*, 15(1): 111–52.

Castro Varela, M. (2011) '"Wir haben das Recht auf kostenlose Geschirrspülmaschine" – Soziale Gerechtigkeit, Recht und Widerstand', in M. Castro Varela and N. Dhawan (eds), *Soziale (Un)Gerechtigkeit: Kritische Perspektiven auf Diversity, Intersektionalität und Antidiskriminierung*, Berlin: LIT, pp 36–61.

Castro Varela, M. (2015) 'Strategisches Lernen. Bildung, Solidarität, soziale Ungleichheit', *Luxemburg – Gesellschaftsanalyse und linke Praxis*, 2: 16–23.

Castro-Gómez, S. and Grosfoguel R. (eds) (2007) *El Giro Decolonial. Reflexiones para una Diversidad Epistémica más allá del Capitalismo Global*, Bogotá: Siglo del hombre editores.

Césaire, A. ([1950]2000) *Discourse on Colonialism*, New York: Monthly Review Press.

Chakrabarty, D. (2000) *Provincializing Europe: Postcolonial Thought and Historical Difference*, Princeton, NJ and Oxford: Princeton University Press.

Chandler, D. (2017) 'The new international paternalism: International regimes', in M.N. Barnett (ed), *Paternalism beyond Borders*, Cambridge: Cambridge University Press, pp 132–58.

Cheney, K.E. (2012) 'Seen but not heard: African orphanhood in the age of HIV/AIDS', in M.O. Ensor (ed), *African Childhoods: Education, Development, Peacebuilding, and the Youngest Continent*, New York: Palgrave Macmillan, pp 95–108.

Cheney, K.E. (2013) 'Malik and his three mothers: AIDS orphans' survival strategies and how children's rights hinder them', in K. Hanson and O. Nieuwenhuys (eds), *Reconceptualizing Children's Rights in International Development: Living Rights, Social Justice, Translations*, New York and Cambridge: Cambridge University Press, pp 152–74.

Cheney, K.E. (2018) 'Decolonizing childhood studies: Overcoming patriarchy and prejudice in child-related research and practice', in S. Spyrou, R. Rosen and D.T. Cook (eds), *Reimagining Childhood Studies*, London and New York: Bloomsbury Academic, pp 91–104.

Childs, P., Weber, J.J. and Williams, P. (2006) *Post-Colonial Theory and Literatures: African, Caribbean and South Asian*, Trier: Wissenschaftlicher Verlag.

Churchill, W. (2004) *Kill the Indian, Save the Man: the Genocidal Impact of American Indian Residential Schools*, San Francisco: City Lights Books.

Claassen, R. (2014) 'Capability paternalism', *Economics and Philosophy*, 30(1): 57–73.

CLAS (2015) *Some Memories Never Fade. Final Report of the Confidential Listening and Assistance Service*, New Zealand: CLAS.

Clavería Cruz, A. (2019) *Escribiendo identidades. La discusión política en torno a la estandarización alfabética y ortográfica de lenguas indígenas en Chile: los casos del mapudungun, jaqi aru y kunsa*, Antofagasta: Qillqa Editorial, Universidad Católica del Norte.

Close, P. (2014) *Child Labour in Global Society*, Sociological Studies of Children and Youth, Vol. 17, Bingley: Emerald.

Cockburn, T. (1998) 'Children and Citizenship in Britain: A Case for a socially interdependent model of citizenship', *Childhood*, 5(1): 99–117.

Cockburn, T. (2005) 'Children as participative citizens: A radical pluralist case for 'child-friendly' public communication', in A. Invernizzi and B. Milne (eds), *Children's Citizenship: An Emergent Discourse on the Rights of the Child? Journal of Social Sciences*, Special Issue N° 9, Delhi: Kamla – RAJ Enterprises, pp 19–29.

Cockburn, T. (2006) 'Global childhood?', in A. Carling (ed), *Globalization and Identity: Development and Integration in a Changing World*, London and New York: Taurus, pp 77–88.

Cockburn, T. (2013) *Rethinking Children's Citizenship*, Basingstoke: Palgrave Macmillan.

Cockcroft, L. (2014) *Global Corruption. Money, Power, and Ethics in the Modern World*, Philadelphia: Pennsylvania University Press.

Cohen, E.F. (2005) 'Neither seen no heard: children's citizenship in contemporary democracies', *Citizenship Studies*, 9(2): 221–40.

Collins, J.-M. (2006) 'Bearing the burden of bastardy: Infanticide, race and motherhood in Brazilian slave society', in B.H. Bechtold and D. Cooper Graves (eds), *Killing Infants: Studies in the Worldwide Practice of Infanticide*, Lewiston, NY, Queenston, Ontario and Lampeter, Wales: The Edwin Mellen Press, pp 199–229.

Collins, T.M. (2017) 'A child's rights to participate: Implications for international child protection', *International Journal of Human Rights*, 21(1): 14–46.

Coloma, R.S. (ed) (2009) *Postcolonial Challenges in Education*, New York: Peter Lang.

Colonna, E. (2012) 'Children who take care of other children in the suburbs of Maputo, Mozambique', in M.O. Ensor (ed), *African Childhoods: Education, Development, Peacebuilding, and the Youngest Continent*, New York: Palgrave Macmillan, pp 81–94.

Coly, H. and Terenzio F. (2007) 'The stakes of children's participation in Africa. The African Movement of Working Children and Youth', in B. Hungerland, M. Liebel, B. Milne and A. Wihstutz (eds), *Working to Be Someone: Child Focused Research with Working Children*, London and Philadelphia: Jessica Kingsley, pp 179–85.

Comaroff, J. and Comaroff, J. (2008) 'The colonization of consciousness', in M. Lambek (ed), *A Reader in the Anthropology of Religion*, Malden, MA: Blackwell, pp 464–78.

Connell, R. (2007) *Southern Theory: The Global Dynamics of Knowledge in Social Science*, Crows Nest, Australia: Allen and Unwin, and Cambridge: Polity Press.

Connolly, M. and Ennew, J. (1996) 'Introduction: Children out of place', *Childhood*, 3(2): 131–47.

Cook, D.T. and Wall, J. (eds) (2011) *Children and Armed Conflict: Cross-Disciplinary Investigations*, Basingstoke: Palgrave Macmillan.

Coons, C. and Weber, M. (eds) (2013) *Paternalism: Theory and Practice*, Cambridge: Cambridge University Press.

Corbett, G.H. (2002) *Nation Builders: Barnardo Children in Canada*, Toronto: Dundurn.

Cordero Arce, M. (2012) 'Towards an emancipatory discourse of children's rights', *International Journal of Children's Rights*, 20: 365–421.

Cordero Arce, M. (2015) 'Maturing children's rights theory: From children, with children, of children', *International Journal of Children's Rights*, 23: 283–331.

Cordero Arce, M. (2018) 'Why is (to be) the subject of children's rights?', in S. Spyrou, R. Rosen and D.T. Cook (eds), *Reimagining Childhood Studies*, London and New York: Bloomsbury Academic, pp 169–82.

Corona Caraveo, Y. (2003) 'Diversidad de infancias. Retos y compromisos', in Y. Corona Caraveo and R.R. Villamil Uriarte (eds), *Tramas. Subjetividad y Procesos Sociales. Diversidad de Infancias*, Mexico City: Universidad Autónoma Metropolitana, Unidad Xochimilco, pp 13–31.

Corona Caraveo, Y, Pérez, C. and Hernández, J. (2010) 'Youth participation in indigenous traditional communities', in B. Percy-Smith and N. Thomas (eds), *A Handbook of Children and Young People's Participation: Perspectives from Theory and Practice*, London and New York: Routledge, pp 141–49.

Coronil, F. (2008) 'Elephants in the Americas? Latin American Postcolonial Studies and Global Decolonization', in M. Moraña, E. Dussel and C. Jáuregui (eds), *Coloniality at Large. Latin America and the Postcolonial Debate*, Durham, NC and London: Duke University Press, pp 396–416.

Costa, S. (2005) 'Postkoloniale Studien und Soziologie. Differenzen und Konvergenzen', *Berliner Journal für Soziologie*, 2: 283–94.

Costa, S. (2013) 'Da mestiçagem à diferença: nexos transnacionais da formação nacional no Brasil', in E.F. Dutra (ed), *O Brasil em dois tempos. História, pensamento social e tempo presente*, Belo Horizonte: UFMG, pp 301–20.

Couzens, M. and Noel Zaal, F. (2009) 'Legal recognition for child-headed households: An evaluation of the emerging South African framework', *International Journal of Children's Rights*, 17: 299–320.

Cowan, J.K., Dembour, M.-D. and Wilson, R.A. (eds) (2001) *Culture and Rights: Anthropological Perspectives*, Cambridge: Cambridge University Press.

Cregan, K. and Cuthbert, D. (2014) *Global Childhoods – Issues and Debates*, London: Sage.

CRIN (2016) *Discrimination and Disenfranchisement. A Global Report on Status Offences* (3rd edn), London: Child Rights International Network, www.crin.org/sites/default/files/crin_status_offences_global_report_0.pdf

CRIN (2018) *What Lies Beneath. A CRIN report – 2018 edition*, London: Child Rights Information Network, www.crin.org/sites/default/files/crin_report_2018_edition.pdf.

Crouch, C. (2005) *Post-Democracy*, Cambridge: Polity Press.

Crouch, C. (2015) *The Knowledge Corrupters: Hidden Consequences of the Financial Takeover of Public Life*, Cambridge: Polity Press.

Crow Dog, M. (1991), with Richard Erdoes, *Lakota Woman*, New York: HarperCollins.

Cussiánovich, A. (2001) 'What does protagonism mean?', in M. Liebel, B. Overwien and A. Recknagel (eds), *Working Children's Protagonism: Social Movements and Empowerment in Latin America, Africa and India*, Frankfurt/M and London: IKO, pp 157–70.

Cussiánovich, A. (2007) *Aprender la Condición Humana: Ensayo sobre Pedagogía de la Ternura*, Lima: Ed. Ifejant.

Cussiánovich, A. (2010) 'Evaluación e incidencia de la Convención sobre los Derechos del Niño a veinte años de su aprobación 1989–2009', *NATs – Revista Internacional desde los Niños/as y Adolescentes Trabajadores*, 18: 15–25.

Cussiánovich, A. and Márquez, A.M. (2002) *Toward a Protagonist Participation of Boys, Girls and Teenagers*, Lima: Save the Children Sweden.

Darian Smith, K. (2013) 'Children, colonialism and commemoration', in K. Darian Smith and C. Pasceo (eds), *Children, Childhood and Cultural Heritage*, London and New York: Routledge, pp 159–74.

Darwin, C. (1845) *Journal of Researches into the Natural History and Geology of the Countries Visited During the Voyage of H.M.S. Beagle Round the World, Under the Command of Capt. Fitz Roy, R.N.* (2nd edn), London: John Murray.

Davies, M. (2008) 'A childish culture? Shared understandings, agency and intervention: an anthropological study of street children in northwest Kenya', *Childhood*, 15(3): 309–30.

De Beauvoir, S. ([1949]1997) *The Second Sex*, London: Vintage.

De Sousa Santos, B. (ed) (2008) *Another Knowledge is Possible: Beyond Northern Epistemologies*, London and New York: Verso.

De Sousa Santos, B. (2009) *Una Epistemología del Sur: La Reinvención del Conocimiento y la Emancipación Social*, Buenos Aires: Siglo XXI Editores.

De Sousa Santos, B. (2016) *Epistemologies of the South: Justice against Epistemicide*, New York and London: Routledge.

De Sousa Santos, B. and Rodríguez-Garavito, C.A. (eds) (2005) *Law and Globalization from Below: Towards a Cosmopolitan Legality*, Cambridge: Cambridge University Press.

De Sousa Santos, B. and Meneses, M.P. (eds) (2014) *Epistemologías del Sur (Perspectivas)*, Madrid: Akal.

Dean, C. (2002) 'Sketches of childhood: Children in colonial Andean art and society', in T. Hecht (ed), *Minor Omissions: Children in Latin American History and Society*, Madison: The University of Minnesota Press, pp 21–51.

Dei, G.J.S. (2016) 'Anti-colonial education', in M.A. Peters (ed), *Encyclopedia of Educational Philosophy and Theory*, Springer Singapore, pp 1–6.

Dei, G.J.S, and Opini, B.M. (2007) 'Schooling in the context of difference: The challenge of post-colonial education in Ghana', in D. Thiessen and A. Cook-Sather (eds), *International Handbook of Student Experience in Elementary and Secondary School*, Springer Netherlands, pp 463–91.

Dei, G.J.S. and Simmons, M. (eds) (2010) *Fanon & Education: Thinking through Pedagogical Possibilities*, New York: Peter Lang.

Dei, G.J.S., Asgharzadeh, A., Babador, S.E. and Shahjahan, R.A. (2006) *Schooling and Difference in Africa: Democratic Challenges in a Contemporary Context*, Toronto, Buffalo and London: University of Toronto Press.

Delpar, H. (2008) *Looking South: The Evolution of Latin American Scholarship in the United States, 1850–1975*, Tuscaloosa: University of Alabama Press.

Dembour, M.-B. (2001) 'Following the Movement of the Pendulum: Between Universalism and Relativism', in J.K. Cowan, M.-B. Dembour and R.A. Wilson (eds), *Culture and Rights: Anthropological Perspectives*, Cambridge: Cambridge University Press, pp 56–79.

Desmet, E. (2017) 'Inspirations for children's rights from indigenous peoples' rights', in E. Brems, E. Desmet and W. Vandenhole (eds), *Children's Rights Law in the Global Human Rights Landscape: Isolation, Inspiration, Integration?* New York: Routledge, pp 129–45.

Dhawan, N. (ed) (2014) *Decolonizing Enlightenment: Transnational Justice, Human Rights and Democracy in a Postcolonial World*, Opladen, Berlin and Toronto: Barbara Budrich.

Díaz Gómez, A. (2005) 'Subjetividad política y ciudadanía juvenil', *Les Cahiers Psychologie Politique*, 7 (July), http://lodel.irevues.inist.fr/cahierspsychologiepolitique/index.php?id=1140

Dieckermann, E. (2018) 'The best interests principle and its relationship to subjectivity, culture and historical injustice', unpublished master's paper, University of Applied Sciences Potsdam.

Dittrich, C. (2013) 'Die Entbergung des Anderen. Enrique Dussels Kritik der Moderne', Introduction to E. Dussel, *Der Gegendiskurs der Moderne*, Vienna and Berlin: Turia + Kant, pp 9–18.

Dorfman, A. and Mattelart, A. ([1971]1975) *How to Read Donald Duck: Imperialist Ideology in the Disney Comic*, New York: International General.

Douglas, M. (2002) *Purity and Danger: An Analysis of Concepts of Pollution and Taboo*, London: Routledge.

Dower, N. and Williams, J. (eds) (2002) *Global Citizenship – A Critical Reader*, Edinburgh: University Press.

Dreyfus, H. and Taylor, C. (2015) *Retrieving Realism*, Cambridge, MA and London: Harvard University Press.

Dübgen, F. and Skupien, S. (eds) (2015) *Afrikanische politische Philosophie: Postkoloniale Positionen*, Berlin: Suhrkamp.

DuBois, W.E.B. ([1903]1996) *The Souls of Black Folk*, New York and London: Penguin.

Durkheim, É. (1934) *L'éducation morale*, Nouvelle Édition, Paris: Presses Universitaires de Paris.

Dussel, E. (1980) *Philosophy of Liberation*, London: Wipf & Stock Publishers.

Dussel, E. (1994) *Historía de la Filosofía latinoamericana y Filosofía de la Liberación*, Bogotá: Nueva América.

Dussel, E. (2007) *Materiales para una Política de la Liberación*, Madrid: Plaza y Valdés.

Dussel, E. (2011) *Politics of Liberation: A Critical Global History*, Norwich: Hymns Ancient & Modern.

Dussel, E. (2013) *Der Gegendiskurs der Moderne. Kölner Vorlesungen*, Vienna and Berlin: Turia + Kant.

Dworkin, R. (1972) 'Paternalism', *The Monist*, 56(1): 64–84.

Dworkin, R. (2017) 'Paternalism', Stanford Encyclopedia of Philosophy, http://plato.stanford.edu/entries/paternalism/

Dzankic, J. (2012) 'The pros and cons of Ius Pecuniae: Investor citizenship in comparative perspective', EUI Working Papers, RSCAS, 2012/14, http://cadmus.eui.eu/handle/1814/21476

Dzankic, J. (2014) 'The Maltese Falcon, or: My Porsche for a Passport', in A. Shachar and R. Bauböck (eds), *Should Citizenship be for Sale?* EUI Working Papers RSCAS, 2014/01, pp 17–18.

Eboussi Buulaga, F. (2015) 'Wenn wir den Begriff "Entwicklung" akzeptieren, sind wir verloren. Von der Notwendigkeit einer gegenseitigen "Dekolonisierung" unseres Denkens!', in F. Dübgen and S. Skupien (eds), *Afrikanische Politische Philosophie. Postkoloniale Positionen*, Berlin: Suhrkamp, pp 115–26.

ECLAC-UNICEF (2010) *La Pobreza Infantil en América Latina y el Caribe*, Santiago de Chile: CEPAL.

Edmonds, R. (2019) 'Making children's "agency" visible: Towards the localisation of a concept in theory and practice', *Global Studies of Childhood*, 9(3): 200–11.

Eichsteller, G. (2009) 'Janusz Korczak – His legacy and its relevance for children's rights today', *International Journal of Children's Rights*, 17: 377–91.

Eisenstadt S.N. (ed) (2002) *Multiple Modernities*, New Brunswick, NJ: Transaction Publications.

Eisenstadt, S.N. (2004) 'The civilizational dimension of modernity: Modernity as a distinct civilization', in S.A. Arjomand and E. Tiryakian (eds), *Rethinking Civilizational Analysis*, London: Sage, pp 48–66.

Ekundayo, O. (2015) 'Does the African Charter on the Rights and Welfare of the Child (ACRWC) only underlines and repeats the Convention on the Rights of the Child (CRC)'s Provisions?: Examining the Similarities and the Differences between the ACRWC and the CRC', *International Journal of Humanities and Social Science*, 5(7): 143–58.

Elias, N. (2000) *The Civilizing Process: Sociogenetic and Psychogenetic Investigations*, revised edition, Oxford: Blackwell.

Ennew, J. (2002) 'Outside childhood. Street children's rights', in B. Franklin (ed), *The New Handbook of Children's Rights*, London and New York: Routledge, pp 388–403.

Ennew, J. (2005) 'Prisoners of childhood: Orphans and economic dependency', in J. Qvortrup (ed), *Studies in Modern Childhood*, Basingstoke: Palgrave MacMillan, pp 128–46.

Ensor, M.O. (ed) (2012) *African Childhoods: Education, Development, Peacebuilding, and the Youngest Continent*, New York: Palgrave Macmillan.

Escobar, A. (2018) *Otro posible es posible: Caminando hacia las transiciones desde Abya Yala/Afro/Latino-América*, Bogotá: ediciones desde abajo.

Esser, F. (2016) 'Neither "thick" nor "thin": Reconceptualising agency and childhood relationally', in F. Esser, M.-S. Baader, T. Betz and B. Hungerland (eds), *Reconceptualising Agency and Childhood. New Perspectives in Childhood Studies*, London and New York: Routledge, pp 48–60.

Esser, F., Baader, M.S., Betz, T. and Hungerland, B. (2016) 'Reconceptualising agency and childhood: An Introduction', in F. Esser, M.-S. Baader, T. Betz and B. Hungerland (eds), *Reconceptualising Agency and Childhood: New Perspectives in Childhood Studies*, London and New York: Routledge, pp 1–16.

Eze, E.C. (ed) (1997a) *Postcolonial African Philosophy: A Critical Reader*, Cambridge, MA: Blackwell.

Eze, E.C. (1997b) 'Introduction: Philosophy and the (Post)colonial', in E.C. Eze (ed), *Postcolonial African Philosophy: A Critical Reader*, Cambridge, MA: Blackwell, pp 1–21.

Fafunwa, A.B. (1974) *History of Education in Nigeria*, London: Allen and Unwin.

Fairchild, H.H. (2017) 'What is Africana Psychology?', in H.H. Fairchild (ed), *Black Lives Matter: Lifespan Perspectives*, Delhi: Indo American Books, pp 3–17.

Fanon, F. ([1952]1986) *Black Skin. White Masks*, London: Pluto Press.

Fanon, F. ([1961]2005) *The Wretched of the Earth*, New York: Grove Press.

Farson, R. (1974) *Birthrights*, New York and London: Macmillan and Collier Macmillan.

Fass, P.S. (2007) *Children of a New World: Society, Culture, and Globalization*, New York: New York University Press.

Fass, P.S. (ed) (2012) *The Routledge History of Childhood in the Western World*, New York and London: Routledge.

Fass, P.S. and Grossberg, M. (eds) (2011) *Reinventing Childhood after World War II*, Philadelphia: University of Pennsylvania Press.

Feinstein, C., Giertsen, A. and O'Kane, C. (2010) 'Children's participation in armed conflict und post-conflict peacebuilding', in B. Percy-Smith and N. Thomas (eds), *A Handbook of Children and Young People's Participation: Perspectives from Theory and Practice*, Abingdon: Routledge, pp 53–62.

Fernández Steinko, A. (2004) *Clase, Trabajo y Ciudadanía. Introducción a la Existencia Social*, Madrid: Biblioteca Nueva.

Fernando, C. and Ferrari, M. (eds) (2013) *Handbook of Resilience in Children of War*, New York: Springer.

Firestone, S. (1970) 'Down with childhood', in S. Firestone (ed), *The Dialectic of Sex: The Case for a Feminist Revolution*, New York: Bantam Books, pp 65–94.

Fitz-Roy, R. (1839) *Narrative of the Surveying Voyages of His Majesty's Ships Adventure and Beagle, Between the Years 1826 and 1836, Describing their Examination of the Southern Shores of South America and the Beagle's Circumnavigation of the Globe*, three volumes, London: Henry Colburn.

Flax, J. (1993) 'The play of justice: Justice as a transitional space', *Political Psychology*, 14(2): 331–46.

Fleischhauer, J. (2008) *Vom Krieg betroffene Kinder: Eine vernachlässigte Dimension von Friedenskonsolidierung. Eine Untersuchung psychosozialer Intervention für Kinder während und nach bewaffneten Konflikten am Beispiel Eritreas*, Opladen and Farmington Hills: Budrich UniPress Ltd.

Flusty, S. (2004) *De-Coca-Colonization: Making the Globe from the Inside Out*, New York and London: Routledge.

Fonseca, C. (1998) *Caminos de adopción*, Buenos Aires: Eudeba.

Fontana, L.B. and Grugel, J. (2016) 'Deviant and Over-compliance: The domestic politics on child labor in Bolivia and Argentina', *Human Rights Quarterly*, 39(3): 631–56.

Forgacs, D. (ed) (2000) *The Gramsci Reader. Selected Writings 1916–1935*, New York: New York University Press.

Foucault, M. ([1969]2002) *Archaeology of Knowledge*, London: Routledge.

Franklin, B. (1994) 'Kinder und Entscheidungen – Entwicklung von Strukturen zur Stärkung von Kinderrechten', in C. Steindorff (ed), *Vom Kindeswohl zu den Kindesrechten*, Neuwied: Luchterhand, pp 43–66.

Franklin, B. (2002) 'Children's rights and media wrongs: Changing representations of children and the developing rights agenda', in B. Franklin (ed), *The New Handbook of Children's Rights*, London and New York: Routledge, pp 15–42.

Frankopan, P. (2015) *The Silk Roads: A New History of the World*, London: Bloomsbury.

Freeman, M. (2002) *Human Rights: An Interdisciplinary Approach*, London: Wiley.

Freeman, M. (2009) 'Children's rights as human rights: Reading the UNCRC', in J. Qvortrup, W.A. Corsaro and M.-S. Honig (eds), *The Palgrave Handbook of Childhood Studies*, Basingstoke: Palgrave Macmillan, pp 377–93.

Freire, P. ([1968]2000) *Pedagogy of the Oppressed*, New York: The Continuum International Publishing Group.

Gade, C.B.N. (2011) 'The historical development of the written discourses on Ubuntu', *South African Journal of Philosophy*, 30(3): 303–29.

Galeano, E. (1971) *Open Veins of Latin America*, New York: Monthly Review Press.

Gallagher, M. (2019) 'Rethinking children's agency: Power, assemblages, freedom and materiality', *Global Studies of Childhood*, 9(3): 188–99.

Gankam Tambo, I. (2013) 'Das Bildungswesen in Nigeria', in C. Adick (ed), *Bildungsentwicklungen und Schulsysteme in Afrika, Asien, Lateinamerika und der Karibik*, Münster: Waxmann, pp 279–99.

Gankam Tambo, I. (2014) *Child Domestic Work in Nigeria: Conditions of Socialisation and Measures of Intervention*, Münster and New York: Waxmann.

Gargallo, F. (2007) 'Hacia una apreciación histórica de la niñez en la calle en América Latina', in P. Rodríguez Jiménez and M.E. Manarelli (eds), *Historia de la Infancia en América Latina*, Bogotá: Universidad Externado de Colombia, pp 535–49.

Garzón Valdés, E. (1988) '¿Es éticamente justificable el paternalismo jurídico?', *DOXA* (Universidad de Alicante), 5: 155–73.

Geiss, I. (1974) *The Pan African Movement: A History Of Pan Africanism In America, Europe, and Africa*, London: Methuen.

Germann, J. (2010) 'Straßenkinder und Child-Headed Households in Guatemala und Zimbabwe', in M. Liebel and R. Lutz (eds), *Sozialarbeit des Südens, Band 3: Kindheiten und Kinderrechte*, Oldenburg: Paulo Freire Verlag, pp 281–96.

Germann, S.E. (2005) *An Exploratory Study of Quality of Life and Coping Strategies of Orphans Living in Child-Headed Households in the High HIV/AIDS Prevalent City of Bulawayo, Zimbabwe*, Pretoria: UNISA – University of South Africa.

Gillard, J. (2013) 'National Apology for Forced Adoptions (21.03.2013)', www.ag.gov.au/About/Forced-AdoptionsApology/Documents/Nationalapologyforforcedadoptions.pdf

Gilliam, Á. (1996) 'O ataque contra a ação afirmativa nos Estados Unidos: Um ensaio para o Brasil', in J. Souza (ed), *Anais do Seminario Internacional "Multiculturalismo e Racismo: O papel da accao afirmativa nos Estados Democráticos Contemporáneos"*, Brasília: Ministerio da Justicia, Secretaria Nacional de a Direitos Humanos.

Gilroy, P. (1993) *The Black Atlantic: Modernity and Double Consciousness*, Cambridge, MA: Harvard University Press.

Girling, F.K. (1960) *The Acholi of Uganda*, London: Her Majesty's Stationery Office.

Go, J. (2016) *Postcolonial Thought and Social Theory*, New York: Oxford University Press.

Go, J. (2017) 'Postcolonial thought as social theory', in C.E. Benzecry, M. Krause and I.A. Read (eds), *Social Theory Now*, Chicago: The University of Chicago Press, pp 130–61.

González Contró, M. (2006) 'Paternalismo jurídico y derechos del niño', *Isonomía*, 25: 101–35.

González Contró, M. (2008) *Derechos Humanos de los Niños: Una Propuesta de Fundación*, Mexico City: Universidad Nacional Autónoma de México.

González Rey, F. (2012) 'La subjetividad y significación para el estudio de los procesos políticos: sujeto, sociedad y política', in C.P. Echandía, A. Díaz Gómez and P. Vommaro (eds), *Subjetividades políticas: desafíos y debates latinoamericanos*, Bogotá: Universidad Distrital Francisco José de Caldas, pp 11–29.

Gottlieb, A. (2004) *The Afterlife is Where We Come From: The Culture of Infancy in West Africa*, Chicago: University of Chicago Press.

Graf, G. (2017) 'Die Menschenrechte von Kindern', in J. Drerup and C. Schickhardt (eds), *Kinderethik. Aktuelle Perspektiven – Klassische Problemvorgaben*, Münster: Mentis, pp 121–32.

Gramsci A. (1971) *Selections from the Prison Notebooks*, edited by Q. Hoare and G. Nowell-Smith, London: Lawrence and Wishart.

Grohs, G. (1967) *Stufen afrikanischer Emanzipation. Studien zum Selbstverständnis westafrikanischer Eliten*, Stuttgart: Kohlhammer.

Grosfoguel, R. (2007a) 'Descolonizando los Universalismos Occidentales: El Pluri-Versalismo Transmoderno Decolonial desde Aimé Césaire hasta los Zapatistas', in S. Castro-Gómez and R. Grosfoguel (eds), *El Giro Decolonial. Reflexiones para una Diversidad Epistémica más allá del Capitalismo Global*, Bogotá: Siglo del hombre editores, pp 63–77.

Grosfoguel, R. (2007b) 'The epistemic turn: Beyond political-economy paradigms', *Cultural Studies*, 21(2–3): 211–23.

Grosfoguel, R. (2016) 'Del "extractivismo económico" al "extractivismo epistémico" y al "extractivismo ontológico": una forma destructiva de conocer, ser y estar en el mundo', *Tabula Rasa*, 24: 123–43.

Grugel, J. and Piper, N. (2007) *Critical Perspectives in Global Governance: Rights and Regulations in Governing Regimes*, London and New York: Routledge.

Grunert, F. (2006) 'Paternalismus in der politischen Theorie der deutschen Aufklärung. Das Beispiel Christian Wolff', in M. Anderheiden, H.M. Heinig, S. Kirste and K. Seelmann (eds) (2006), *Paternalismus und Recht. In Memoriam Angela Augustin (1968–2004)*, Tübingen: Mohr Siebeck, pp 9–27.

Gstettner, P. (1981) *Die Eroberung des Kindes durch die Wissenschaft. Aus der Geschichte der Disziplinierung*, Hamburg: Rowohlt.

Guest, E. (2003) *Children of AIDS: Africa's Orphan Crisis*, London: Pluto Press.

Guha, R. (1997) *Dominance without Hegemony: History and Power in Colonial India*, Cambridge, MA: Harvard University Press.

Guttiérrez, N. (1995) 'Miscegenation as nation-building: Indian and immigrant women in Mexico', in D. Stasiulis and N. Yuval-Davis (eds), *Unsettling Settler Societies: Articulations of Gender, Ethnicity and Class*, London, Thousand Oaks and New Delhi: Sage, pp 161–87.

Gyekye, K. (1995) *An Essay on African Philosophical Thought: The Akan Conceptual Scheme* (2nd edn), Philadelphia: Temple University Press.

Gyekye. K. (1997) *Tradition and Modernity: Philosophical Reflections on the African Experience*, New York and Oxford: Oxford University Press.

Habermas, J. ([1973]1976) *Legitimation Crisis*, London: Heinemann

Habermas, J. ([1981]1985) *The Theory of Communicative Action, Vol. 2. Lifeworld and System: The Critique of Functionalist Reason*, Boston: Beacon.

Habermas, J. (2003) *The Future of Human Nature*, Cambridge: Polity.

Haebich, A. (2002) 'Imagining assimilation', *Australian Historical Studies*, 33(118): 61–70.

Haebich, A. (2011) 'Forgetting indigenous histories: Cases from the history of Australia's Stolen Generation', *Journal of Social History*, 44(4): 1033–46.

Hall, S. (1992) 'The West and the Rest: Discourse and Power', in S. Hall and B. Giebens (eds), *Formations of Modernity*, Oxford: Polity, in association with Open University, pp 276–95.

Hanson, K. and Nieuwenhuys, O. (eds) (2013) *Reconceptualizing Children's Rights in International Development: Living Rights, Social Justice, Translations*, New York and Cambridge: Cambridge University Press.

Hanson, K. and Ruggiero, R. (2013) *Child Witchcraft Allegations and Human Rights*, Brussels: European Commission, Policy Department DG External Politics.

Harper, S. (2008) 'Text of Prime Minister Stephen Harper's residential schools apology', *The Canadian Press*, 11 June, www.ctvnews.ca/text-of-stephen-harper-s-residential-schools-apology-1.301820

Harris-Short, S. (2003) 'International human rights law: Imperialist, inept and ineffective? Cultural relativism and the UN Convention on the Rights of the Child', *Human Rights Quarterly*, 35: 130–81.

Hecht, T. (ed) (2002) *Minor Omissions: Children in Latin American History and Society*, Madison: The University of Minnesota Press.

Hegel, G.W.F. ([1837]2001) *The Philosophy of History*, Ontario: Kitchener – Batoche Books.

Heidenreich, F. (2011) *Theorien der Gerechtigkeit. Eine Einführung*, Opladen and Farmington Hills: Barbara Budrich.

Heissler, K. (2010) 'Migrating with honor: Sites of agency and power in child's Labor migration in Bangladesh', in M.O. Ensor and E. Gozdziak (eds), *Children and Migration: At the Crossroads of Resiliency and Vulnerability*, Basingstoke: Palgrave Macmillan, pp 209–29.

Held, D. (1989) 'Citizenship and Autonomy', in D. Held and J.B. Thompson (eds), *Social Theory of Modern Societies: Anthony Giddens and his Critics*, Cambridge: Cambridge University Press, pp 162–84.

Held, D. (1995) *Democracy and Global Order*, London: Polity.

Held, D. (2002) 'Law of states, law of peoples', *Legal Theory*, 8: 1–44.

Henderson, P.C. (2013) 'Ukugana: "Informal marriage" and children's rights discourse among rural "AIDS orphans" in KwaZulu-Natal, South Africa', in K. Hanson and O. Nieuwenhuys (eds), *Reconceptualizing Children's Rights in International Development: Living Rights, Social Justice, Translations*. New York and Cambridge: Cambridge University Press, pp 29–47.

Henderson, P.C. (2006) 'South African AIDS orphans: Examining assumptions around vulnerability from the perspective of rural children and youth', *Childhood*, 13(3): 303–27.

Hendricks, H. (2011) 'The Evolution of Childhood in Western Europe c. 1400 – c. 1750', in J. Qvortrup, W.A. Corsaro and M.-S. Honig (eds), *The Palgrave Handbook of Childhood Studies*, Basingstoke: Palgrave Macmillan, pp 114–26.

Hengst, H. (2013) *Kindheit im 21. Jahrhundert: Differenzielle Zeitgenossenschaft*, Weinheim and Munich: Beltz-Juventa.

Henley & Partners (2014) 'Why you need alternative citizenship', www.henleyglobal.com/why-alternative-citizenship/

Herriger, N. (1997) *Empowerment in der Sozialen Arbeit*, Stuttgart: Kohlhammer.

Hill, M., Davis, J., Prout, A. and Tisdall, K. (2004) 'Moving the participation agenda forward', *Children & Society*, 18: 77–96.

Himmelbach, N. and Schröer, W. (2014) 'Die transnationale Kindheit', in M.S. Baader, F. Eßer and W. Schröer (eds), *Kindheiten in der Moderne. Eine Geschichte der Sorge*, Frankfurt/M. and New York: Campus, pp 492–509.

Himonga, C. (2008) 'African customary law and children's rights: Intersections and domains in a new era', in J. Sloth-Nielsen (ed), *Children's Rights in Africa: A Legal Perspective*, Aldershot: Ashgate, pp 73–90.

Holt, L. (2011) *Geographies of Children, Youth and Families: International Perspectives*, London: Routledge.

Holzscheiter, A. (2010) *Children's Rights in International Politics: The Transformative Power of Discourse*, Basingstoke: Palgrave Macmillan.

Honwana, A. (2005) 'Innocent and guilty: child soldiers as interstitial and tactical agents', in A. Honwana and F. de Boeck (eds), *Makers and Breakers. Children and Youth in Postcolonial Africa*, Oxford: James Currey; Trenton: Africa World Press; Dakar: CODESRIA, pp 31–52.

Hopgood, S. (2017) 'Modernity at the cutting edge: Human rights meets FGM', in M.N. Barnett (ed), *Paternalism beyond Borders*, Cambridge: Cambridge University Press, pp 256–91.

Horkheimer, M. and Adorno, T.W. ([1947]2002) *Dialectic of Enlightenment*, Stanford, CA: Stanford University Press.

Hountondji, P. (ed) (1994) *Les Savoirs Endogènes: Pistes pour une Recherche*, Dakar: CODESRIA.

Howard, N.P. (2012) 'A critical appraisal of anti-child trafficking discourse and policy in Southern Benin', *Childhood*, 19(4): 554–68.

HREOC (1997) *Bringing Them Home: Report of the National Inquiry into the Separation of Aboriginal and Torres Strait Islander Children from Their Families 1997*, Sydney: Human Rights and Equal Opportunity Commission.

Huijsmans, R. (2016) 'Decentring the history of the idea of children's rights', *International Journal of Children's Rights*, 24: 924–9.

Human Rights Commission New Zealand (2017) *E Kore Ano: Never Again*, 13 February, www.hrc.co.nz/news/e-kore-ano-never-again/

Hunner-Kreisel, C. and Bohne, S. (eds) (2016) *Childhood, Youth and Migration: Connecting Global and Local Perspectives*, Cham: Springer International Publishing Switzerland.

Huynh, K., D'Costa, B. and Lee-Koo, K. (2015) *Children and Global Conflict*, Cambridge: Cambridge University Press.

Inksater, K. (2010) 'Transformative juricultural pluralism: Indigenous justice systems in Latin America and international human rights', *Journal of Legal Pluralism*, 42(60): 105–42.

Inosemzew, W. and Lebedew, A. (2016) 'Der Dritte Kolonialismus', *Le Monde Diplomatique* (German edition), November, p 3.

Institut für Sozialforschung (1956) *Soziologische Exkurse*, Frankfurt/M.: Europäische Verlagsanstalt.

Invernizzi, A. and Milne, B. (eds) (2005) *Children's Citizenship: An Emergent Discourse on the Rights of the Child? Journal of Social Sciences,* Special Issue N° 9, Delhi: Kamla – RAJ Enterprises.

Invernizzi, A. and Williams, J. (eds) (2011) *The Human Rights of Children: From Visions to Implementation*, Farnham: Ashgate.

Invernizzi, A., Liebel, M., Milne, B. and Budde, R. (eds) (2017) *'Children out of Place' and Human Rights. In Memory of Judith Ennew*, Cham: Springer International Switzerland.

Isin, E.F. and Turner, B.S. (eds) (2003) *Handbook of Citizenship Studies*, London: Sage.

Jacobs, M.D. (2009) *White Mother to a Dark Race: Settler Colonialism, Maternalism, and the Removal of Indigenous Children in the American West and Australia, 1880–1940*, Lincoln and London: University of Nebraska Press.

Jacobs, M.D. (2013) 'Remembering the forgotten child: The American child welfare crisis of the 1960s and 1970s', *American Quarterly*, 70(1–2): 136–59.

Jacquemin, M. (2006) 'Can the language of rights get hold of the complex realities of child domestic work? The case of young domestic workers in Abidjan, Ivory Coast', *Childhood*, 13(3): 389–406.

James, A. (2011) 'Agency', in J. Qvortrup, W.A. Corsaro and M.-S. Honig (eds), *The Palgrave Handbook of Childhood Studies*, Basingstoke and New York: Palgrave Macmillan, pp 34–45.

James, A., Jenks, C. and Prout, A. (1998) *Theorizing Childhood*, Cambridge: Polity Press.

James, C.L.R. ([1938]1980) *The Black Jacobins: Tousaint L'Ouverture and the San Domingo Revolution*, London: Allison & Busby.

Jans, M. (2004) 'Children as citizens. Towards a contemporary notion of child participation', *Childhood*, 11(1): 27–44.

Jensen, S.Q. (2011) 'Othering, identity formation and agency', *Qualitative Studies*, 2(2): 63–78.

Jijon, I. (2019) 'The priceless child talks back: How working children respond to global norms against child labor', *Childhood*, DOI: 10.1177/0907568219870582

Jullien, F. (2017) *Il n'y pas d'identité culturelle. Mais nous défendons les ressources culturelles*, Paris: Éditions de l'Herne.

Kaime, T. (2009) *The African Charter on the Rights and Welfare of the Child: A Socio-Legal Perspective*, Pretoria: Pretoria University Law Press.

Kallio, K.P. and Hakli, J. (eds) (2015) *The Beginning of Politics: Youthful Political Agency in Everyday Life*, London and New York: Routledge.

Kam Kah, H. (2015) *The Sacred Forest: Gender and Matriliny in the Laimbwe History (Cameroon), C. 1750–2011*, Introduction by Bea Lundt, Zurich and Berlin: LIT.

Katz, C. (2004) *Growing Up Global: Economic Restructuring and Children's Everyday Lives*, Minneapolis: University of Minnesota Press.

Katz, C. (2012) 'Work and Play: Economic restructuring and children's everyday learning in rural Sudan', in G. Spittler and M. Bourdillon (eds), *African Children at Work: Working and Learning in Growing Up for Life*, Zurich and Berlin: LIT, pp 227–48.

Kendrick, M. and Kakuru, D. (2012) 'Funds of knowledge in child-headed households: A Ugandan case study', *Childhood*, 19(3): 397–413.

Kerner, I. (2012) *Postkoloniale Theorien zur Einführung*, Hamburg: Junius.

Kershaw, R. and Sacks, J. (2008) *New Lives for Old: The Story of Britain's Child Migrants*, Kew, Richmond, Surrey: National Archives.

Key, E. (1909) *The Century of the Child*, New York and London: G.P. Putnam and Sons.

Kimiagar, B. and Hart, R. (2017) 'Children's free association and the collective exercise of their rights', in M.D. Ruck, M. Peterson-Badali and M. Freeman (eds), *Handbook of Children's Rights*, New York and London: Routledge, pp 498–514.

Kipling, R. (1899) 'The White Man's Burden', https://sourcebooks. fordham.edu/mod/kipling.asp

Ki-Zerbo, J. (1990) *Educate or Perish: Africa's Impass and Prospects*, Dakar: BREDA with WCARO (UNESCO-UNICEF, Western Africa).

Klein, N. (2012) 'Dancing the world into being: A conversation with Idle-No-More's Leanne Simpson', *Yes Magazine*, 5 March, www. yesmagazine.org/peace-justice/dancing-the-world-into-being-a-conversation-with-idle-no-more-leannesimpson

Kleinhans, M.-M. and Macdonald, R.A. (1997) 'What is critical legal pluralism?', *Canadian Journal of Law and Society*, 12(2): 25–46.

Klocker, N. (2007) 'An example of "thin" agency: Child domestic workers in Tanzania', in R. Panelli, S. Punch and E. Robson (eds) *Global Perspectives on Rural Childhood and Youth*, New York and London: Routledge, pp 83–93.

Konetzke, R. (ed) (1958–1962) *Colección de Documentos para la Historia de la Formación Social de Hispanoamérica, 1493–1810*, Vol. III, Madrid: Consejo Superior de Investigaciones Científicas.

Korczak, J. ([1919]1999a) 'Fröhliche Pädagogik', in F. Beiner and E. Dauzenroth (eds), *Janusz Korczak, Sämtliche Werke*, Vol. 4, Gütersloh: Gütersloher Verlagshaus, pp 316–93.

Korczak, J. ([1919–20]1999b) 'Wie liebt man ein Kind', in F. Beiner and E. Dauzenroth (eds), *Janusz Korczak, Sämtliche Werke*, Vol. 4, Gütersloh: Gütersloher Verlagshaus, pp 7–315.

Korczak, J. (2007) *Selected works of Janusz Korczak*. Originally published for the National Science Foundation by the Scientific Publications Foreign Cooperation Center of the Central Institute for Scientific, Technical and Economic Information, Warsaw, 1967, edited by M. Wolins. Digital reprint in 2007 by University of Michigan: www. januszkorczak.ca/legacy/CombinedMaterials.pdf

Korczak, J. (2009) *The Child's Right to Respect*, Strasbourg: Council of Europe, Commissioner for Human Rights.

Kovach, M. (2010) *Indigenous Methodologies: Characteristics, Conversations, and Contexts*, Toronto, Buffalo and London: University of Toronto Press.

Kraftl, P. and Horton, J. (2018) 'Children's geographies and the "New Wave" of childhood studies', in S. Spyrou, R. Rosen and D.T. Cook (eds), *Reimagining Childhood Studies*, London and New York: Bloomsbury Academic, pp 105–20.

Kultgen, J. (1995) *Autonomy and Intervention: Parentalism in the Caring Life*, New York and Oxford: Oxford University Press.

Kuwali, D. (2014) 'Decoding Afrocentrism: Decolonizing legal theory', in O. Onazi (ed), *African Legal Theory and Contemporary Problems. Critical Essays*, Dordrecht: Springer, pp 71–92.

Kwan, S.S.-M. (2014) *Postcolonial Resistance and Asian Theology*, London and New York: Routledge.

Kymlicka, W. and Norman, W. (1995) 'Return of the citizen: A survey of recent work on citizenship theory', in R. Beiner (ed), *Theorizing Citizenship*, Albany: SUNY Press, pp 283–322.

Lajo, J. (2010) 'Sumaq Kaway-Ninchik o Nuestro Vivir Bien', *Revista de la Integración,* 5: 112–25.

Lancy, D.F. (2012) 'Unmasking children's agency', SSWA Faculty Publications, Paper 277, https://digitalcommons.usu.edu/sswa_facpubs/277

Lander, E. (ed) (2000) *La colonialidad del saber: eurocentrismo y ciencias sociales*, Buenos Aires: CLACSO.

Lang, M. and Mokrani, D. (eds) (2013) *Beyond Development: Alternative visions from Latin America*, Quito: Fundación Rosa Luxemburg and Amsterdam: Transnational Institute.

Lansdown, G. (2002) 'Children's Rights Commissioners for the UK', in B. Franklin (ed), *The New Handbook of Children's Rights*, London and New York: Routledge, pp 285–97.

Lansdown, G. (2005) *The Evolving Capacities of the Child*, Florence: UNICEF Innocenti Research Centre.

Laraña, E. Johnston, H. and Gusfield, J.R. (eds) (1995) *New Social Movements: From Ideology to Identity*, Philadelphia: Temple University Press.

Larkins, C. (2019) 'Excursions as corporate agents: A critical realist account of children's agency', *Childhood*, 26(4): 414–29.

Latour, B. (1993) *We Have Never Been Modern*, Cambridge, MA: Harvard University Press.

Latour, B. (2005) *Reassembling the Social: An Introduction to Actor-Network-Theory*, Oxford: Oxford University Press.

LeFrançois, B. (2014) 'Adultism', in T. Teo (ed) *Encyclopedia of Critical Psychology*, New York: Springer, pp 47–49.

Levinas, E. (1968) *Totalité et Infinit. Essai sur l'extériorité*, Den Haag: Nijhoff.

Liebel, M. (2004) *A Will of Their Own: Cross-Cultural Perspectives on Working Children*, London and New York: ZED Books.

Liebel, M. (2007a) 'Paternalism, participation and children's protagonism', *Children, Youth and Environments*, 17(3): 56–73.

Liebel, Manfred (2007b) 'Between prohibition and praise: Some hidden aspects of children's work in affluent societies', in B. Hungerland, M. Liebel, B. Milne and A. Wihstutz (eds) *Working to Be Someone: Child Focused Research with Working Children*, London and Philadelphia: Jessica Kingsley, pp 123–32.

Liebel, M. (2008) 'Citizenship from below', in A. Invernizzi and J. Williams (eds) *Children and Citizenship*, London: Sage, pp 32–43.

Liebel, M. (2012a), in cooperation with K. Hanson, I. Saadi and W. Vandenhole, *Children's Rights from Below: Cross-Cultural Perspectives*, Basingstoke: Palgrave Macmillan.

Liebel, M. (2012b) 'Child-led organizations and the advocacy of adults. Experiences from Bangladesh and Nicaragua', in M. Freeman (ed), *Law and Childhood Studies: Current Legal Issues 2011*, Vol. 14, Oxford: Oxford University Press, pp 92–103.

Liebel, M. (2014) 'Adultism and age-based discrimination against children', in D. Kutsar and H. Warming (eds), *Children and Non-Discrimination. Interdisciplinary Textbook*, Tartu: University Press of Estonia, pp 119–43.

Liebel, M. (2015) 'Protecting the rights of working children instead of banning child labour: Bolivia tries a new legislative approach', *International Journal of Children's Rights*, 23(3): 529–47.

Liebel, M. (2016) 'The Moscow Declaration on the Rights of the Child (1918): A contribution from the hidden history of children's rights', *International Journal of Children's Rights*, 24(1): 3–28.

Liebel, M. (2017) '"Children without childhood"? Against the postcolonial capture of childhoods in the Global South', in A. Invernizzi, M. Liebel, B. Milne and R. Budde (eds) *'Children Out of Place' and Human Rights. In Memory of Judith Ennew*, Cham: Springer International Switzerland, pp 99–117.

Liebel, M. (2018a) 'Janusz Korczak's understanding of children's rights as agency rights', in M. Michalak (ed), *The Rights of the Child Yesterday, Today and Tomorrow – the Korczak Perspective, Part I*, Warsaw: Office of the Ombudsman for Children – Poland, pp 204–39.

Liebel, M. (2018b) 'Welfare of agency? Children's interests as foundation of children's rights', *International Journal of Children's Rights*, 26: 597–625.

Liebel, M. and Invernizzi, A. (2018) 'The movements of working children and the International Labour Organization: A lesson on enforced silence', *Children & Society*, 33(2): 142–53.

Liebel, M. and Saadi, I. (2012) 'Cultural variations in constructions of children's participation', in M. Liebel (ed) *Children's Rights from Below: Cross-Cultural Perspectives*, Basingstoke: Palgrave Macmillan, pp 162–82.

Liebel, M., Overwien, B. and Recknagel, A. (eds) (2001) *Working Children's Protagonism: Social Movement and Empowerment in Latin America, Africa and India*, Frankfurt/M. and London: IKO.

Lifton, B.J. (1994) *The King of Children: The Life and Death of Janusz Korczak*, London: Pan Books.

Lister, R. (2003) *Citizenship: Feminist Perspectives*, Basingstoke: Palgrave.

Lister, R. (2006) 'Children and citizenship', *Childright – A Journal of Law and Policy Affecting Children and Young People*, 223, February: 22–5.

Lister, R. (2007) 'Why citizenship: Where, how and why children?', *Theoretical Inquiries in Law*, 8(2): 693–718.

Lloyd, A. (2002) 'Evolution of the African Charter on Rights and Welfare of the Child and the African Committee of Experts: Raising the gauntlet', *International Journal of Children's Rights*, 10: 179–98.

Lloyd, A. (2008) 'The African regional system for the protection of children's rights', in J. Sloth-Nielsen (ed), *Children's Rights in Africa: A Legal Perspective*, Aldershot: Ashgate, pp 33–52.

Locke, J. ([1690]1995) *An Essay Concerning Human Understanding*, Amherst and New York: Prometheus Books.

Long, M. and Sephton, R. (2011) 'Rethinking the "best interests" of the child: Voices from Aboriginal child and family welfare practitioners', *Australian Social Work*, 64(1): 96–112.

Loomba, A. (2005) *Colonialism/Postcolonialism* (2nd edn), London and New York: Routledge.

Lundt, B. (2016) 'Ich bin dann mal da! Vom schwierigen Ankommen weißer Lehramtsstudierender in Ländern Afrikas und von der Aufgabe des Faches Geschichte angesichts der Agenda 2030', *Zeitschrift für Geschichtsdidaktik*, 15: 31–45.

Lundt, B. and Marx, C. (eds) (2016) *Kwame Nkrumah 1909–1972: A Controversial African Visionary*, Stuttgart: Franz Steiner.

Mackert, J. (1999) *Kampf um Zugehörigkeit. Nationale Staatsbürgerschaft als Modus sozialer Schließung*, Opladen and Wiesbaden: Westdeutscher Verlag.

Mackert, J. and Müller, H.-P. (eds) (2007) *Moderne (Staats)Bürgerschaft. Nationale Staatsbürgerschaft und die Debatten der Citizenship-Studies*, Wiesbaden: VS.

Marshall, T.H. (1950) *Citizenship and Social Class*, Cambridge: Cambridge University Press.

Martin, E. (2001) *Sozialpädagogische Berufsethik. Auf der Suche nach dem richtigen Handeln*, Weinheim and Munich: Juventa.

Martínez Muñoz, M. and Cabrerizo Sanz, L. (2015) *Guía para la Evaluación. Herramienta Prota-Estela*, Lima: Save the Children International and Enclave de Evaluación.

Martínez-Alier, V. (1989) *Marriage, Class and Colour in Nineteenth-Century Cuba*, Ann Arbor: University of Michigan Press.

Marx, K. ([1867]1960) *Das Kapital. Kritik der Politischen Ökonomie. Erster Band*, Berlin: Dietz.

Masferrer León, C.V. (2010) 'Hijos, huérfanos y expósitos. Un recorrido por la niñez de la época colonial novohispana', in L. Márquez Morfín (ed), *Los Niños, Actores Sociales Ignorados. Levantando el Velo, una Mirada al Pasado*, Mexico City: Escuela Nacional de Antopología e Historia and Consejo Nacional para la Cultura y las Artes, pp 305–23.

Mayall, B. (2015) 'The sociology of childhood and children's rights', in W. Vandenhole, E. Desmet, D. Reynaert and S. Lembrechts (eds), *Routledge International Handbook of Children's Rights Studies*, London and New York: Routledge, pp 77–93.

Mbembe, A. (2001) *On the Postcolony*, Berkeley and Los Angeles, CA: University of California Press.

Mbembe, A. (2003) 'Necropolitics', *Public Culture*, 15 : 11–40.

Mbembe, A. (2010) *Sortir de la Grande Nuit. Essai sur l'Afrique Décolonisée*, Paris: La Découverte.

Mbembe, A. (2013) *Critique de la Raison Nègre*, Paris: La Découverte.

Mehta, U.S. (1999) *Liberalism and Empire: A Study in Nineteenth-Century British Liberal Thought*, Chicago and London: University of Chicago Press.

Meintjes, H. and Giese, S. (2006) 'Spinning the epidemic: The making of mythologies of orphanhood in the context of AIDS', *Childhood*, 13(3): 407–30.

Mendel, G. (1971) *Pour Décoloniser l'Enfant. Sociopsychanalyse de l'Autorité*, Paris: Payot.

Menke, C. and Pollmann, A. (2007) *Philosophie der Menschenrechte zur Einführung*, Hamburg: Junius.

Merry, S. (2001) 'Changing Rights, Changing Culture', in J.K. Cowan, M.-B. Dembour and R.A. Wilson (eds), *Culture and Rights: Anthropological Perspectives*, Cambridge: Cambridge University Press, pp 31–55.

Messner, C. (2012) 'Living law: performative, not discursive', *International Journal for the Semiotics of Law*, 25(4): 537–52.

Metge, J. and Ruru. J. (2013) 'Kua Tutū Te Pūehu, Kia Mau: Māori Aspirations and Family Law Policy', in M. Henagan and B. Atkin (eds), *Family Law Policy in New Zealand*, Wellington: LexisNexis, pp 47–80.

Metz, T. (2007) 'Toward an African moral theory', *The Journal of Political Philosophy*, 15: 321–41.

Mies, M. (2005) *Krieg ohne Grenzen. Die neue Kolonisierung der Welt*, Cologne: PapyRossa.

Miescher, S.F. (2009) 'Masculinities and Transcultural Perspectives in African History', in M. Ineichen, A. Rathmann-Lutz, S. Wenger and A.K. Liesch (eds), *Gender in Trans-lt: Transkulturelle und Transnationale Perspektiven / Transcultural and Transnational Perspectives*. Zurich: Chronos, pp 69–83.

Mignolo, W.D. (1993) 'Colonial and postcolonial discourses: Cultural critique or academic colonialism', *Latin American Research Review*, 28: 120–31.

Mignolo, W.D. (2000) *Local Histories / Global Designs: Coloniality, Subaltern Knowledges, and Border Thinking*, Princeton, NJ: Princeton University Press.

Mignolo, W.D. (2001) *Capitalismo y Geopolítica del Conocimiento*, Buenos Aires: Ediciones del Signo.

Mignolo, W.D. (2005) *The Idea of Latin America*, Malden, MA and Oxford: Blackwell.

Mignolo, W.D. (2006) 'Citizenship, knowledge, and the limits of humanity', *American Literary History*, 18(2): 312–31.

Mignolo, W.D. (2009) 'Epistemic disobedience, independent thought and de-colonial freedom', *Theory, Culture & Society*, 26(7–8): 1–23.

Milanich, N. (2002) 'Historical perspectives on illegitimacy and illegitimates in Latin America', in T. Hecht (ed), *Minor Omissions: Children in Latin American History and Society*, Madison: The University of Minnesota Press, pp 72–101.

Milanich, N. (2007) 'Informalidad y extralegalidad de los niños en América Latina. Del período colonial hasta el presente', in P. Rodríguez Jiménez and M.E. Manarelli (eds), *Historia de la Infancia en América Latina*, Bogotá: Universidad Externado de Colombia, pp 591–614.

Milanović, B. (2012) *The Haves and the Have-Nots: A Brief and Idiosyncratic History of Global Inequality*, New York: Basic Books.

Mill, J.S. ([1859]2001) *On Liberty*, Ontario: Kitchener Batoche Books.

Milloy, J.S. (1999) *A National Crime: The Canadian Government and the Residential School System, 1879 to 1986*, Winnipeg: University of Manitoba Press.

Milne, B. (2007) 'Do the participation articles in the Convention on the Rights of the Child (CRC) present us with a recipe for children's citizenship?', in B. Hungerland, M. Liebel, B. Milne and A. Wihstutz (eds), *Working to Be Someone: Child Focused Research with Working Children*, London and Philadelphia: Jessica Kingsley, pp 205–09.

Ministry of Education (2018) *Our Schooling Futures: Stronger Together*, Wellington, New Zealand.

Ministry of Social Development (2015) *Expert Panel Final Report: Investing in New Zealand's Families and their Children*, Wellington, New Zealand.

Mizen, P. and Ofosu-Kusi, Y. (2010) 'Asking, giving, receiving: Friendships as survival strategies among Accra's street children', *Childhood*, 17(4): 441–54.

Mizen, P. and Ofosu-Kusi, Y. (2013) 'Seeing and knowing? Street children's lifeworlds through the camera's lens', in K. Hanson and O. Nieuwenhuys (eds), *Reconceptualizing Children's Rights in International Development: Living Rights, Social Justice, Translations*, New York and Cambridge: Cambridge University Press, pp 48–70.

Montgomery, H. (2001) *Modern Babylon? Prostituting Children in Thailand*, Oxford: Berghahn.

Montgomery, H. (2017) 'Anthropological perspectives on children's rights', in M.D. Ruck, M. Peterson-Badali and M. Freeman (eds), *Handbook of Children's Rights*, New York and London: Routledge, pp 97–113.

Moosa-Mitha, M. (2005) 'A difference-centred alternative to theorization of children's citizenship rights', *Citizenship Studies*, 9(4): 369–88.

Moraña, M., Dussel, E. and Jáuregui, C. (eds) (2008) *Coloniality at Large: Latin America and the Postcolonial Debate*, Durham, NC and London: Duke University Press.

Morris, A. (2015) *The Scholar Denied: W.E.B. DuBois and the Birth of Modern Sociology*, Berkeley: University of California Press.

Morris, R.C. (ed) (2010) *Can the Subaltern Speak? Reflections on the History of an Idea*, New York: Columbia University Press.

Morrison, H. (2015) *Childhood and Colonial Modernity in Egypt*, Basingstoke: Palgrave Macmillan.

Morrison, H. (ed) (2012) *The Global History of Childhood Reader*, London and New York: Routledge.

Morrow, V. and Pells, K. (2012) 'Integrating children's human rights and child poverty debates: examples from young lives in Ethiopia and India', *Sociology*, 46(5): 906–20.

Moses, A.D. (ed) (2004) *Genocide and Settler Society: Frontier Violence and Stolen Indigenous Children in Australian History*, New York: Berghahn Books.

Moumouni, A. (1968) *Education in Africa*, New York: Praeger.

Mudimbe, V.Y. (1988) *The Invention of Africa: Gnosis, Philosophy and the Order of Knowledge*, Bloomington and Indianapolis: Indiana University Press.

Mühlbacher, S. and Sutterlüty, F. (2019) 'The principle of child autonomy: A rationale for the normative agenda of childhood studies', *Global Studies of Childhood*, 9(3): 249–60.

Müller, S. and Otto, H.-U. (eds) (1984) *Verstehen oder Kolonialisieren? Grundprobleme sozialpädagogischen Handelns und Forschens*, Bielefeld: Kleine.

Munyakho, D. (1992) *Kenya: Child Newcomers in the Urban Jungle*, Florence: UNICEF – Innocenti Studies.

Mutua, M. (2002) *Human Rights: A Political and Cultural Critique*, Philadelphia: University of Pennsylvania Press.

Mutua, M. (2009) 'Human rights NGOs in East Africa: Defining the Challenges', in M. Mutua (ed), *Human Rights NGOs in East Africa: Political and Normative Tensions*, Philadelphia: University of Pennsylvania Press, pp 11–36.

Mutua, M. (2016) *Human Rights Standards. Hegemony, Law, and Politics*, New York: State University of New York Press.

Myers-Scotton, C. (1993) 'Elite closure as a powerful language strategy: the African case', *International Journal of the Sociology of Language*, 103(1): 149–64

Nandy, A. (1983) *The Intimate Enemy: Loss and Recovery of Self under Colonialism*, New Delhi: Oxford University Press.

Nandy, A. (1987) *Traditions, Tyranny and Utopias: Essays in the Politics of Awareness*, New Delhi: Oxford University Press.

National Foster Care Coalition (2007) *Disproportionately: Addressing the Disproportionate Number of Children and Youth of Color in Foster Care and the Inequitable Outcome They Experience*, Washington DC: National Foster Care Coalition.

Nazzari, M. (1996) 'Concubinage in colonial Brazil: The inequalities of race, class, and gender', *Journal of Family History*, 21(2): 107–24.

Ndaba, W.J. (1994) *Ubuntu in Comparison to Western Philosophies*, Pretoria: Ubuntu School of Philosophy.

Ndulo, M. (2011) 'African customary law, customs, and women's rights', *Indiana Journal of Global Legal Studies*, 18(1): 87–120.

Negt, O. (1997) *Kindheit und Schule in einer Welt der Umbrüche*, Göttingen: Steidl.

Nelson, E. (1927) 'El problema de la ilegitimidad', *Boletín del Instituto Internacional Americano de Protección a la Infancia*, 1(2): 221–48.

Nestvogel, R. (1996) 'Traditionelle afrikanische Erziehungsmuster und ihre Darstellung zwischen Idealisierung und Abwertung', *Zeitschrift für internationale Bildungsforschung und Entwicklungspädagogik (ZEP)*, 19(2): 15–24.

Newman, J. (2005) 'Protection through Participation. Young People Affected by Forced Migration and Political Crisis', *RSC Working Paper* N° 20, Refugee Studies Centre, University of Oxford, UK.

Ngalim, V.B. (2014) 'A conflict of colonial cultures in the educational sub-systems in Africa: celebrating fifty years of political and not educational sovereignty in Cameroon', *European Scientific Journal*, 1: 622–35.

Nieuwenhuys, O. (2007) 'Embedding the global womb: Global child labour and the new policy agenda', *Children's Geographies*, 5(1–2): 149–63.

Nieuwenhuys, O. (2009) 'From child labour to working children's movements', in J. Qvortrup, W.A. Corsaro and M.-S. Honig (eds) *The Palgrave Handbook of Childhood Studies*, Basingstoke: Palgrave Macmillan, pp 289–300.

Nieuwenhuys, O. (2013) 'Theorizing childhood(s): Why we need postcolonial perspectives', *Childhood*, 20(1): 3–8.

Nizza da Silva, M.B. (1993) *Vida Privada e Quotidiano no Brasil: Na Época de D. Maria I e D João VI*, Lisbon: Editorial Estampa.

Nkrumah, K. (1964) *Consciencism: Philosophy and Ideology for Decolonization and Development with Particular Reference to the African Revolution*, New York: Monthly Review Press.

Nnaemeka, O. (ed) (1998) *Sisterhood, Feminisms and Power: From Africa to the Diaspora*, Trenton, NJ: African World Press.

Nolan, A. (2010) 'The child as "democratic citizen": challenging the "participation gap"', *Public Law*, 4: 767–82.

Nsamenang, A.B. and Lamb, M.E. (1994) 'Socialization of Nso children in the Bamenda grassfields of Northwest Cameroon', in P. Marks Greenfield and R.R. Cockling (eds), *Cross-Cultural Roots of Minority Child Development*, Hillsdale, NJ: L. Erlbaum, pp 133–46.

Nsamenang, A.B. (2008) 'Agency in early childhood learning and development in Cameroon', *Contemporary Issues in Early Childhood Education*, 9(3): 211–23.

Nsamenang, A.B. (2010) 'Childhoods within Africa's triple heritage', in G.S. Cannella and L. Diaz Soto (eds), *Childhoods: A Handbook*, New York: Peter Lang, pp 39–54.

Nussbaum, M. (2011) *Creating Capabilities: The Human Development Approach*, Cambridge, MA: Belknap Press.

Nzegwu, N. (1994) 'Gender equality in a dual-sex system: The case of Onitsha', *Canadian Journal of Law & Jurisprudence*, 7: 73–96.

Odera Oruka, H. (1981) 'Four trends in current African philosophy', in A. Diemer (ed), *Symposium on Philosophy in the Present Situation of Africa*, Wiesbaden: Steiner, pp 1–7.

Odera Oruka, H. (1988) 'Grundlegende Fragen der afrikanischen "Sage-Philosophy"', in F.M. Wimmer (ed), *Vier Fragen zur Philosophie in Afrika, Asien und Lateinamerika*, Vienna: Passagen, pp 35–53.

Odera Oruka, H. ([1989]1997) 'The philosophy of foreign aid: A question of the right to a human minimum', *Praxis International*, 8(4).

Odera Oruka, H. (ed) (1990) *Sage Philosophy: Indigenous Thinkers and Modern Debate on African Philosophy*, London: Brill Academic.

Ofosu-Kusi, Y. and Mizen, P. (2012) 'No longer willing to be dependent: Young people moving beyond learning', in G. Spittler and M. Bourdillon (eds), *African Children at Work: Working and Learning in Growing Up for Life*, Zurich and Berlin: LIT, pp 279–302.

Ogundipe-Leslie, M. (1994) *Recreating Ourselves: African Women and Critical Transformation*, Trenton, NJ: African World Press.

Ogunyemi, C.O. (1985) 'Womanism: The dynamics of the contemporary black female novel in English', *Signs*, 11: 63–80.

Okonyo, K. (1976) 'The dual-sex political system in operation: Igbo-Women and the community politics in Midwestern Nigeria', in N.J. Hafkin and E.G. Bay (eds), *Women in Africa: Studies in Social and Economic Change*, Stanford, CA: Stanford University Press, pp 45–85.

Okri, B. (1993) *The Famished Road*, New York: Anchor Books.

Oliver, C.M. and Dalrymple, J.E. (eds) (2008) *Developing Advocacy for Children and Young People: Current Issues in Research, Policy and Practice*, London: Jessica Kingsley.

Olowu, D. (2002) 'Protecting children's rights in Africa: a critique of the African Charter on the Rights and Welfare of the Child', *International Journal of Children's Rights*, 10(2): 127–36.

Olsen, F. (1995) 'Children's Rights: Some feminist approaches to the United Nations Convention on the Rights of the Child', in P. Alston, S. Parker and J. Seymour (eds), *Children's Rights and the Law*, Oxford: Oxford University Press, pp 192–220.

Omolo, A. (2015) *Violence against Children in Kenya. An Ecological Model of Risk Factors and Consequences, Responses and Projects*, Münster: Waxmann.

Onazi, O. (ed) (2014) *African Legal Theory and Contemporary Problems. Critical Essays*, Dordrecht: Springer.

Osterhammel, J. (2005) *Colonialism: A Theoretical Overview*, Princeton, NJ: Markus Wiener.

Oswell, D. (2013) *The Agency of Children: From Family to Global Human Rights*, Cambridge: Cambridge University Press.

Oswell, D. (2016) 'Re-aligning children's agency and re-socialising children in Childhood Studies', in F. Esser, M.-S. Baader, T. Betz and B. Hungerland (eds), *Reconceptualising Agency and Childhood. New Perspectives in Childhood Studies*, London and New York: Routledge, pp 19–33.

Ousmane, S. (1995) *Xala*, Paris: Présence africaine.

Oxfam (2017) 'An economy for the 1%. How privilege and power in the economy drive extreme inequality and how this can be stopped', Oxfam Briefing Paper, 18 January, www.oxfam.de/system/files/bp210-economy-one-percent-tax-havens-180116-en.pdf

Oyèwùmi, O. (ed) (1997) *The Invention of Women: Making an African Sense of Western Gender Discourses*, Minneapolis: The University of Minnesota Press.

Özerdem, A. and Podder, S. (2015) *Youth in Conflict and Peace Building: Mobilization, Reintegration and Reconciliation*, Basingstoke: Palgrave Macmillan.

Özerdem, A., Thiessen, C. and Qassoum, M. (eds) (2017) *Conflict Transformation and the Palestinians: The Dynamics of Peace and Justice under Occupation*, London and New York: Routledge.

Pal, A. (2008) 'Makkala Panchayats: Institutionalization of children's participation in local decision-making', *Children, Youth and Environments*, 18(2): 197–205.

Palmeri, A. (1980) 'Childhood's end: Toward the liberation of children', in W. Aiken and H. LaFollette (eds), *Whose Child? – Children's Rights. Parental Authority and State Power*, Totowa, NJ: Rowman and Littlefield, pp 105–23.

Parry, B. (2004) *Postcolonial Studies: A Materialist Critique*, London and New York: Routledge.

Parsons, T. (1951) *The social system*, fourth edition, New York: Free Press.

Parsons, T. (1965) 'Full citizenship for the Negro American? A sociological problem', *Daedalus*, 94(4): 1009–54.

Parsons, T. (1971) *The System of Modern Societies*, Englewood Cliffs: Prentice Hall.

Patterson, O. (1982) *Slavery and Social Death: A Comparative Study*, Cambridge, MA.: Harvard University Press.

Payne, R. (2012a) 'Agents of support: intra-generational relations and the role of agency in the support of child-headed households in Zambia', *Children's Geographies*, 10(3): 293–306.

Payne, R. (2012b) '"Extraordinary survivors" or "ordinary lives"? Embracing "everyday agency" in social interventions with child-headed households in Zambia', *Children's Geographies*, 10(4): 399–411.

Penn, H. (2005) *Unequal Childhoods: Young Children's Lives in Poor Countries*, London and New York: Routledge.

Peterson, A.L. and Almere Read, K. (2002) 'Victims, heroes, enemies. Children in Central American wars', in T. Hecht (ed), *Minor Omissions: Children in Latin American History and Society*, Madison: The University of Wisconsin Press, pp 215–31.

Piketty, T. (2014) *Capital in the Twenty-First Century*, Cambridge, MA and London: The Belknap Press of Harvard University Press.

Plavgo, I. and de Milliano, M. (2014) 'Multidimensional child deprivation in sub-Saharan Africa', *Innocenti Working Paper N° 2014–19*, Florencia: UNICEF.

Postman, N. (1982) *The Disappearance of Childhood*, New York: Vintage Books.

Prah, K.K. (2005) 'Language of Instruction for Education, Development and African Emancipation', in B. Brock-Utne and R.K. Hopson (eds), *Languages of Instruction for African Emancipation: Focus on Postcolonial Contexts and Considerations*, Dar es Salaam: Mkuki na Nyota Publishers and Cape Town: Centre for Advanced Studies of African Society (CASAS), pp 23–49.

Pridmore, P. and Stephens, D. (2000) *Children as Partners for Health: A Critical Review of the Child-to-Child Approach*, London: Zed Books.

Prout, A. (2000) 'Childhood bodies, construction, agency and hybridity', in A. Prout (ed), *The Body, Childhood and Society*, Basingstoke: Macmillan, pp 1–18.

Prout, A. (2003) 'Participation, policy and the changing conditions of childhood', in C. Hallet and A. Prout (eds), *Hearing the Voices of Children: Social Policy for a New Century*, London and New York: Routledge-Falmer, pp 11–25.

Prout, A. (2005) *The Future of Childhood*, London and New York: Routledge-Falmer.

Puao-te-Ata-tu (1988) *The Report of the Ministerial Committee on a Māori Perspective of the Department of Social Welfare* (September 1988), Wellington, New Zealand.

Punamäki, R.-L., Quota, S. and El-Sarraj, E. (1997) 'Models of traumatic experiences and children's psychological adjustment: the role of perceived parenting and the children's own resources and activity', *Child Development*, 64(4): 718–28.

Punamäki, R.-L., Quota, S. and El-Sarraj, E. (2001) 'Resiliency factors predicting psychological adjustment after political violence among Palestinian children', *International Journal of Behavioral Development*, 25(3): 256–67.

Pupavac, V. (1998) 'The infantilisation of the South and the UN Convention on the Rights of the Child', *Human Rights Law Review*, 3(2): 1–6.

Pupavac, V. (2001) 'Misanthropy without borders: The international children's rights regime', *Disasters*, 25(2): 95–112.

Quijano, A. (2000) 'Colonialidad del Poder y Classificación Social', *Journal of Worlds System Research*, 6(2): 342–86.

Quijano, A. (2008) 'Coloniality of power, Eurocentrism, and social classification', in M. Moraña, E. Dussel and C. Jáuregui (eds), *Coloniality at Large. Latin America and the Postcolonial Debate*, Durham, NC and London: Duke University Press, pp 181–224.

Qvortrup, J. (2005) 'Varieties of childhood', in J. Qvortrup (ed), *Studies in Modern Childhood: Society, Agency, Culture*, Basingstoke: Palgrave, pp 1–20.

Radcliffe, S.A. (1995) 'Five Centuries of Gendered Settler Society: Conquerors, Natives and Immigrants in Peru', in D. Stasiulis and N. Yuval-Davis (eds), *Unsettling Settler Societies: Articulations of Gender, Ethnicity and Class*, London: Sage, pp 188–206.

Raithelhuber, E. (2016) 'Extending agency: the merit of relational approaches for childhood studies', in F. Esser, M.-S. Baader, T. Betz and B. Hungerland (eds), *Reconceptualising Agency and Childhood: New Perspectives in Childhood Studies*, London and New York: Routledge, pp 89–101.

Rajagopal, B. (2003) *International Law from Below: Development, Social Movements and Third World Resistance*, Cambridge: Cambridge University Press.

Rashed, H. and Short, D. (2014) 'Genocide and settler colonialism: Can a Lemkin-inspired genocide perspective aid our understanding of the Palestinian situation', in P. Hynes, M. Lamb, D. Short and M. Waites (eds), *New Directions in the Sociology of Human Rights*, London and New York: Routledge, pp 20–47.

Read, P. (1998) *The Stolen Generations: The Removal of Aboriginal Children in New South Wales 1883 to 1969*, Sydney: New South Wales Department of Aboriginal Affairs.

Read, P. (2002) 'Clio or Janus? Historians and the stolen generations', *Australian Historical Studies*, 33(118): 54–62.

Real Academia Española ([1726–1739]1987) *Diccionario de Autoridades*, Vol. D–Ñ, Barcelona: Editorial Herder.

Reddy, N. (2017) 'Working children in an increasingly hostile world', in A. Invernizzi, M. Liebel, B. Milne and R. Budde (eds), *'Children out of Place' and Human Rights. In Memory of Judith Ennew*, Cham: Springer International Switzerland, pp 63–78.

Reed, J.-P. (2013) 'Theorist of subaltern subjectivity: Antonio Gramsci, popular beliefs, political passion, and reciprocal learning', *Critical Sociology*, 39(4): 561–91.

Renan, E. (1891) *The Future of Science*, London: Chapman and Hall.

Rensink, B. (2011) 'Genocide of Native Americans: Historical facts and historiographical debates', in S. Totten and R.K. Hitchcock (eds), *Genocide of Indigenous Peoples*, New Brunswick and London: Transaction Publishers, pp 15–36.

Reynaert, D. and Rose, R. (2017) 'Children's rights: A framework to eliminate social exclusion?', in M.D. Ruck, M. Peterson-Badali and M. Freeman (eds), *Handbook of Children's Rights*, New York and London: Routledge, pp 36–52.

Reynaert, D., Desmet E., Lembrechts, S. and Vandenhole, W. (2015) 'Introduction: A critical approach to children's rights', in W. Vandenhole, E. Desmet, D. Reynaert and S. Lembrechts (eds), *Routledge International Handbook of Children's Rights Studies*, London and New York: Routledge, pp 1–23.

Richter, E. and Lehmann, T. (2016) 'Partizipation in der Kita zwischen deliberativer und Expertendemokratie', in R. Mörgen, P. Rieker and A. Schnitzer (eds), *Partizipation von Kindern und Jugendlichen in vergleichender Perspektive*, Weinheim and Basel: Beltz-Juventa, pp 39–63.

Richter, J. (2016) *Human Rights Education Through Ciné Debat: Film as a Tool to Fight against Female Genital Mutilation in Burkina Faso*, Wiesbaden: Springer VS.

Ritzer, G. (2007) *The McDonaldization of Society*, Los Angeles: Sage.

Rivas, A. (2010) 'Modern research discourses constructing the postcolonial subjectivity of (Mexican) American children', in G.S. Cannella and L. Diaz Soto (eds), *Childhoods: A Handbook*, New York: Peter Lang, pp 245–64.

Rivera Cusicanqui, S. (2010) *Ch'ixinakak utxiwa: una reflexión sobre prácticas y discursos descolonizadores*, Buenos Aires: Tinta Limón Ediciones.

Rizvi, F. (2007) 'Postcolonialism and globalization in education', *Cultural Studies & Critical Methodologies*, 7(3): 256–63.

Roberts, D. (2002) *Shattered Bonds: The Color of Child Welfare*, New York: Basic Books.

Robertson, J.A. (1996) *Children of Choice: Freedom and the New Reproductive Technologies*, Princeton, NJ: Princeton University Press.

Robson, E., Bell, S. and Klocker, N. (2007) 'Conceptualizing agency in the lives and actions of rural young people', in R. Panelli, S. Punch and E. Robson (eds), *Global Perspectives on Rural Childhood and Youth*, New York and London: Routledge, pp 135–48.

Roche, J. (1999) 'Children: Rights, participation and citizenship', *Childhood*, 6(4): 475–93.

Rodgers, D. (2005) 'Children as social movement participants', in D.A. Kinney and K. Brown Rosier (eds), *Sociological Studies of Children and Youth*, Vol. 11, Bingley: Emerald, pp 239–59.

Rodríguez, I. (2001) 'Reading subalterns across texts, disciplines, and theories: From representation to recognition', in I. Rodríguez (ed) *The Latin American Subaltern Studies Reader*, Durham, NC and London: Duke University Press, pp 1–32.

Rodríguez, S. ([1828]1990) *Sociedades Americanas*, Caracas: Biblioteca Ayacucho.

Rogers, A. (2001) 'Problematising literacy and development', in B.V. Street (ed), *Literacy and Development: Ethnographic Perspectives*, London and New York: Routledge, pp 205–22.

Rojas Flores, J. (2010) *Historia de la Infancia en el Chile Republicano 1810–2010*, Santiago de Chile: Ocho Libros Editores.

Rojas Suárez, N.D. (2012) *Movimientos sociales de niños, niñas, adolescentes y jóvenes de Colombia: Comprensión de una experiencia*, Manizales: Universidad de Manizales – CINDE.

Rosen, D.M. (2005) *Armies of the Young: Child Soldiers in War and Terrorism*, New Brunswick, NJ and London: Rutgers University Press.

Rosen, D.M. (2014) 'Reflections on the well-being of child soldiers', in A. Ben-Arieh (ed) *Handbook of Child Well-Being*, Dordrecht: Springer, pp 3071–100.

Rosen, D.M. (2015) *Child Soldiers in the Western Imagination: From Patriots to Victims*, New Brunswick, NJ and London: Rutgers University Press.

Rousseau, J.-J. ([1762]1979) *Emile, or on Education*, New York: Basic Books.

Rubio, S. (1928) *Cámara de Diputados* (Chile), 2a Sesión Ordinaria, 28 May.

Rudd, K. (2008) 'Text of the Apology to the Stolen Generations', 13 February, www.dfat.gov.au/indigenous/apology-to-stolen-generations/national_apology.html

Rudd, K. (2009) Transcript of Apology to the Forgotten Australians and former child migrants, Great Hall, Parliament House, 16 November, http://pandora.ula.gov.au/pan/110625/20091116-1801/www.pm.gov.au/node/6321.html

Rües, N. and Jones, A. (2016) 'The implementation of earth jurisprudence through substantive constitutional rights of nature', *Sustainability*, 8(2): 1–19.

Rwezaura, B. (1998) 'The duty to hear the child: A view from Tanzania', in N. Welshman (ed) *Law, Culture, Tradition and Children's Rights in Eastern and Southern Africa*, Dartmouth: Ashgate, pp 57–84.

Saavedra, C.M. and Camicia, S.P. (2010) 'Transnational childhoods: Bodies that challenge boundaries', in G.S. Cannella and L. Diaz Soto (eds), *Childhoods: A Handbook*, New York: Peter Lang, pp 27–37.

Sacchi, S. (1994) 'Politische Aktivierung und Protest in Industrieländern – Stille Revolution oder Kolonisierung der Lebenswelt?' *Zeitschrift für Soziologie*, 23(4): 323–38.

Said, E.W. (1978) *Orientalism*, New York: Vintage.

Said, E.W. (1985) 'Orientalism reconsidered', in F. Barker, P. Hulme, M. Iverson and D. Loxley (eds), *Europe and its Others*, Colchester: University of Essex, pp 27–50.

Sall, E. (2002) 'Kindheit in Afrika – Konzepte, Armut und die Entwicklung einer Kinderrechtskultur', in K. Holm and U. Schulz (eds), *Kindheit in Armut weltweit*, Opladen: Leske + Budrich, pp 81–101.

Sánchez Santoyo, H.M. (2003) 'La percepción sobre el niño en el México moderno (1810–1930)', in Y. Corona Caraveo and R.R. Villamil Uriarte (eds), *Tramas. Subjetividad y Procesos Sociales. Diversidad de Infancias*, Mexico City: Universidad Autónoma Metropolitana, Unidad Xochimilco, pp 33–59.

Sandel, M.J. (2007) *The Case against Perfection: Ethics in the Age of Genetic Engineering*, Cambridge, MA and London: The Belknap Press in Harvard University Press.

Sarr, F. (2016) *Afrotopia*, Paris: Philippe Rey.

Sarra, C. (2011a) *Strong and Smart – Towards a Pedagogy for Emancipation: Education for First Peoples*, London and New York: Routledge.

Sarra, C. (2011b) 'Time for a high-expectations relationship between Indigenous and non-Indigenous Australia', https://chrissarra. wordpress.com/2011/10/19/time-for-a-high-expectations-relationship-between-indigenous-and-non-indigenous-australia/

Sarra, C. (2014) 'Beyond victims: The challenge of leadership', *2014 Griffith Review Annual Lecture*, State Library of Queensland, https:// griffithreview.com/wp-content/uploads/Chris-Sarra-Beyond-Victims.pdf

Savyasaachi and Mandel Butler, U. (2014) 'Decolonizing the notion of participation of children and young people', in E.K.M. Tisdall, A.M. Gadda and U. Mandel Butler (eds), *Children and Young People's Participation and Its Transformative Potential. Learning from across Countries*, Basingstoke: Palgrave Macmillan, pp 44–60.

Scheid, D.P. (2016) *The Cosmic Common Good: Religious Grounds for Ecological Ethics*, Oxford and New York: Oxford University Press.

Scheper-Hughes, N. and Sargent, C. (1998) 'Introduction: The cultural politics of childhood', in N. Scheper-Hughes and C. Sargent (eds), *Small Wars: The Cultural Politics of Childhood*, Berkeley: University of California Press, pp 1–33.

Schibotto, G. (2015) 'Saber Colonial, Giro Decolonial e Infancias Múltiples de América Latina', *NATs – Revista Internacional desde los Niños/as y Adolescentes Trabajadores*, XIX(25): 51–68.

Schickhardt, C. (2012) *Kinderethik. Der moralische Status und die Rechte der Kinder*, Münster: Mentis.

Schmitt, C. and Witte, M.D. (2017) '"You are special": Othering in biographies of "GDR children from Namibia"', *Ethnic and Racial Studies*, February, pp 1–18.

Scholz, G. (1994) *Die Konstruktion des Kindes: Über Kinder und Kindheit*, Opladen: Westdeutscher Verlag.

Scott, C. (2002) 'Citizenship education: who pays the piper?', in B. Franklin (ed), *The New Handbook of Children's Rights*, London and New York: Routledge, pp 298–310.

Sen, A. (1999) *Development as Freedom*, Oxford: Oxford University Press.

Senghor, L.S. (1964) *On African Socialism*, New York: Praeger.

Shachar, A. (2009) *The Birthright Lottery: Citizenship and Global Inequality*, Cambridge, MA: Harvard University Press.

Shachar, A. (2014) 'Dangerous liaisons: Money and citizenship', in A. Shachar and R. Bauböck (eds), *Should Citizenship be for sale?* EUI Working Papers RSCAS, 2014/01, pp 3–8.

Shachar, A. and Hirschl, R. (2007) 'Citizenship as inherited property', *Political Theory*, 35(3): 253–87.

Shiffrin, S. (2000) 'Paternalism, unconscionability doctrine, and accommodation', *Philosophy and Public Affaires*, 29: 205–50.

Shizha, E. (2014) 'Rethinking contemporary sub-Saharan African school knowledge: Restoring the indigenous African cultures', *International Journal for Cross-Disciplinary Subjects in Education (IJCDSE)*, 4(1): 1870–78.

Skidmore, P. (2012) *Marjorie – To Afraid to Cry: A Home Child Experience*, Toronto: Dundurn.

Smallwood, G. (2015) *Indigenous Critical Realism. Human Rights and the First Australians' Wellbeing*, Abingdon and New York: Routledge.

Smith, A.-M. (2007) 'The children of Loxicha, Mexico: Exploring ideas of childhood and the rules of participation', *Children, Youth and Environments*, 17(2): 33–55.

Smith, K. (2010) 'Gramsci at the margins: subjectivity and subalternity in a theory of hegemony', *International Gramsci Journal*, 1(2): 39–50.

Smith, N., Lister R., Middleton, S. and Cox, L. (2005) 'Young people as real citizens: towards an inclusionary understanding of citizenship', *Journal of Youth Studies*, 8(4): 425–43.

Solinger, R. (2002) *Beggars and Choosers: How the Politics of Choice Shapes Adoption, Abortion and Welfare in the United States*, New York: Hill and Wang.

Solinger, R. (2013) *Reproductive Politics*, Oxford and New York: Oxford University Press.

Sommerville, C.J. (1982) *The Rise and Fall of Childhood*, Los Angeles: Sage.

Sorgner, S.L. (2015) 'The future of education: Genetic enhancement and metahumanities', *Journal of Evolution and Technology*, 25: 31–48.

Soysal, Y.N. (1994) *Limits of Citizenship: Migrants and Postnational Membership in Europe*, Chicago: The University of Chicago Press.

Spivak, G.C. (1985) 'The Rani of Sirmur: an essay in reading the archives', *History and Theory*, 24(3): 247–72.

Spivak, G.C. (1988) 'Can the subaltern speak?', in C. Nelson and L. Grossberg (eds), *Marxism and the Interpretation of Culture*, Urbana, IL: University of Illinois Press, pp 66–111.

Spivak, G.C. (1990) *The Post-Colonial Critique. Interviews, Strategies, Dialogues*, edited by S. Harsym, New York and London: Routledge.

Spivak, G.C. (1999) *A Critique of Postcolonial Reason*, Cambridge, MA: Harvard University Press.

Spivak, G.C. (2004) 'Righting wrongs', *South Atlantic Quarterly*, 103(2/3): 523–81.

Spivak, G.C. (2008) *Other Asias*, Malden, MA and Oxford: Blackwell.

Spyrou, S. (2018) *Disclosing Childhoods: Research and Knowledge Production for a Critical Childhood Studies*, Basingstoke: Palgrave Macmillan.

Squires, P. (ed) (2008) *ASBO Nation: The Criminalisation of Nuisance*, Bristol: Policy Press.

Stainton Rogers, W. (2004) 'Promoting better childhoods: constructions of child concern', in M.J. Kehily (ed), *An Introduction to Childhood Studies*, Maidenhead: Open University Press, pp 125–44.

Stammers, N. (2009) *Human Rights and Social Movements*, London and New York: Pluto Press.

Stammers, N. (2013) 'Children's rights and social movements' reflections from a cognate field', in K. Hanson and O. Nieuwenhuys (eds), *Reconceptualizing Children's Rights in International Development: Living Rights, Social Justice, Translations*, New York and Cambridge: Cambridge University Press, pp 275–92.

Stearns, P.N. (2005) *Growing Up. The History of Childhood in a Global Context*, Waco, TX: Baylor University Press.

Stearns, P.N. (2006) *Childhood in World History*, New York and London: Routledge.

Stephens, S. (ed) (1995) *Children and the Politics of Culture*, Princeton, NJ: Princeton University Press.

Stephens, S. (2012) 'Children and the politics of culture in "late capitalism"', in H. Morrison (ed), *The Global History of Childhood Reader*, London and New York: Routledge, pp 375–93.

Stern, J. (2011) 'Ius Pecuniae – Staatsbürgerschaft zwischen ausreichendem Lebensunterhalt, Mindestsicherung und Menschenwürde', in J. Dahlvik, H. Fassmann and W. Sievers (eds), *Migration und Integration – wissenschaftliche Perspektiven aus Österreich, Jahrbuch 1/2011*, Vienna and Göttingen: Vienna University Press.

Stoecklin, D. and Fattore, T. (2018) 'Children's multidimensional agency: Insights into the structuration of choice', *Childhood*, 25(1): 47–62.

Stoecklin, D. (2013) 'Theories of action in the field of child participation: In search of explicit frameworks', *Childhood*, 20(4): 443–57.

Street, B.V. (ed) (2001) *Literacy and Development: Ethnographic perspectives*, London and New York: Routledge.

Sunstein, C.R. and Thaler, R.H. (2008) *Nudge: Improving Decisions about Health, Wealth and Happiness*, New Haven, CT: Yale University Press.

Sutterlüty, F. and Tisdall, E.K.M. (2019) 'Agency, autonomy and self-determination: Questioning key concepts of childhood studies', *Global Studies of Childhood*, 9(3): 182–7.

Syria Revolt (2013) 'Air Strike While a Young Syrian Girl Sings for Freedom' (Video), 19 December, www.youtube.com/watch?v=NLfRkLMchcY

Taft, J.K. (2019) *The Kids Are in Charge: Activism and Power in Peru's Movement of Working Children*, New York: New York University Press.

Tai, T.V. (1988) *The Vietnamese Tradition of Human Rights*, Berkeley, CA: Institute of East Asian Studies, University of California.

Tai, T.V. (2004–05) 'Buddhism and human rights in traditional Vietnam', *Review of Vietnamese Studies 2004–05*, http://hmongstudies.org/TaVanTaiBUDDHISM_AND_HUMAN_RIGHTS.pdf

Tamanaha, B.Z. (2011) 'A vision of social-legal change: Rescuing Ehrlich from "living law"', *Law and Social Inquiry*, 36(1): 297–318.

Taylor, G. (2016) 'The Fire within Syria tire burning' (video), 14 September, www.youtube.com/watch?v=MsQnfSzBqck

terre des hommes (ed) (2014) *Convención de los Derechos del Niño (CDN). Cultura Andino-Amazónica y Buen Vivir. Auditoría a la CDN desde la Mirada de los Niños y Niñas Indígenas*, Lima: Plataforma peruana de co-partes de terre des hommes – Alemania.

Thiong'o, N. (1986) *Decolonising the Mind: The Politics of Language in African Literature*, London: James Currey.

Thomas, N. (2007) 'Towards a theory of children's participation', *International Journal of Children's Rights*, 15: 1–20.

Tisdall, E.K.M. and Punch, S. (2012) 'Not so "new"? Looking critically at childhood studies', *Children's Geographies*, 10(3): 249–64.

Tolfree, D. (2004) *Whose Children? Separated Children's Protection and Participation in Emergencies*, Stockholm: Save the Children Sweden.

Tomberg, F. (2003) *Habermas und der Marxismus. Zur Aktualität einer Rekonstruktion des historischen Materialismus*, Würzburg: Königshausen & Neumann.

TRCC (2012) *Truth and Reconciliation Commission of Canada: Interim Report*, Winnipeg, Manitoba, www.falconers.ca/wp-content/uploads/2015/07/TRC-Interim-Report.pdf

TRCC (2015) *Honouring the Truth, Reconciling for the Future: Summary of the Final Report of the Truth and Reconciliation Commission of Canada*, Winnipeg, Manitoba, www.trc.ca/assets/pdf/Honouring_the_Truth_Reconciling_for_the_Future_July_23_2015.pdf

Trouillot, M.-R. (1995) 'A unthinkable history: The Haitian revolution as a non-event', in M.-R. Trouillot, *Silencing the Past: Power and the Production of History*, Boston: Beacon Press, pp 70–107.

Twum-Danso, A. (2005) 'The political child', in A. McIntyre (ed), *Invisible Stakeholders: Children and War in Africa*, Pretoria: Institute for Security Studies, pp 7–30.

Twum-Danso Imoh, A., Bourdillon, M. and Meichsner, S. (eds) *Global Childhoods beyond the North-South Divide*, Cham: Palgrave Macmillan/ Springer Nature Switzerland.

UN (2015) *Transforming our World: The 2030 Agenda for Sustainable Development*, New York: United Nations, https:// sustainabledevelopment.un.org/content/documents/21252030%20 Agenda%20for%20Sustainable%20Development%20web.pdf

UNDP (1999) *Human Development Report 1999*, published for the United Nations Development Programme, New York and Oxford: Oxford University Press.

UNICEF (2002) *State of the World's Children 2003*, New York: UNICEF.

UNICEF (2005) *The State of the World's Children 2005: Childhood under Threat*, New York: UNICEF.

UNICEF (2006) *Zur Situation der Kinder in der Welt 2006. Kinder ohne Kindheit*, Frankfurt/M.: Fischer.

UNICEF (2014) *UNICEF Report 2014. Jedes Kind hat Rechte. Mit allen Daten zur Situation der Kinder in der Welt*, Frankfurt/M.: Fischer.

UNICEF (2016a) *The State of the World's Children 2016: A Fair Chance for Every Child*, New York: UNICEF.

UNICEF (2016b) *Clear the Air for Children: The impact of Air Pollution on Children*, New York: UNICEF.

Valentine, K. (2011) 'Accounting for agency', *Children & Society*, 25(5): 347–58.

Valentine, K. and Meinert, L. (2009) 'The adult North and the young South: Reflections on the civilizing mission of children's rights', *Anthropology Today*, 25(3): 23–8.

Van Breda, A.D. (2010) 'The phenomenon and concerns of child-headed households in South Africa', in M. Liebel and R. Lutz (eds), *Sozialarbeit des Südens, Band 3: Kindheiten und Kinderrechte*, Oldenburg: Paulo Freire Verlag, pp 259–79.

Van Daalen, E., Hanson, K. and Nieuwenhuys, O. (2016) 'Children's rights as living rights. The case of street children and a new law in Yogyakarta, Indonesia', *International Journal of Children's Rights*, 24: 803–25.

Van Daalen, E. and Mabillard, N. (2019) 'Human rights in translation: Bolivia's law 584, working children's movements, and the global child labour regime', *The International Journal of Human Rights*, 26(4): 596–614.

Vandenhole, W. (2012) 'Localizing the human rights of children', in M. Liebel (eds), *Children's Rights from Below: Cross-Cultural Perspectives*, Basingstoke: Palgrave Macmillan, pp 80–93.

Vandenhole, W., Desmet, E., Reynaert, D. and Lembrechts, S. (eds) (2015) *Routledge International Handbook of Children's Rights Studies*, London and New York: Routledge.

Vinyamata i Camp, E. and Benavides Vanegas, F.S. (eds) (2011) *El largo camino hacia la paz. Procesos e iniciativas de paz en Colombia y Ecuador*, Barcelona: Editorial UOC.

Vittachi, A. (1989) *Stolen Childhood: In Search of the Rights of the Child*, Cambridge: Polity Press.

Von Werlhof, C., Mies, M. and Bennholdt-Thomsen, V. (1988): *Frauen – die letzte Kolonie. Zur Hausfrauisierung der Arbeit*, Hamburg: Rowohlt.

Wagner, C.M., Lyimo, E.D. and Lwendo, S. (2012) 'Matches but not fire: Street children in Dar es Salaam, Tanzania', in M.O. Ensor (ed), *African Childhoods: Education, Development, Peacebuilding, and the Youngest Continent*, New York: Palgrave Macmillan, pp 33–46.

Wagnleitner, R. (1994) *Coca-Colonization and the Cold War*, Chapel Hill, NC: University of North Carolina Press.

Wallace, J.-A. (1994) 'De-scribing *The Water Babies*: the child in postcolonial theory', in C. Tiffin and A. Lawson (eds), *De-scribing Empire*, London and New York: Routledge, pp 171–84.

Wallerstein, Immanuel (2006) *European Universalism: The Rhetoric of Power*, New York and London: The New Press.

Walsh, C. (2007) 'Interculturalidad y Colonialidad del Poder. Un pensamiento y posicionamiento "otro" desde la diferencia colonial', in S. Castro-Gómez and R. Grosfoguel (eds), *El giro decolonial. Reflexiones para una diversidad epistémica más allá del capitalismo global*, Bogotá: Siglo del hombre editores, pp 47–62.

Walsh, C. (2010) 'Development as Buen Vivir', *Development*, 53(1): 15–21.

Warren, A. (1998) 'The orphan train.' *The Washington Post*, November, www.washingtonpost.com/wp-srv/national/horizon/nov98/orphan.htm

Weaver, K.K. (2006) ' "She made to crush the child's fragile skull": Disease, infanticide, and enslaved women in 18th-century Saint-Domingue', in B.H. Bechtold and D. Cooper Graves (eds), *Killing Infants: Studies in the Worldwide Practice of Infanticide*, Lewiston, NY, Queenston, Ontario and Lampeter, Wales: The Edwin Mellen Press, pp 25–44.

Webber, J. (2006) 'Legal pluralism and human agency', *Osgoode Hall Law Journal*, 44(1): 167–98.

Weber, M. ([1921/22]2013) *Economy and Society: An Outline of Interpretive Sociology*, Berkeley, CA: University of California Press.

Weisner, T.S. (1997) 'Support for children and the African family crisis', in T.S. Weisner, C. Bradley and C.P. Kilbride (eds), *African Families and the Crisis of Social Change*, Westport, CT: Bergin and Garvey, pp 22–44.

Wells, K. (2009) *Childhood in a Global Perspective*, Cambridge and Malden, MA: Polity Press.

Wessels, M. and Kostelny. K. (2017) 'Child rights and practitioner wrongs: Lessons from interagency research', in M.D. Ruck, M. Peterson-Badali and M. Freeman (eds), *Handbook of Children's Rights*, New York and London: Routledge, pp 579–96.

White, M.D. (2013) *The Manipulation of Choice. Ethics and Libertarian Paternalism*, New York: Palgrave Macmillan.

Wihstutz, A. (2016) 'Children's agency: contributions from feminist and ethic of care theories to sociology of childhood', in F. Esser, M.-S. Baader, T. Betz and B. Hungerland (eds), *Reconceptualising Agency and Childhood: New Perspectives in Childhood Studies*, London and New York: Routledge, pp 61–74.

Winn, M. (1984) *Children without Childhood*, Harmondsworth: Penguin.

Wiredu, K. (1996) *Cultural Universals and Particulars: An African Perspective*, Bloomington: Indiana University Press.

Wohlgemuth, L. and Sall, E. (eds) (2006) *Human Rights, Regionalism and the Dilemmas of Democracy in Africa*, Dakar: CODESRIA.

Woldeslase, W., Berhe, M. and Belay, A. (2002) *Pilot Study on Indigenous Knowledge on Child Care in Eritrea*. Asmara.

Wolf, A. (2010) 'Geschwisterliche Bande: Zugehörigkeit, Verwandtschaft und Verbundenheit von Kindern in Waisenhaushalten im Kontext von AIDS in Malawi', in M. Liebel and R. Lutz (eds), *Sozialarbeit des Südens, Band 3: Kindheiten und Kinderrechte*, Oldenburg: Paulo Freire Verlag, pp 185–202.

Wolf, J.-C. (2006) 'Die liberale Paternalismus-Kritik von John Stuart Mill', in M. Anderheiden, H.M. Heinig, S. Kirste and K. Seelmann (eds), *Paternalismus und Recht. In Memoriam Angela Augustin (1968–2004)*, Tübingen: Mohr Siebeck, pp 55–68.

Wyness, M. (2015) *Childhood*, Cambridge and Malden, MA: Polity.

Wyness, M., Harrison, L. and Buchanan, I. (2004) 'Childhood, politics and ambiguity: Towards an agenda for children's political inclusion', *Sociology*, 38(1): 81–99.

Young Lives (2016) *Towards a Better Future? Hopes and Fears from Young Lives*, Oxford: Young Lives.

Young, I. (1989) 'Polity and group difference: A critique of the ideal o universal citizenship', *Ethics*, 99: 250–74.

Young, R. (1980) 'In the interests of children and adolescents', in W. Aiken and H. LaFollette (eds), *Whose Child? – Children's Rights. Parental Authority and State Power*, Totowa, NJ: Rowman and Littlefield, pp 177–98.

Young, R.J.C. (2003) *Postcolonialism: A Very Short Introduction*, Oxford: Oxford University Press.

Zeiher, H.J. and Zeiher, H. (1994) *Orte und Zeiten der Kinder. Soziales Leben im Alltag von Großstadtkindern*, Weinheim and Munich: Juventa.

Zemelman, H. (2007) *El Ángel de la Historia: Determinación y Autonomía de la Condición Humana*, Barcelona: Anthropos.

Zemelman, H. (2009) *Pensar Teórico y Pensar Epistémico: Los Retos de las Ciencias Sociales Latinoamericanas*, Mexico City: IPECAL.

Zimba, R.F. (2002) 'Indigenous conceptions of childhood development and social realities in southern Africa', in H. Keller, Y.P. Poortinga and A. Scholmerish (eds), *Between Cultures and Biology: Perspectives on Ontogenic Development*, Cambridge: Cambridge University Press, pp 89–115.

Zude, H.U. (2010) *Paternalismus. Fallstudien zur Genese des Begriffs*, Freiburg: Alber.

Index

Note: The abbreviation 't' refers to a table.

A

Abebe, T. 108
Acosta, Alberto 55
Actor-Network-Theory 25
Adichie, Chimamanda Ngozi 99, 105
Adick, C. 106
Adorno, T.W. 132
adulthood 11, 12t 13, 15
  separation of childhood from *v*, 13,
    14, 23–4, 34, 38, 48–50, 118,
    137, 180–1
  see also paternalism
adultism/adult-centrism 136, 154, 157,
  164, 167, 175
advocacy 56, 123, 127, 146, 154, 188
Africa 2, 19, 26, 34, 67, 99–100, 123
  children's rights 108–17, 123,
    131, 209
  civilization and 59, 60, 62
  contribution to postcolonial
    theory 59–63
  education and childcare 100–8
  paternalism and children's
    participation 117–22
African Charter of the Rights and
  Welfare of the Child 123
African Movement of Working
  Children and Youth
  (AMWCY) 219
agency 108, 123, 187, 191
  children's rights 137, 141, 153,
    157, 192
  postcolonialism 5, 9, 11, 13,
    17, 23–30
Alderson, Priscilla 26, 204
Aldridge, J. 202
AMWCY *see* African Movement of
  Working Children and Youth
anticolonialism 42, 55, 58, 59, 61, 64,
  102, 140, 198
antisocial behaviour 95–6, 209
Arendt, Hannah 132, 194
Arewa, A. 100
Ariès, Philippe 24, 45
Ashcroft, Bill 36–7, 37–8, 40, 42, 70
Asia 19, 22
Atkinson-Sheppard, Sally 27–8
Australia 6, 77, 78, 80, 81–2, 84,
  139, 141
authoritarianism 54, 68, 163

autonomy 11, 12, 23, 25, 49–50, 51,
  205, 207
  paternalism 165, 171, 175, 178,
    181–4, 188
Azri, Khairul 191

B

Balagopalan, Sarada 70–1, 143–5, 146
Bangladesh 27–38, 211
Barber, C.L. 39
Barnardo's Believe in Children 79
Barnett, Michael N. 133, 161
Becker, S. 202
Bell, Avril 85
Benin 110–11
Bennholdt-Thomsen, Veronika 44
best interest principle 138–42, 154–5,
  162, 176, 177, 188
Bhabha, Homi K. 58
The Black Atlantic (Gilroy) 57–8
Black Skin. White Masks
  (Fanon) 33, 57
Boatcă, M. 194
Bolivia 150–2
Bordonaro, Lorenzo 17, 27
Boyden, Jo 110–11
Brazil 90
Bringing Them Home Report
  (1997) 84
British Empire 6, 78, 79–80, 81
Brock-Utne, Ute 108
Buckingham, David 15
Burke, Ronald 140, 141
Burr, Rachel 142–3

C

Cabrerizo Sanz, L. 178
Camicia, Steven 23
Canada 6, 78, 80, 81, 82, 83, 84–5
Cannella, Gaile S. 47–9, 70
Capability Approach 25
capitalist world market *see* globalization
Caribbean 20, 59, 64
Carneiro, Sueli 91
CASAS *see* Centre for Advanced
  Studies of African Society
Castro Varela, Maria do Mar 35
Castro-Gómez, S. 65
Centre for Advanced Studies of African
  Society (CASAS) 106

Centre for HIV/ AIDS Networking
(HIVAN) (South Africa) 112
Césaire, Aimé 59
Chakrabarty, Dipesh 69
Chandler, David 133
Cheney, Kristen 10, 11
child ethics 171, 172, 173
child labour *see* working children
child movement *see* migration
child neglect 82, 84, 97, 139
child protagonism 29, 180–8, 189
child protection 6, 13, 48, 50, 77, 80,
91, 120, 165
children's rights 28, 135, 149,
152, 156
citizenship 200, 201, 207
paternalism and participation 170,
173, 175–80, 184, 188, 189
Child Welfare Act (1925) (New
Zealand) 82
child-headed households 28, 113–14,
115, 116–17, 123
childcare 25, 27, 28, 100–8,
139, 166–7
'Children in adult roles' (UNICEF) 13
children and childhoods 1, 2–3, 4, 10,
15, 18, 20, 92
citizenship and 198–207
concept/history of 33–4, 37–8, 48
modern conception of 11, 12t, 13,
23, 137
separation from adulthood v 13,
14, 23–4, 34, 38, 48–50, 118,
137, 180–1
as 'victims' 2, 27–8, 110–11, 113,
122, 130, 147
children on the move *see* migration
Children and Young Persons Act (1974)
(New Zealand) 82
Children and Young Persons
Amendment Act (1983) (New
Zealand) 85
Children's and Adolescents' Code
(*Código Niña, Niñoy Adolescente*)
(Bolivia) 151–2
children's movements 6, 123, 178, 179,
190, 207–12, 218
children's rights 6, 10, 16–17, 49, 86,
97, 185
'Children's Rights: Some feminist
approaches to the United Nations
Convention on the Rights of the
Child' (Olsen) 127
children's rights
Africa 108–17, 123, 131, 209
agency 137, 141, 153, 157, 192
ambivalences of human rights 129–34

case studies on dilemmas of 142–52
citizenship 200, 201, 208–10, 212
exploitation 131, 150, 156, 220
human dignity 131, 133, 134, 145,
151, 152, 153, 154, 155–6
indigenous people 139, 140,
141–2, 151
inequality 132–3, 134, 135, 147–52,
153–4, 156, 157
minimalist/maximalist understanding
of 153–4
paternalism 133, 136, 153, 154, 155,
156, 170–5, 181–2
postcolonialism and 127–9, 155–8,
217–18, 221
poverty 137, 153–4, 156
social responsibility 137, 143, 154,
156, 185, 192
universality and cultural
relativism 128, 135–42, 154
working children 151, 152, 211,
211–12, 219, 221
world order 132, 133–4, 135,
155, 156
Chile 88, 94–5
chronological age 50–1, 88, 118,
136–8, 155, 192
paternalism 174, 184–5, 186
citizenship 6, 77, 132, 179, 190
ambivalences/contradictions of 193–6
children and 198–207
children's movements in Global
South 207–12, 218
'citizenship from
below' 191–3, 205–7
inequality 193, 195, 208
liberal/republican citizenship 196–8
poverty 195, 201, 202, 208, 209
Civil and Political Covenant
(1966) 131
civilization 3, 6, 10, 136, 140
Africa and 59, 60, 62
colonialization and 36, 37–8, 47
'illegitimate' children 6, 89–94
indigenous/'irregular' children 80,
81, 94–6
race and racism and 87–9, 94–6
Coca-Colaization 18
Cockburn, Tom 199–200, 205
colonial languages 39, 62, 63, 64,
69–70, 105–6
*The Coloniality of Knowledge.
Eurocentrism and Social Sciences.
Latin American Perspectives*
(Lander) 65
colonialization 1, 4, 5–6, 13, 16, 17,
33, 43–8, 65–6

as a childhood project 36–9
civilization and 36, 37–8, 47
decolonization of childhoods 49–51
definition of 34–5
dialectic of education and
power 40–3
Committee on the Rights of the Child
(United Nations) 135
communitarianism 22, 28, 59, 60, 65,
139, 186, 197
education and childcare 101–3,
107–8, 114, 118–19, 121–2
conceptual decolonization 61, 62–3
conquest
colonialism v 4, 5, 21, 34, 36, 37, 39,
40, 43, 47
postcolonialism 54, 65, 66, 78–80,
87
Convention on the Rights of
the Child *see* United Nations
Convention on the Rights of
the Child
Corona Caraveo, Yolanda 96
Coronil, Fernando 53
Cregan, Kate 21–2
Critique de la Raison Nègre
(Mbembe) 60
Crow Dog, Mary 83
cultural traditions and
networks 80–5, 122
children's rights 128, 135–42, 154,
156, 157
postcolonialism 55, 58, 59, 60, 62
Cussiánovich, Alejandro 70
Cuthbert, Denise 21–2

D

Darian Smith, Kate 81
Darwin, Charles 89
Das Kapital (Marx) 87
Davies, Matthew 111
De Sousa Santos, Boaventura 67, 70
de Weert, Sebald 88
'de-centre-ing': children's rights
128–9
Dean, Carolyn 88
*The Decolonial Turn. Reflections on an
Epistemic Diversity beyond Global
Capitalism* (Castro-Gómez and
Grosfoguel) 65
decolonization 4–5, 10, 11, 35,
49–51, 182
Africa 59, 61, 62
Latin America 63, 65, 67
Dembour, Marie-Benedicte 139–40
dependency 51, 53, 80, 120, 146, 165
citizenship 200, 204, 207

postcolonialism 12, 13, 14, 15,
17, 18, 25
deportation of children 78–80
Descartes, René 29
development psychology 24–5, 39, 41,
46–7, 47–8, 49, 184
developmentalism (economic) 40–1,
62, 82, 85
children's rights 184, 195, 217
colonialism 10, 11, 17, 18, 20, 28
education and childcare 100,
132, 133
postcolonialism 54–5, 64, 67, 68
Dictionary of Authorities (*Diccionario
de Autoridades*) (Royal Spanish
Academy) 92
digital communication
technologies 14–15, 16, 22, 40, 43,
140, 210
domination 22, 82, 88, 206
colonialism 35, 37, 39, 40
postcolonial theories 55, 59, 62, 64,
65–6, 130, 135
Du Bois, W.E.B. 57
Dussel, Enrique 67–8, 69
Dworkin, Ronald 162

E

Eboussi Boulaga, Fabien 61–2
ecology of knowledge (*ecología de
saberes*) 67
Economic, Social and Cultural Rights
Covenant (1966) 131
Ecuador 194
Edmonds, Ruth 28–9
Educación Popular 41
education 50–1, 70–1, 81, 83, 95,
154, 156
Africa 100–8, 219–20
colonialism 14, 15, 16, 22, 34, 37–9
communitarianism 101–3, 107–8,
114, 118–19, 121–2
dialectic of power and 40–3
families 101–3, 104, 107
participation 107–8, 117–22, 123,
201, 203
paternalism 168, 178–9, 181
power relations and structures 40–3,
109–10, 120–1, 122
Egypt 128–9, 191
'Elephants in the Americas? Latin
American Postcolonial Studies
and Global Decolonization'
(Coronil) 53
Emile, or on education
(Rousseau) 37, 38
equal citizenship 199–202

Eritrea 121–2
Die Eroberung des Kindes durch die Wissenschaft. Aus der Geschichte der Disziplinierung ('The conquest of the child by science: From the history of discipline') (Gstettner) 46–7, 49
Escobar, Arturo 56
Essay Concerning Human Understanding (Locke) 37, 38
Eurocentric-Western-bourgeois
  childhood pattern 27, 59, 88, 153
  children's rights 127–8, 135–6, 138, 139, 140, 141–2, 151, 154, 182
  dominant understanding of childhood 1, 4, 5, 13, 14, 15, 16–17, 23, 85
  education in Africa 100–8, 109, 110, 118, 122
  limitations of 9, 11, 12t, 13–15
  model for development of 'traditional' societies 54–5, 64, 67, 68, 82, 85, 184
  postcolonialism 34, 36, 37, 43, 47, 49, 50
European Enlightenment 4, 37, 47, 49, 65, 66, 69, 127, 131, 132
European Union 21, 134, 197, 201
exclusion 6, 38, 62, 68, 78, 91, 119
  children's rights 141, 150, 157, 179, 185, 202, 208
exploitation 14, 46, 50, 51, 88, 105, 110
  children's rights 131, 150, 156, 220
  world resources 44, 55, 87, 109, 134
Eze, Emmanuel Chukwudi 59, 61

F

Fafunwa, A.B. 106–7
Fairbridge Society 79
families *v*, 16, 17, 19–20, 22, 23, 34
  education/childcare 101–3, 104, 107
  racism and 90, 91, 92, 93–4, 95
  state violence 81–3, 85
The Famished Road (Okri) 9
Fanon, Frantz 33, 57
Fattore, Tobia 25
Female Genital Mutilation (FGM) 141, 156
FGM *see* Female Genital Mutilation
Final Report of the Modernising Child, Youth and Family Panel (Ministry of Social Development) (New Zealand) 85
Firestone, Shulamith 14, 24, 44–5
Fitz-Roy, Captain Robert 88–9
France 57, 59, 131–2
Franklin, Bob 11–12, 118

Freire, Paulo 70
The Future of Science (Renan) 37

G

Galeano, Eduardo 64
Gallagher, Michael 27
Gankam Tambo, Ina 107–8
Gargallo, Francesca 90, 91
Geneva Declaration on the Rights of the Child (1924) 170
genocide 78, 82, 94, 115
Gerakan Kaum Jalanan Merdeka (independent street movement) (Indonesia) 148
Ghana 26, 111–12, 120
Giese, Sonja 113
Gilliam, Ángela 91
Gilroy, Paul 57–8
global childhood 15–23
global justice 63, 132–4
Global North 63, 104, 122, 130, 135
  colonialism 2, 3, 5, 9, 18, 21–2, 23
Global South 55, 109, 130, 132
  agency of children 23–7, 202
  children's movements in 207–12
  colonialism 2, 5, 6, 9, 11, 20, 21–2
  globalization 5, 156, 193, 217
  education and 103, 104, 105, 109
  postcolonialism 15–23, 39, 40, 61, 66
González Contró, Mónica 171–2, 175, 189
good childhood 5, 11, 16
Gottlieb, Alma 103
Graf, Gunter 171
Gramsci, Antonio 208
Grohs, Gerhard 102
Grosfoguel, R. 65
Grunert, F. 164
Gstettner, Peter 46–7, 49
Guha, Ranajit 63

H

Habermas, Jürgen 43–4
Haebich, Anna 81–2
Half of a Yellow Sun (Adichie) 99
Hall, Stuart 54
Happy Education (Korczak) 169
Hegel, G.W.F. 99
Heidenreich, Felix 133, 134
Henderson, Patricia 112–13
Hengst, Heinz 15
Herriger, N. 203–4
HIV/ AIDS 112–13, 114
HIVAN *see* Centre for HIV/ AIDS Networking (HIVAN) (South Africa)

Horkheimer, M. 132
Hountondji, Paulin 62
How to Love a Child (Korczak) 167
Howard, Neil 110–11
Huijsmans, Roy 128–9
Human Development Report *see*
    United Nations Human
    Development Report (UNDP)
human dignity iv 86, 97, 112, 120,
    162–3, 172, 220, 221
  children's rights 131, 133, 134, 145,
    151, 152, 153, 154, 155–6
  human rights 129–34, 135, 136, 138,
    140, 142, 157, 192, 193
*Human Rights of Children: A Proposal
    for Grounds* (González
    Contró) 171–2
Human Rights Commission (New
    Zealand) 85

I

'illegitimate' children 6, 89–94
ILO *see* International Labour
    Organization
IMF *see* International Monetary Fund
income and wealth distribution 18, 20,
    195, 198
independent national states 21, 55,
    66–7, 87, 91, 196
India 71, 128–9, 143–7
Indian Child Welfare Act (1978) 84
indigenous people 62, 87, 88,
    210, 212
  children's rights 139, 140, 141–2, 151
  civilization of children 94–6
  paternalism 184–5, 186–7
  removal/assimilation of
    children 78, 80–5
Indonesia 147–50
inequality 5, 6, 42, 50, 85, 175, 189
  children's rights 132–3, 134, 135,
    147–52, 153–4, 156, 157
  citizenship 193, 195, 208
  global childhood and 15–23
  postcolonialism and 10, 15–23, 55,
    58, 217
infantalization v 38, 39, 48, 87–8, 118,
    136, 137
inferiority 11, 45, 48, 83, 199
  paternalism 164, 165, 166, 167, 169,
    185, 188
  postcolonialism 53, 57, 66
INGOs *see* International Non-
    Governmental Organizations
Institut für Sozialforschung 183
intergenerational relations 25, 28,
    119–20, 177, 184–5, 194

International Labour Organization
    (ILO) 110, 151
International Monetary Fund
    (IMF) 21, 65, 132
International Non-Governmental
    Organizations (INGOs) 130
international relief organizations 39,
    79, 109–10, 133, 142, 143–5, 147
The Invention of Africa (Mudimbe) 33
Invernizzi, A. 199
invisibility 2, 21, 24, 103, 122,
    217, 218
  postcolonialism 51, 65, 67, 68, 70,
    217, 218
'irregular' children 94–6

K

Kakuru, Doris 113–14
Katz, Cindi 22
Kendrick, Maureen 113–14
Kenya 26, 102, 111
Kerner, Ina 66
Ki-Zerbo, Joseph 104
Kinderöffentlichkeit (children's
    public) 206–7
Klocker, Natascha 26
knowledge production and
    retention 10, 11, 22, 23, 41,
    48, 105
  postcolonialism 62, 65, 67, 70
Korczak, Janusz 167, 168–9, 170

L

labour markets *see* working children
Lander, Edgardo 65
language *see* colonial languages
Latin America 6, 20, 26, 42, 87–8, 97,
    196, 209
  civilization of indigenous/'irregular'
    children 94–6
  contribution to postcolonial
    theory 63–8
  racism and 'illegitimate'
    children 89–94
Latin American Subaltern Studies
    Group 63–4, 65
Latour, Bruno 25
*Law on Child Protection, Care, and
    Education* (1991) (UNICEF) 142–3
Law on the Protection of Children
    Living on the Street (2011)
    (Indonesia) 148–9
legal paternalism 164–5, 166, 167,
    172, 189
Lehmann, T. 168
Levinas, Emmanuel 68
liberal citizenship 196–8, 201

liberation movements 42–3, 55, 58, 59, 61, 64–5, 68, 102, 140, 198
life expectancy 18–20, 85, 92
Lister, Ruth 199, 204–5
living rights 128, 149, 150, 153
The Location of Culture (Bhabha) 58
Locke, John 37, 38
Loomba, Ania 56

M

McDonaldization 18
majority world see Global North
Malawi 116–17
Mandel Butler, U. 182
Mapuche people 94–5
marginalization 5, 6, 34, 57, 65, 77, 82, 96, 185
  children's rights 147, 150, 157
  citizenship 198, 199–200, 202, 212
  education and childcare 113, 114, 123
Mariátegui, José Carlos 64
Marshall, Thomas H. 199–200, 200–1
Martínez Muñoz, M. 178
Marx, Karl 87
Masferrer León, Cristina 92
maturity 23, 38, 39, 77, 136, 169, 171, 181, 192
Mbembe, Achille 60
Mehta, Uday Singh 38
Meintjes, Helen 113
Mendel, Gérard 46, 47
Menke, C. 127
mestizo children 90
Mexico 26–7, 64, 95–6, 186–8
Middle East 26
Mies, Maria 44
Mignolo, Walter 56, 64, 66, 195
migration 5, 22–3, 27, 87, 194, 195
  deportation of children 78–80
  education and childcare 109, 110, 112, 117, 123
Milanich, Nara 89–90, 91, 93
Mill, John Stuart 163–4
Milne, B. 199
Ministry of Education (New Zealand) 85
Ministry of Social Development (New Zealand) 85
minority world see Global South
Mizen, Phillip 111–12
modernity and modernization
  history of childhood and 33–4
  "Western" narrative 2, 3, 10, 54–5, 60, 64, 67, 68, 69, 83
  'Modernity/ Coloniality' (*modernidad/ colonialidad*) 65, 66

moral rights 172–3
Moscow Declaration on the Rights of the Child (1918) 170
Moses, Dirk 83
Mudimbe, V.Y. 33
multidimensional agency 25
Mutua, Makau 130–1

N

Nandy, Ashis 36
nation states 6, 54, 77, 79, 82, 133
  citizenship 192, 193, 194, 195, 196, 203
  independence and 21, 55, 66–7, 87, 91, 196
Négritude 59–60
Negt, Oskar 206
neo-Zapatist movement 64
Nestvogel, Renate 107
New Childhood Studies 12
New Zealand 6, 78, 80, 82, 85
Nieuwenhuys, Olga 9, 10, 11, 24
Nigeria 107–8
Nkrumah, Kwame 61
Nsamenang, Bame 100–2

O

Odera Oruka, Henry 60, 70, 133
Ofosu-Kusi, Yaw 111–12
Okri, Ben 9
Olsen, Frances 127
On Liberty (Mill) 163
On Postcolonial Futures (Ashcroft) 36–7, 37–8, 40, 42, 70
Open Veins of Latin America (Galeano) 64
oppression 6, 14, 24, 42, 45, 77, 208, 217
  postcolonialism and 53, 55, 62, 65
Orientalism (Said) 56, 64, 130
orphans 79, 110, 112, 113, 114, 117
Osterhammel, J. 34–5
Oswell, David 28
Our Schooling Futures: Stronger Together Report (Ministry of Education) (New Zealand) 85
'outside childhood' 21–2
Oxfam 21

P

Palestine 27, 42
Pan-Africanism 59, 61
Pan-American Child Congresses 96
parentalism/parentification 139, 164
participation 155, 156, 169
  citizenship and 191, 192, 193, 196, 203, 205, 208, 209, 210

education 107–8, 117–22, 123
paternalism and child
    protection 175–80
paternalism and
    protagonism 180–8, 189
passivity 13, 51, 111, 113, 197–8
paternalism 3, 6, 13, 38, 42, 51
    Africa 109–10, 117–22
    against children 166–70
    autonomy 165, 171, 175, 178,
        181–4, 188
    beyond paternalism 188–90, 217–21
    child protection and
        participation 175–80, 189
    children's rights 133, 136, 153, 154,
        155, 156, 170–5, 181–2
    chronological age 174, 184–5, 186
    indigenous people 184–5, 186–7
    inferiority 164, 165, 166, 167, 169,
        185, 188
    participation and
        protagonism 180–8, 189
    social responsibility 176–7, 177–8,
        186, 187, 188
    understanding 161–6
    see also adulthood
Paternalism beyond Borders
    (Barnett) 161
Payne, Ruth 17, 27, 28, 114
Peru 26, 87–8
Philosophie der Menschenrechte (Menke
    and Pollmann) 127
The Philosophy of History (Hegel) 99
Philosophy of Liberation (Dussel) 67–8
Piketty, Thomas 20–1
pluralism 56, 65, 67
political rights 200, 203, 204, 205,
    206, 207
    voting rights 174, 179, 186, 192,
        193, 194
Pollmann, A. 127
Portugal 87
postcolonialism 1, 2–4, 6, 9–11, 30–1,
    53–8, 69–71
    African contributions to 59–63
    agency 5, 9, 11, 13, 17, 23–30
    children's rights 127–9, 155–8,
        217–18, 221
    inequality 10, 15–23, 55, 58, 217
    inferiority 53, 57, 66
    Latin American contributions
        to 63–8
    limitations of Euro-centric childhood
        pattern 9, 11, 12t, 13–15
    poverty 18, 19–20, 21, 26, 27
    subalternity 53, 56–7, 63–4, 69, 71
    two-dimensional understanding 54

unequal global childhoods 15–23
Postman, Neil 15
poverty 54, 80, 85, 95, 109, 113
    children's rights 137, 153–4, 156
    citizenship 195, 201, 202, 208, 209
    postcolonialism and 18, 19–20,
        21, 26, 27
power relations and structures 3, 5, 6,
    21–2, 35, 190, 197
    children's rights 147–52
    citizenship 202–5
    education and 40–3, 109–10,
        120–1, 122
    postcolonialism 55, 57, 58, 65–6
precolonial cultures 22, 60, 61, 65, 68,
    100–1, 106
privatization of assets 20–1
production methods 19, 22, 33, 34, 51,
    59, 87, 212
    education and 101, 103, 108, 109
productive work 14, 34, 50–1, 201
Prout, Alan 12t, 15
Puao-te-Ata-tu 85
Purple Hibiscus (Adichie) 105

Q

Quijano, Aníbal 65
Qvortrup, Jens 199

R

race and racism 6, 36–7, 46, 156,
    208, 217
    civilization of indigenous/'irregular'
        children 94–6
    families 90, 91, 92, 93–4, 95
    'illegitimate' children 89–94, 96
    postcolonialism and 54, 57–8, 60, 69
    state violence 82, 83, 84, 85–6
    women 87, 90, 91, 93–4, 95
rationality 29, 65, 88, 167–8
religious influences 79, 81, 89, 95, 100
Renan, Ernest 37
Report of the Ministerial Committee
    on a Maori Perspective of the
    Department of Social Welfare
    (Puao-te-Ata-tu) 85
reproduction 22, 23, 33, 34, 51,
    78, 184
republican citizenship 196–8
respect 119–21
Retamar, Roberto Fernandez 64
Reynaert, Didier 153–4
Rhodesia 78
Ribeiro, Darcy 64
Richter, E. 168
Roche, J. 202
Rodgers, Diane 208

Rogers, A. 41
Rose, Rudi 153–4
Rousseau, Jean-Jacques 37, 38
Royal Spanish Academy 92
rural areas 18, 22, 113–14, 210
Rwanda 115

S

Saavedra, Cinthya 23
Sacchi, Stefan 44
Said, Edward W. 56, 64, 130
Sargent, Carolyn 113
Save the Children 148
Savyasaachi 182
Scheper-Hughes, Nancy 113
Schibotto, Giangi 70, 71
Schickhardt, Christoph 172–3,
    174, 175
Scholz, Gerold 49
Senegal 218–21
Senghor, Léopold 59, 61
Sierra Leone 18
slavery 57, 58, 59, 60–1, 67, 83,
    87, 90, 92
Smith, Anne-Marie 187–8
social difference 204–5
social movements 6, 24, 29, 45–6,
    56, 68, 70
social responsibility 13, 15, 17, 24, 50,
    106, 107, 114
  children's rights 137, 143, 154, 156,
    185, 192
  citizenship and 192, 197, 202
  paternalism 176–7, 177–8, 186,
    187, 188
South Africa 27, 42, 59–60, 78, 117
South America 29, 56, 137–8
South Asia 18
South Asian Subaltern Studies
    Group 63
Spain 87
Spivak, Gayatri 56, 69, 70, 132
state violence 77–8, 86
  deportation of children 78–80
  removal/assimilation of indigenous
    children 80–5
Stearns, Peter 16
Stoecklin, Daniel 25
Street, B.V. 41
street children 2, 26, 27, 78, 79, 90, 95
  children's rights 143–50, 187, 209
  education and childcare 110, 111–12,
    117, 220
sub-Saharan Africa 18, 20, 100, 106
subalternity 10, 34, 50, 195, 208
  postcolonialism and 53, 56–7,
    63–4, 69, 71

subjectivities 29–30, 156, 168, 196
subordination 10, 17, 24, 44, 48, 49,
    88, 162, 211
  education and 105, 118, 120
Sumak Kawsay/ Buen Vivir 29
Sunstein, Cass 163
superiority 35, 48, 54, 56, 62, 85, 91,
    96, 130, 164
Sustainable Development Goals (United
    Nations) 134
Syria 27

T

Tanzania 26, 115–16
Thaler, Richard 163
Thiong'o, Ngũgĩ wa 62
Tolfree, David 116
Tomberg, Friedrich 43–4
transportation of children 78–80
Truth and Reconciliation Commission
    (Canada) 84–5
Twum-Danso, Afua 119

U

Ubuntu 59–60, 63
UDHR *see* Universal Declaration of
    Human Rights
Uganda 113–14
UNICEF 12–13, 18, 19, 20,
    142–3, 191
United Nations 109, 134
United Nations Committee on the
    Rights of the Child 135, 154
United Nations Convention on the
    Rights of the Child (UNCRC) 12,
    16–17, 97
  children's rights 127–8, 135, 136–7,
    138, 142–3, 154
  citizenship 192, 202, 205,
    207, 208–29
  education 110, 113, 123
  paternalism 170–1, 181, 189
United Nations Human Development
    Report (UNDP) 20
United States (USA) 6, 23, 46,
    47–8, 127
  postcolonialism 56, 57, 59, 66
  state violence 78, 79, 80, 81, 82, 84
Universal Declaration of Human Rights
    (UDHR) (1948) 131
universality 128, 135–42, 154
urban areas 19, 193, 211–12

V

Van Daalen, E. et al 149–50, 154
van Noort, Olivier 88
Vietnam 142–3

violence 6, 39, 48, 55, 56, 57, 67, 90–1, 210–11
  state deportation of children 78–80
  state removal/assimilation of indigenous children 80–5
Viruru, Radhika 47–9, 70
von Werlhof, Claudia 44

W

Wallace, Joe-Ann 36
Wallerstein, Immanuel 129–30
Walsh, Catherine 67
Wells, Karen 16
Western childhood pattern *see* Eurocentric-Western-bourgeois childhood pattern
'white' people 24, 29, 87, 90, 127
  postcolonialism 55, 57, 59, 60
  state violence 78, 79, 81–3
Wilder, LeRoy 84
Wiredu, Kwasi 61, 62, 120
Woldeslase, W. et al 121
Wolf, Angelika 116–17
Wolf, Jean-Claude 163–4

women 34, 44–5, 63, 70–1, 194, 220, 221
  childcare 101–3
  race and racism 87, 90, 91, 93–4, 95
  state violence 80, 81, 83–4
working children 14, 23, 49, 51
  children's rights 151, 152, 211, 211–12, 219, 221
  postcolonialism 78, 83, 88, 110
World Bank 19, 21, 41, 65, 133
World Health Organization (WHO) 19
world order 50, 55, 105, 155, 156
  children's rights 132, 133–4, 135, 155, 156
World Trade Organization (WTO) 21, 65, 133
Wyness, M. 24

Y

Yoshida, T. 26
youth movements 46

Z

Zambia 114
Zemelman, Hugo 70